PUBLIC, PRIVATE, SECRET
ON PHOTOGRAPHY & THE CONFIGURATION OF SELF

By Charlotte Cotton
With Marina Chao and Pauline Vermare

aperture

PUBLIC, PRIVATE, SECRET
ON PHOTOGRAPHY & THE CONFIGURATION OF SELF

Front
6 Foreword, Mark Lubell
8 Introduction, Charlotte Cotton

David Reinfurt, O-R-G
21 *"Clock"* (2016)

Essays
38 What's in an Image, Marisa Olson
43 Artist, Detective, Accomplice, Lucas Wrench
48 Citizen Selfie, David A. Banks
52 Photography in the Age of Communicative Capitalism, Ben Burbridge
56 Wired! Expanding!, Dan Bustillo
60 Watching Murder Online, Sarah Tuck
65 Keeping Up with the Cartesians: On the Culture of the Selfie with Continual Reference to Kim Kardashian, Daniel Rubinstein

Gallery 01
69 *Public, Private, Secret*, ICP Museum, 250 Bowery, NY, June 2016–January 2017

Interviews
86 Zach Blas with Lucas Wrench
90 Ann Hirsch with Marina Chao
97 Martine Syms with Lucas Wrench
102 Shelly Silver with Marina Chao
109 Nancy Burson with Pauline Vermare
113 John Houck with Pauline Vermare
118 Kate Cooper with Marina Chao
124 Stefan Ruiz with Pauline Vermare
128 Merry Alpern with Pauline Vermare
132 Trevor Paglen with Paula Kupfer
136 Doug Rickard with Paula Kupfer
142 Jon Rafman with Marina Chao

147 Natalie Bookchin with Paula Kupfer
154 Lyle Ashton Harris (as told by Parissah Lin) with Marina Chao

Gallery 02
161 *Public, Private, Secret*, ICP Museum, 250 Bowery, NY, June 2016–January 2017

Reflections
178 Transparent and Opaque, common room
182 Correspondence, David Reinfurt
188 Every Image Found, Mark Ghuneim
193 Students in the New Media Narratives Program Curate Real-Time Social-Media Collections for *Public, Private, Secret*, Elizabeth Kilroy
198 Making *Public/Private/Portrait*, Romke Hoogwaerts
202 Urgent Archives, Paul Soulellis
206 Belonging in the Mess, Johanna Hedva
210 Spooky Action from a Distance, Lucas Wrench
213 Pictures without Words, Joseph Maida
219 Redefining What and Who We See and Don't See, Lacy Austin

Back
225 Poster Wall Displays
227 Live Events
231 Acknowledgments
232 Colophon

Front

Foreword, Mark Lubell

Introduction, Charlotte Cotton

FOREWORD, MARK LUBELL

The International Center of Photography was founded by Cornell Capa in 1974 as an institution dedicated to "concerned photography," his term for socially engaged work that has the capacity to change the way people see the world, understand one another, and react to the circumstances and events that challenge our shared humanity. Since then, we have been dedicated to serving this urgent mission while navigating the expansive and ever-changing nature of photography, a medium uniquely linked to technology and its giddy promises and alienating discontents.

While ICP was preparing for the summer 2016 opening of the museum's new space on the Bowery, the critical conversation of how to address the contemporary state of photography—and its changes in the last decade alone—was occurring across the institution. In 2015, the ICP School welcomed its first class in the newly established New Media Narratives (NMN) program, chaired by Elizabeth Kilroy, which focuses on the use of new digital platforms to tell immersive visual stories. The program, now in its third year, is crucial to our institution's understanding of the shifts in the communicative potential of photography. It is also central to our view of future possibilities for an artistic medium that took a century to be canonized by the museum world, only to explode as part of an unstoppable technological revolution in recent years. ICP's celebrated educational outreach initiative—our Community Programs, helmed by Lacy Austin for the past fifteen years—is likewise critical to facilitating the public discussion about photography and its evolving meaning directly with diverse audiences throughout the city and with our photography community.

So it was fitting that Charlotte Cotton—invited to be ICP's first curator in residence and to organize the inaugural exhibition on the Bowery, *Public, Private, Secret*—was determined from the start to fully engage with both the NMN and our Community Programs as key partners. Along with artist and technologist Mark Ghuneim, she developed an original, real-time technology component in collaboration with New Media Narratives students. In addition, ICP's Community Programs played an integral role in the exhibition and its reach beyond the gallery walls, through Teen Academy classes, tours and workshops, and the Museum's poster wall initiative, all of which brought the questions and concerns of the exhibition project to bear in a broader, inclusive community context.

Public, Private, Secret is an exploration of the singular relationship between photography and contemporary social mores, framed within a discussion of personal privacy; the images we circulate of our reality—increasingly self-constructed—are artifacts of our society's values and desires. But with hundreds of millions of photographs shared and consumed every day, in a millions-to-millions model, a cohesive message becomes nearly impossible to parse. *Public, Private, Secret* looked at this fundamental, large-scale social shift in recent decades, examined the ways it intersects with the history of photography and visual culture, and highlighted the intimate and impersonal ways in which we communicate visually and how these interactions shape our relationships.

We've seen over the last twenty years how our increased connectedness and the ubiquity of handheld cameras have brought image making and language closer and closer together, with the constant exchange of pictures becoming a surrogate for other forms of conversation. The social and psychological ramifications of being so connected, even remotely, are yet to be seen; it is a subject to which ICP will certainly return in the years to come. They form part of the very human questions that have concerned ICP for over four decades, and we intend to continue this inquiry into what photography tells us about ourselves and the world.

The publication of this book allows all of those involved in *Public, Private, Secret* to reflect on the highly collaborative and discursive process of working on the exhibition and the questions, both practical and philosophical, real-time and speculative, that it raised.

Thank you to Charlotte Cotton for taking risks and exploring these new societal constructs in which we are now living. We thank all of the artists, scholars, teachers, and makers who were involved in the project and this volume. Thanks go to Merry Alpern, Zach Blas, Natalie Bookchin, Nancy Burson, Kate Cooper, Lyle Ashton Harris, Ann Hirsch, John Houck, Trevor Paglen, Jon Rafman, Doug Rickard, Stefan Ruiz, Shelly Silver, and Martine Syms for sharing both their work and their words. We are grateful to our close partners who have authored reflection pieces in this publication: Lacy Austin, common room, Mark Ghuneim, Johanna Hedva, Romke Hoogwaerts, Elizabeth Kilroy, Joseph Maida, David Reinfurt, Paul Soulellis, and Lucas Wrench. Thanks go to Geoff Han for conceiving the graphic design for 250 Bowery; *Public, Private, Secret*; and this publication. Thank you to common room for developing an elegant and thoughtful museum and exhibition design. Finally, this exhibition and the accompanying public programming could not have been realized without Pauline Vermare, Marina Chao, and Africia Heiderhoff.

This publication was made possible through the generous support of the Metabolic Studio. The exhibition would not have been possible without support from the ICP Exhibitions Committee, the John and Annamaria Phillips Foundation, the Robert Mapplethorpe Foundation, and the New York City Department of Cultural Affairs in partnership with the City Council. Sincerest thanks also go to Aperture Foundation—including Lesley A. Martin, Samantha Marlow, and their publications colleagues—for being an invaluable partner, both on this volume in particular and in our institutions' shared dedication to photography more broadly.

We are indebted to every one of the many friends of ICP who made our museum's launch at 250 Bowery a success. Thank you.

Mark Lubell
Executive Director, ICP

INTRODUCTION, CHARLOTTE COTTON

The exhibition and programming *Public, Private, Secret* drew together a spectrum of ideas addressing the complex intersections between visual culture and personal privacy. *Public, Private, Secret* opened in June 2016, consciously proclaiming the affinities between our experiences and those of others—and inviting its viewers, as well as its collaborators, to take the issue of privacy very personally. For the run of the exhibition and its related programs, until January 2017, its proclamation was that this cultural moment is one for critical observation and identification of how we are implicated within the currents of visual culture, and of collectively articulating our rights to be seen and heard while claiming the privilege of privacy.

For better and for worse, network culture provides a broad platform for direct address, an unmediated outlet for image creation and distribution. Within this context, our visual creations and online activities blur and remove conventional delineations between public and private (and sometimes secret) expression; in fact, they multiply and expand the number of potential selves. Photography and video are implicated in the crafting of identity and in the reconfiguration of the social conventions that define our public and private selves. Consciously framed by our present era, the works on view in *Public, Private, Secret* signaled how our image-making and consumption patterns are embedded in a wider matrix of online behavior and social codes, which in turn give images a life of their own.

The genesis of *Public, Private, Secret* occurred in the midst of a period of change for the ICP Museum, with its relocation from Midtown Manhattan to the Bowery on the Lower East Side. As curator in residence, my task was to curate the first exhibition and program for ICP's new public space, one that would reanimate the taproots of this fifty-year-old institution in ways that would speak to the present-day climate of visual culture. What I channeled from ICP's conception in the late 1960s and early 1970s was abstract in nature but significant in shaping *Public, Private, Secret*: like many photography-centric galleries and museum departments around the world, the ICP participated in the first concerted wave that defined photography as a bona fide cultural subject in and around 1970. Perhaps romantic in bent, I think of this period of cultural appraisal as a time when enthusiasts came, implicitly, from other places to forge a critical framework for photography for the first time. From a distance, I had observed the ICP's program over the past twenty-five years as an ongoing dialogical questioning of photography's scope and purpose, its alternate histories, its social counterarguments, and its prescient manifestations. The ICP

School and Community Programs are where this institution's fundamental beliefs—in photography's capacities to provide a critical vantage point, and to narrate the underrepresented, and visualize alterity—are lived out. Each of these encounters with the actual and symbolic histories of ICP had immense bearing on the scope of *Public, Private, Secret* and my sense of the permissions that its history was giving us at this pivotal moment—another open field—in the story of photography and visual culture.

As the first curatorial statement to be made within the ICP Museum's new home on the Lower East Side, it was not only important that *Public, Private, Secret* offer a tangibly new curatorial approach to photography but also one that could be readily differentiated from the photographic stories told by other institutions in New York's boroughs. It felt quite natural, given the institution's exhibition trajectory, to draw together historical and contemporary works from the medium's broad terrain, to build a framework that would apply equal intelligence to quotidian visual culture as it does to artists' practices, and articulate that collective social meaning is embedded within photography's full spectrum. To forego the safety of the typical institutional hierarchy applied to photography—and instead to flatten and cross-fertilize it—was a conscious gesture intended to reveal where our sense of personal privacy is demonstrably at stake.

Within weeks of my joining ICP in August 2015, after establishing with my curatorial collaborators Marina Chao and Pauline Vermare that we would investigate the theme of privacy for the inaugural exhibition, our colleagues would ask how "the surveillance show" was coming along. In retrospect and on a number of levels, what I took as an unwelcome simplification of our curatorial research was pretty accurate. As I started meeting with the artists and thinkers shaping the creative discourses in and around surveillance—taking their reading recommendations of texts by Fred Moten and Stefano Harney, Simone Browne, Brian Massumi, and Karen Barad—the heated expanse of the subject we had identified began to appear in relief. Like any ambitious curatorial theme, once you start work in earnest, your chosen subject makes its presence known loudly and continually, and every day seemingly brought a news story or personal anecdote that reinforced the frailty of individual privacy. In one of my first meetings with Dan Bustillo and Lucas Wrench, their idea that we will come to see "surveillance" as the nomenclature of this era did not seem out of scope. I am indebted to Trevor Paglen for talking through *Public, Private, Secret* with me at an early stage and for offering moral support at the right moment to create an exhibition that did not place state surveillance at its central axis. At this stage in the cultural assessment of surveillance, there have been substantial and sentient narrations—through monographic and thematic exhibitions—about the unseen and seemingly unimpeachable degrees to which state surveillance impacts upon our civil liberties. I was mindful that our exhibition not fetishize the visual languages of state surveillance—especially its militaristic drive—and consequently, not to repeat existing, vocalized creative perspectives on the subject of surveillance. I also wanted to avoid a disconnect between the impact

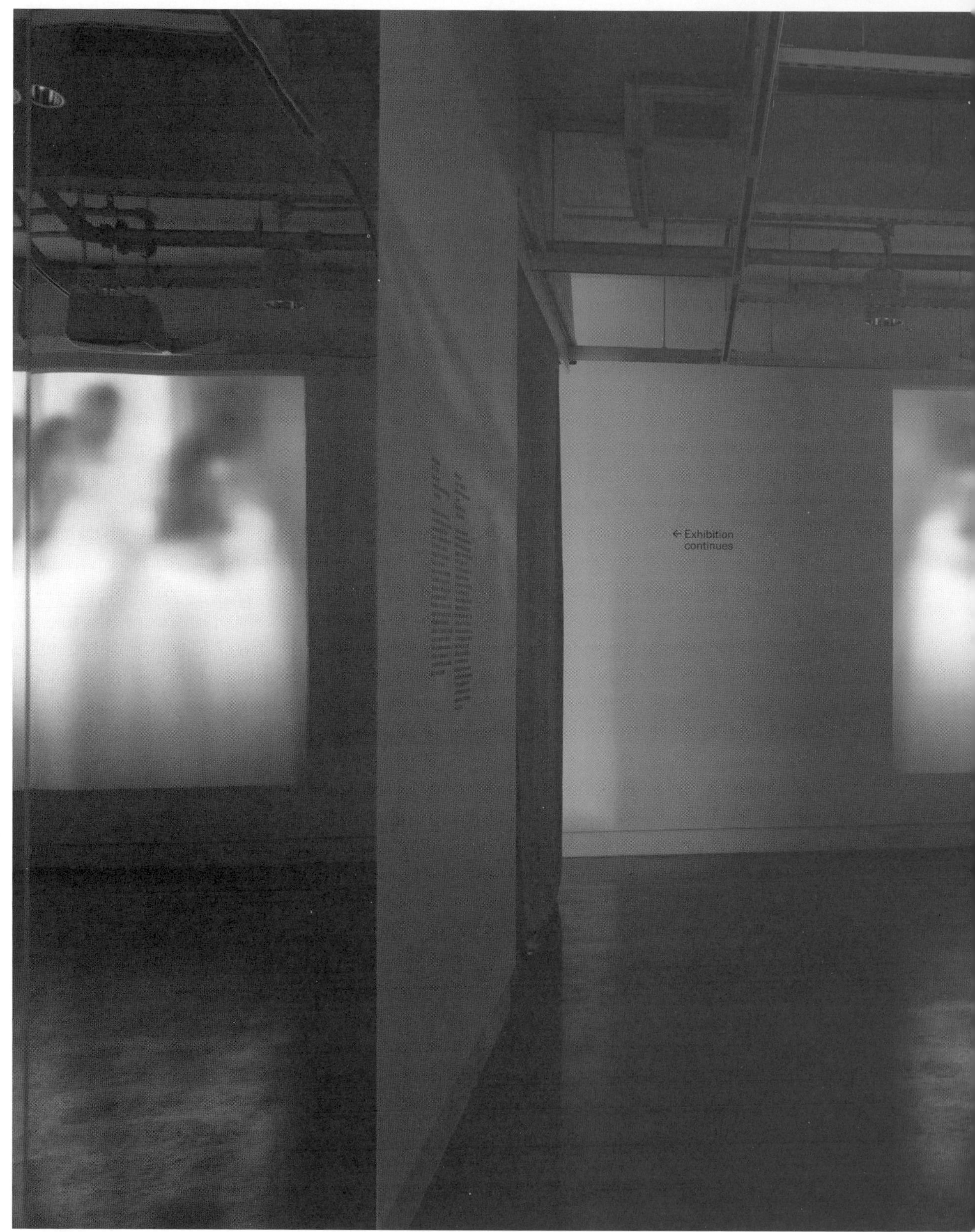
← Exhibition
continues

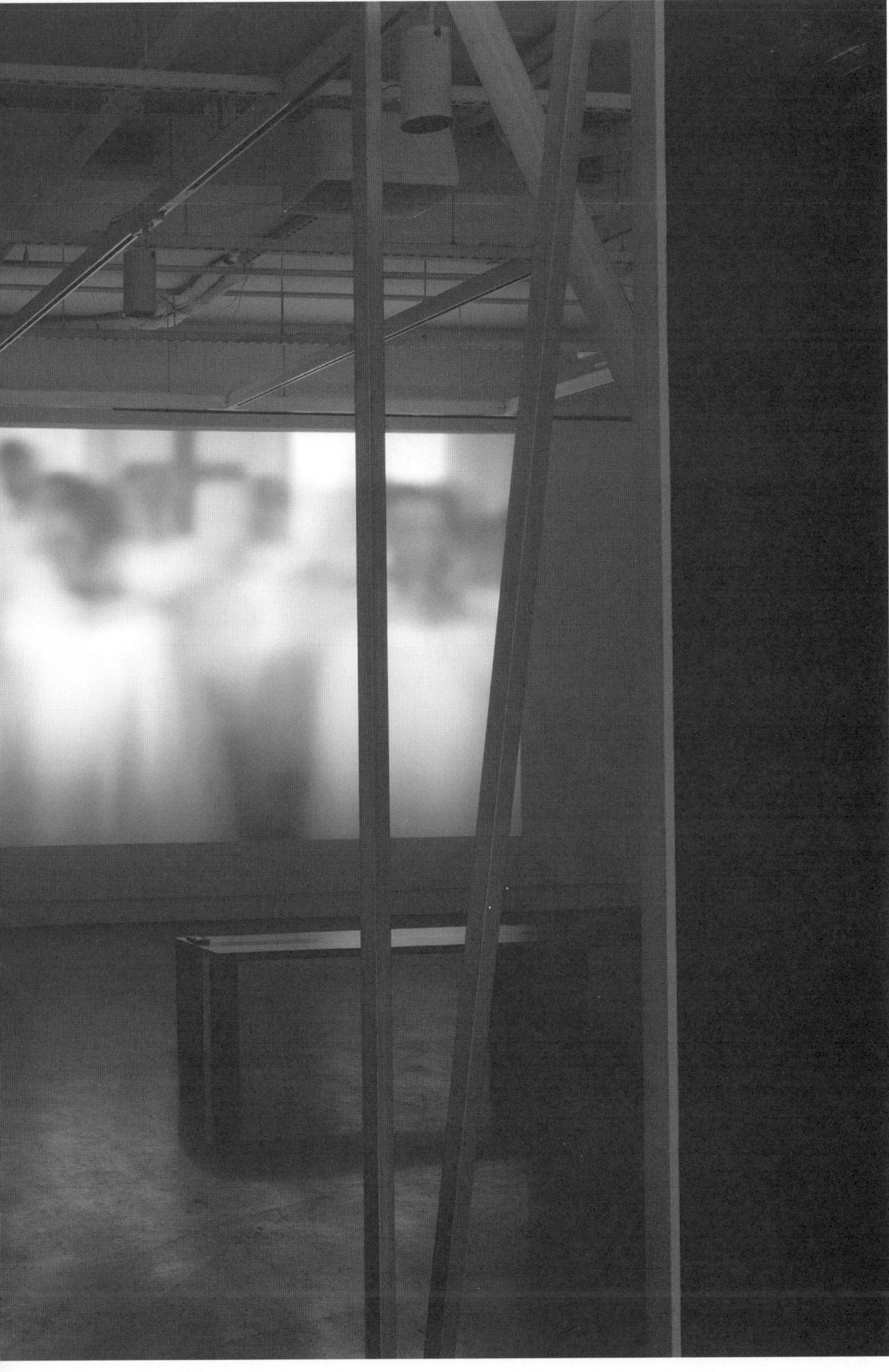

Martine Syms, *Lessons I–LXVIII*, 2014–16. Photo © John Berens

of our daily acquiescence to, and enactment of, more pedestrian forms of surveillance and othering, and the overbearing presence of state surveillance that inevitably shadows it.

Public, Private, Secret's central tenet concerned how we adopt different behaviors within the networked systems in which we labor and recreate, whose built-in mechanisms ensure that any notion of privacy is surrendered. What follows is that any behavior within these systems becomes fair play to be mined for data by for-profit as well as state organizations. This status quo of exposure without recourse is militated further by the pressure to participate in and labor for the culture of public visibility, now an established form of social currency and a prime aspect of "being social." This exhibition was intentionally staged against the backdrop of the many factors that define our media environment, which we internalize and naturalize through our own image usage and behaviors.

After *Public, Private, Secret* opened, Los Angeles Contemporary Exhibitions republished the catalogue for their 1987 exhibition *Surveillance*, curated by Deborah Irmas and Branda Miller, possibly the first substantial exhibition in the US to address the subject of surveillance from artists' perspectives and highlight the ways in which surveillance was becoming naturalized within society. It was heartening to see that the genesis of this theme in exhibition-making had also been pluralistic in its reading of its media and political time, and invited a still-noticeable emphasis on the self-reflection and participation of its viewers. My greatest fear was that our potentially heavy curatorial hand would flatten artists' contributions into illustrations for the exhibition's themes; it was thus in the exhibition's best interest to create open discussion with valued peers and cohorts about these nuanced concerns. Artists are the sentient tribe—they ingest, translate, mediate, subvert, and question the militating social factors that shape our lives in collective and singular ways. Artists also respond to—and carry the weight of—the way in which their practice is read within the collective consciousness, and can be radically re- and misread at moments of profound instability, such as these. Artists are our cultural interlocutors: They confront the world that we live in, some in explicit ways that we recognize as activism, others by bringing their visual skills into the service of communicating our human rights and what is at stake at this troubling political juncture. Some put down their artistic tools and choose to participate in civil action, and some brave souls continue to go to their studio to make sense of it all through their true means. The wise counsel and sheer generosity of Marisa Olson, and the Camerawork network of women artists and curators of photography initiated by Sara VanDerBeek and Eva Respini, helped me and my co-curators enormously with the somewhat daunting task of positioning contemporary artists' works within an increasingly prescriptive exhibition plan.

It was important to me that the first gallery of *Public, Private, Secret* show four artists' video works with no contextualization within the history of photography, or the curation of default media sources by ICP. The aim here was to place the viewer immediately and with certainty into the vantage points that artists are providing onto the both defined and boundaryless terrain between public and private versions of self. This gallery was given over to Natalie Bookchin, Jon Rafman, Doug Rickard, and Martine Syms, four artists whose articulations and observations are drawn from aggregations of visual material. Their authorship is held in their reconfiguring and recontextualizing of existing video imagery—most of it native to online platforms—to create highly subjectivized and alternate readings of human identity as it plays out in visual culture. Through their works, they ask that we pay attention to the profound and deeply social urges that underpin our collective versions of identity, and how these enable different readings of our image world, ever a proxy for the actual world.

Perhaps the most direct way that *Public, Private, Secret* addressed the extent to which the virtual game of seeing and being seen creates slippages between our physical bodies and behaviors was through the inclusion of six curated streams of real-time social media. Their instigator, Mark Ghuneim, and Elizabeth Kilroy, whose New Media Narratives first graduating class developed our research queries, reflect upon the process and durational viewership of the real-time media streams in their contributions to this book. Our intention was to bring the unending, constantly updating operation of online platforms into the exhibition as a definite signifier of the porous boundaries between our public and private selves online. From the construction of popularity and celebrity to the shame of "send all" mistakes, and the chorus of othering, social media has proven itself as the perfect medium for contradictions: it allows us to preempt our fear of intimacy through exhibitionism while answering our desire to live outside of real experience by turning into a voyeur of others' lives. At the same time, the relentlessness of the real-time social-media streams throughout the exhibition butted up against artists' declarations of their freedoms to address and subvert the ways in which automated imagery—captured and interpreted for surveillance purposes—is now used as the standard of restrictive identification to digitally measure and objectify us.

The other material components of *Public, Private, Secret* were historical photographs that we attempted to reanimate as both foundations and markers of change within image culture. Collectively, and alongside contemporary artists' works and the real-time image streams, photography's history was engaged to heighten viewers' attention toward the roots of our image-centric world, underscoring the controls and liberations embedded in photography's histories. For some, I suspect that this iconoclastic approach to the often-considered separatist history of photography was an anathema. But within the context of *Public, Private, Secret*, it was a necessary device for drawing from these historical, material photographs their most incendiary and contemporaneous affect by eradicating the institutionalized hierarchy that placed the medium's history on an unreachable, out-of-time plateau, unconnected to the ways in which we gather and use imagery on our desktops and social-media feeds today. Putting aside the strongly connoisseur-like and authorial approach to historical photography in favor of a mutable contingency of meaning allowed for the underlying dynamic of *Public, Private, Secret* to come to the fore. By constellating historical precedents, contemporary artists' expressions, and real-time media streams in ICP Museum's Gallery 02, the aim was to generate a dynamic form of viewership, one that hinged on viewers' individualized experiences and visual "muscle memory." The invitation was for visitors to assess for themselves the contingent meaning at play; to rethink iconic photography in light of the contemporary visual landscape; to see more deeply and acutely the positions adopted by artists who purposely interject counterarguments into the course of image culture at large; and to imagine how the streams of media that wash over us daily shape our reading of ourselves and others, whether we actively participate or avoid this now-ubiquitous form of quotidian communication.

Public, Private, Secret identified and navigated what we saw as the militating factors that impact on our sense of personal privacy; they were not spelled out but acted as the base beats for self-governed exploration. It was important for an exhibition that framed real personal investment by its viewers in its narrative not to undermine itself by spelling out its tenets in a didactic way. It was also important to me that we provide a critical cultural context and not dismantle, through conventional exhibition "didactics" (as exhibition texts are called in the exhibition trade), the essential invitation for us all to apply our visual and emotional intelligence to the idea of privacy. Instead, the layout of photographs and videos in Gallery 02 was structured with the outer walls touching on the complicity of image making's structure in shaping contemporary privacy—privacy considered here as the quantifiable evidence of celebrity; the ever-present, deeply voyeuristic modality within photography's DNA; the pervasive power of state surveillance; and the biases of commercial data-mining that so readily turns our bodies and ostensibly private behaviors into metadata.

The center of Gallery 02 presented counterarguments to these militating factors, centering on a winding and elliptical journey that artists and their human subjects have proposed to the limited versions of race, gender, sexuality, and autonomy populating the disseminating dynamic of popular visual culture. Utilizing sightlines and the potential routes to be taken by viewers, *Public, Private, Secret* created trajectories of "being seen." Perhaps the most explicit narrative was seeded by three small carte-de-visite photographs of Sojourner Truth with their printed declaration, "I sell the shadow to support the substance," a remarkably resonant statement from over 150 years ago. Behind her repeated image was a video documenting the turning pages of Kim Kardashian's 2015 *Selfish* book. Truth faced a large Vik Muniz photograph of his drawing in ink of Frederick Douglass, recently confirmed as the most photographed American of the mid-nineteenth century. Alongside hung Rashid Johnson's 2003 self-portrait with his hair parted in honor of Douglass, opposite Lyle Ashton Harris's collage that magnificently narrates black identity through personal and public imagery, including a postcard image of a unique photograph on glass of Frederick Douglass. Whether historical or contemporary, creative practices and their authors were positioned to counter the restraints on our identities established by society, and provide alternate versions of the potency of representation. In so doing, and by invoking photography, these independent creative practices were foregrounded as the anticipation of an image future rich with diversity and alterity, one that can be shaped and influenced through self-representation.

The invitation to viewers made by *Public, Private, Secret* could not have been realized without the collaboration with its spatial designers—common room—and graphic designer Geoff Han. Their mission was doubly challenging because it was not only to design an exhibition for a space that was still under construction, but also to conceptualize the design and orientation within the entire museum, including the open, street-level space. In its simplest terms, the exhibition design manifested our aims of implicating its viewers within the visual story of privacy that it told—not simply on an imaginative and intellectual way but in a bodily sense. At its most literal, this led us to using one- and two-way mirrors, and transparent, temporary wall surfaces, which meant that viewers and their movements were present and multiplied through the exhibition. In addition, the individual object "labels" were positioned in large print at an unconventionally low position on the exhibition walls, acting as captions that created a parallel—rather than an integrated—textual narrative of privacy that consciously did not interrupt the visual connections between the different types of visual material. It was crucial that the front space of the new ICP Museum—what would be typically called a lobby—have its own design logic, as a threshold through which you entered *Public, Private, Secret* but also as a genuinely communal space. Despite their often elegant designs, museum lobbies tend to be spatially designed series of instructions: put your bag here, buy a ticket, buy a gift, wait quietly here. My notion for the design of the front space was that it operate like a village square—a time-honored commons—inviting you to make use of it. Our "village square" had its defining features: a café and a library, with its knowledgeable "librarian" Sarah Goldberg, and curated by Spaces Corners's Melissa Catanese and Ed Panar with a thoughtful selection of photobooks. Common room also designed a "notice board"—a wall of designed posters that changed every week and allowed us to extend the thematic of *Public, Private, Secret* to include published and new projects, many created in direct response to the exhibition. It also felt important that our commons have a clock, and for this we turned to David Reinfurt, who created his *"Clock"* to mark out continuous time in a resonant way. Closest to the Bowery sidewalk, a digital monitor was fixed to a free-standing pole. It showed an analog clock face with a pair of projections behind it, visible from the street. The wall-mounted projections streamed live-video data drawn from cameras positioned within the ICP Museum by artist Sean Donovan. Custom software intercepted the CCTV camera feeds, enlarging their pixilation, adjusting coloration, and then organizing the remaining data into an abstracted grid of reorganized pixels. The effect of this durational work was to beautifully and subtly allow

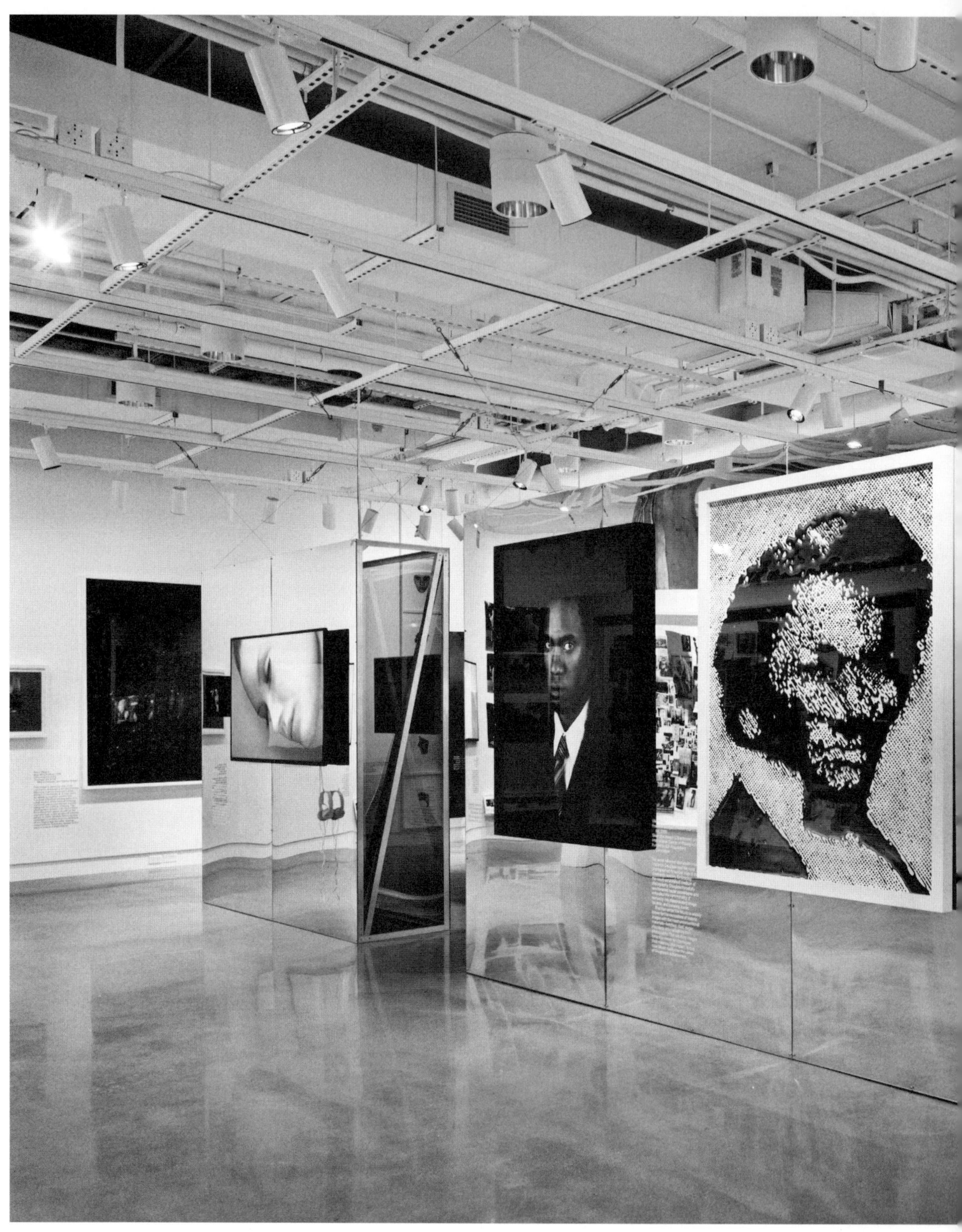

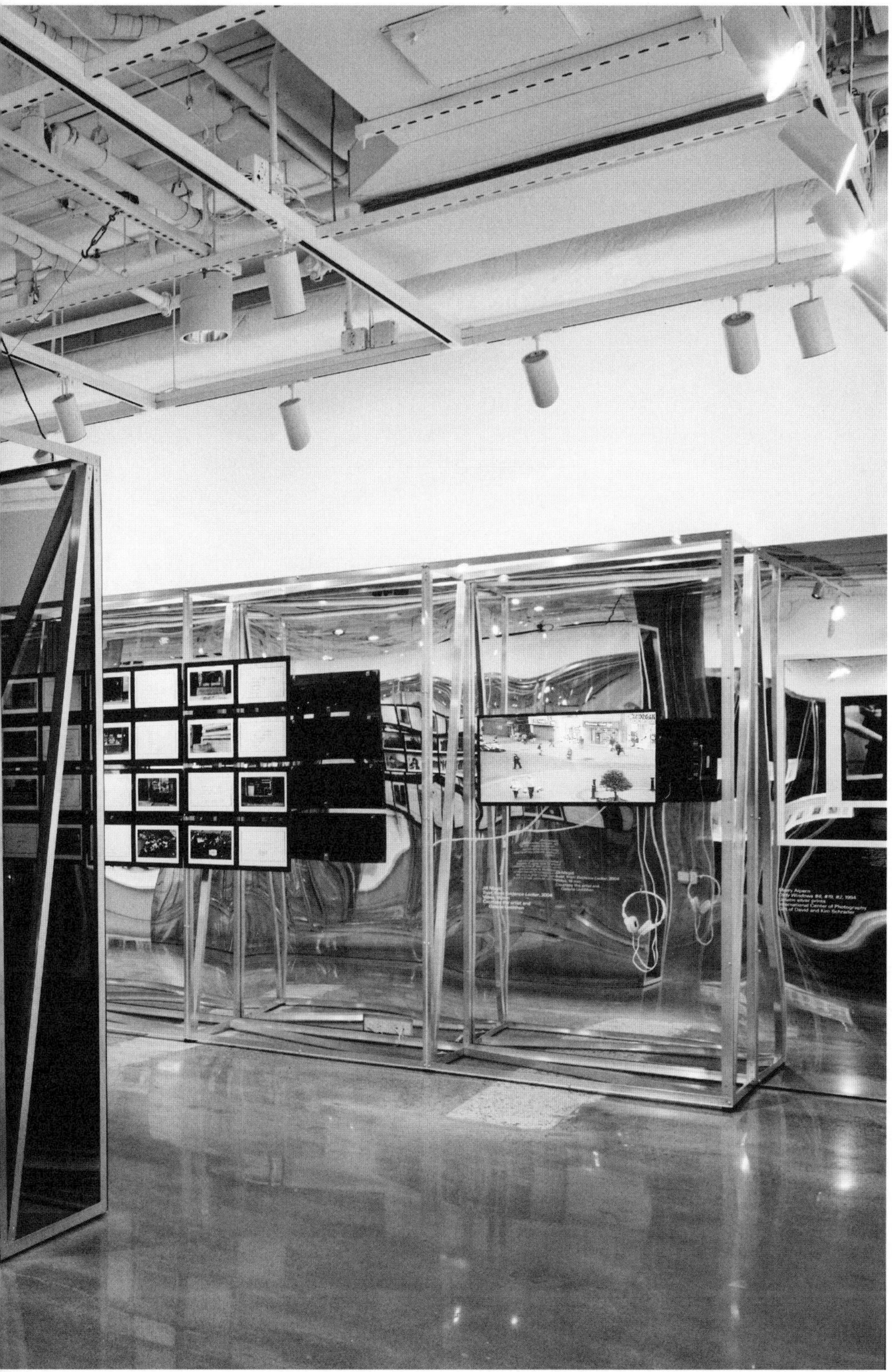

Left: Rashid Johnson, *Self-Portrait with My Hair Parted Like Frederick Douglass*, 2003. Right: Vik Muniz, *Frederick Douglass*, from *Pictures of Ink*, 2000. Photo © Amanda Fitzpatrick

the theme of privacy to permeate the threshold into *Public, Private, Secret*. It graphically and structurally spoke to the permissions that we all give to be surveilled when moving through public space, and to the implication that our bodies are public, algorithmically read, metadata.

Public, Private, Secret actively embodied the modalities of ICP as a school, community program, and museum. It was apparent from the outset of its curatorial development that the traditional museological pyramid that places exhibitions and collections at its summit, with events, pedagogy, and publishing seen as ancillary activities, needed to be flattened in order to engage fully with the issue of personal privacy. The live-events program—which ranged from intense two- to three-hour discussions, book launches courtesy of our resident bookstore Spaces Corners, celebrations to launch the weekly poster-wall displays, to day-long workshops, and ICP's Community Education classes—was the most direct way for the durational and generative spirit of *Public, Private, Secret* to be elaborated upon. We had an exceptional collaborator in director of ICP's Community Education programs Lacy Austin, who used the context of *Public, Private, Secret* to amplify her programs' inclusive and participatory model. Johanna Hedva brought the Processing Foundation's new concepts and research on diverse modes of access to technology through the presentations of its 2016 fellows. Lucas Wrench curated workshops, demonstrations, and performances in partnership with Machine Project that galvanized discussion and action for protecting personal privacy through heightened collective consciousness.

Early in the curatorial process, we decided to wait until the close of the *Public, Private, Secret* exhibition and program before embarking on this publication—its subject called for a textual reader with its own constellation of ideas rather than an exhibition catalogue that by inference would lock down the meaning and outcomes of this viewer-centered experience before it had begun. For the opening of *Public, Private, Secret*, we collaborated with two independent publishers: Romke Hoogwaerts, whose *Mossless* publications had brought prescient photographic practices into his thematically curated volumes, of which *Public/Private/Portrait* was the fourth; and Paul Soulellis, whom we similarly invited to apply his own train of thought and curatorial approach to the theme of personal privacy in a special edition of his *Printed Web*. During the run of *Public, Private, Secret*, real-time media curator Mark Ghuneim published his book *Surveillance Index Edition One*, launched at the ICP Museum in September 2016, which provided an essential compendium of artists' books since the 1980s that have recalibrated and recast the deep shadow of surveillance culture in astute and creative ways.

While there is something quasi-definitive to a printed book, I am grateful to its many authors for maintaining the pluralism of vantage points also present in the exhibition and program, and for entering into a multilayered conversation about what is at stake in this era of surveillance. Each of the contributors to this volume has given a personal account of their perspective upon the issue of privacy. Collectively, and not unlike the *Public, Private, Secret* exhibition, they weave a framework that can serve as a point of departure to make speculations about the impact of visual culture upon the very idea of personhood. My own reflections on *Public, Private, Secret* after it became a public entity in the summer of 2016 have stemmed from my anecdotal experiences, perhaps the most significant of which revolve around the troubling and threatening global events that continue the erosion of the boundaries around our public and private lives. At the opening of the exhibition and ICP Museum's new home there was understandable concern that the hypothesis of *Public, Private, Secret* was too troublesome and pessimistic. I accept that the exhibition's sparse moments of levity bordered on wry irony, and that it could feel tireless in its conceit to implicate its viewers in the pervasive labor of surveillance. But in light of recent world events, *Public, Private, Secret*'s overall narrative matured to be closer to realism than some had initially judged. If the contributions and constellations we brought together acknowledged the collective instability of personhood and the privilege of privacy, they did so within the curatorial intention that its incumbent social lack or loss was one of illusion. I hope that *Public, Private, Secret* served as a visceral proclamation that all we have lost is a false sense of security and that we are made resilient by such knowledge. I also locate hope in the exhibition's and this book's internal counterargument that our capacity to face our realities is not lost. We are left with the knowledge that our shared creative powers and intelligence are perhaps our only tools to resist and subvert threats to our civil liberties, and to assert our right to see and be seen.

In addition to being the first curator in residence at the International Center of Photography (2015–16), Charlotte Cotton has also held curatorial positions at institutions, including the Victoria and Albert Museum and The Photographers' Gallery in London; the Wallis Annenberg Photography Department at the Los Angeles County Museum of Art; Katonah Museum of Art, New York; California Museum of Photography, Riverside; and Metabolic Studio in Los Angeles. She has been a visiting scholar and critic at institutions, including the New School and NYU, New York; California College of the Arts, San Francisco; and Otis College, Los Angeles. She is the author of Photography Is Magic *(Aperture, 2015) and* The Photograph as Contemporary Art *(2004), and cofounder of Words Without Pictures and Eitherand.org.*

DAVID REINFURT, O-R-G

"Clock" (2016)

"Clock" was commissioned for *Public, Private, Secret* as a piece of social furniture at 250 Bowery. It consists of two parts: a pair of projections in the rear of the main public space and a digital monitor at the front, facing the street. The wall-mounted projections streamed live-video data drawn from cameras in the lobby and in the exhibition spaces. Custom software strips the position information (x and y coordinates) from this image stream and reorganizes the remaining low-resolution data in an abstracted grid of sorted pixels. By dropping the ordered pixel positions, any immediate reading of the space is frustrated and, instead, these new images register more forcefully what has changed—the resulting, scrambled images are pictures of that changing data, more readable by a machine than a person. Instead of pictures of the space, these are images of what has changed in it.

"Clock" fed a stream of pixel-sorted camera images from the ICP Museum to an automated Twitter bot which would release one image per hour through the @pblcprvtscrt handle. Although this bot didn't have a huge following, these abstract images, released as incremental tweets, are still kicking around the back alleys of the internet where they will remain on redundant servers, cloud backups, and in the tangled and distributed databases of likes, retweets, repostings, and so on.

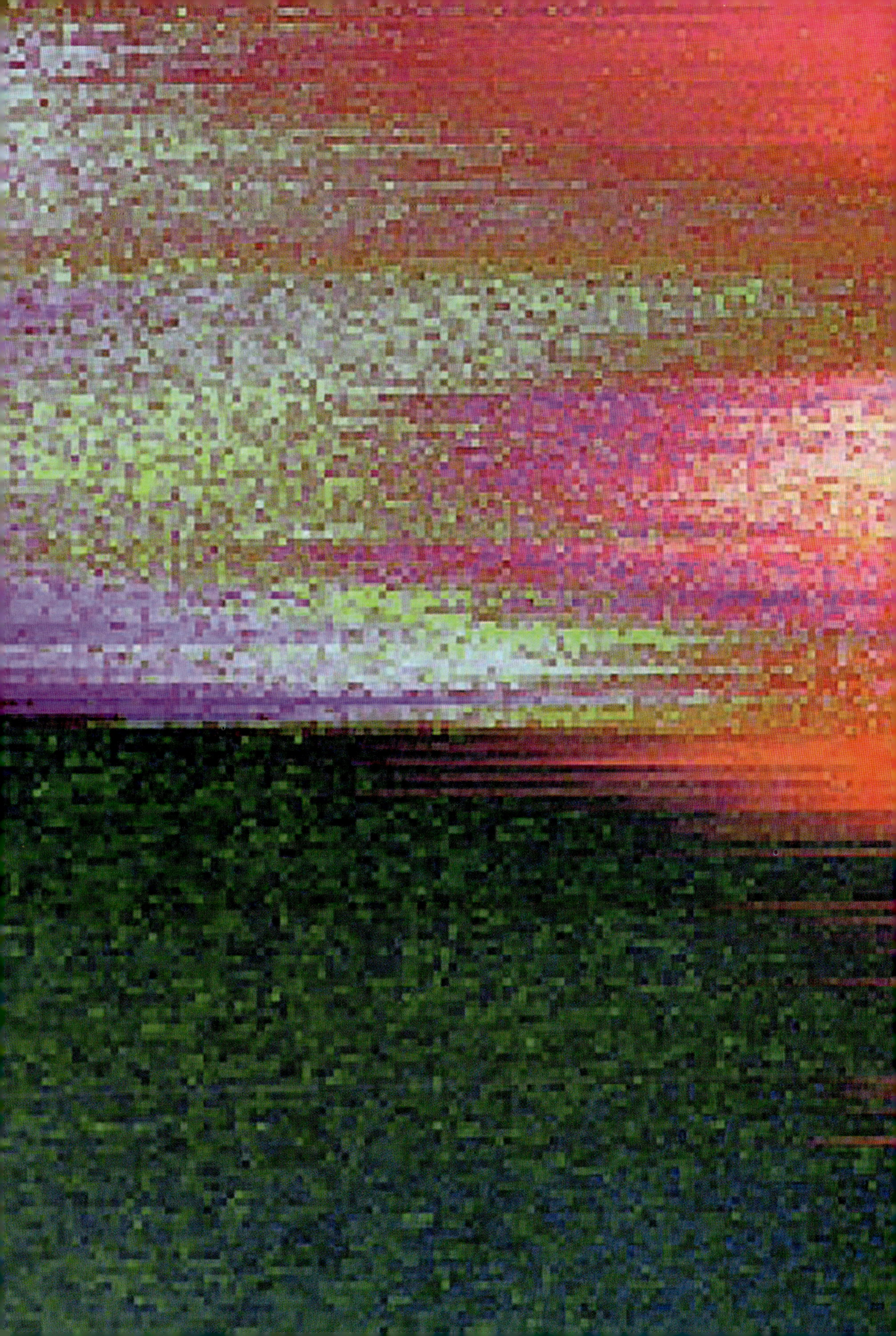

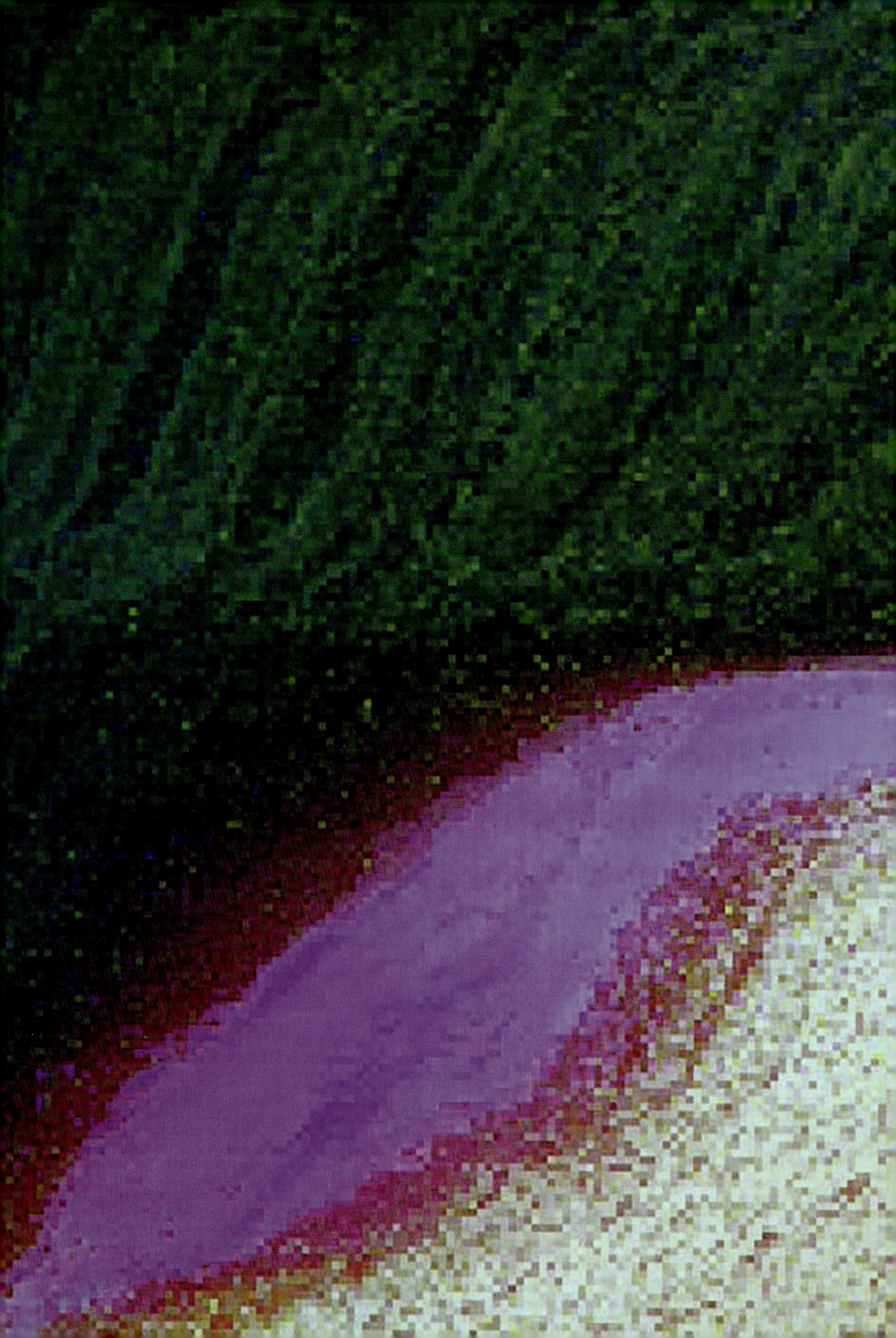

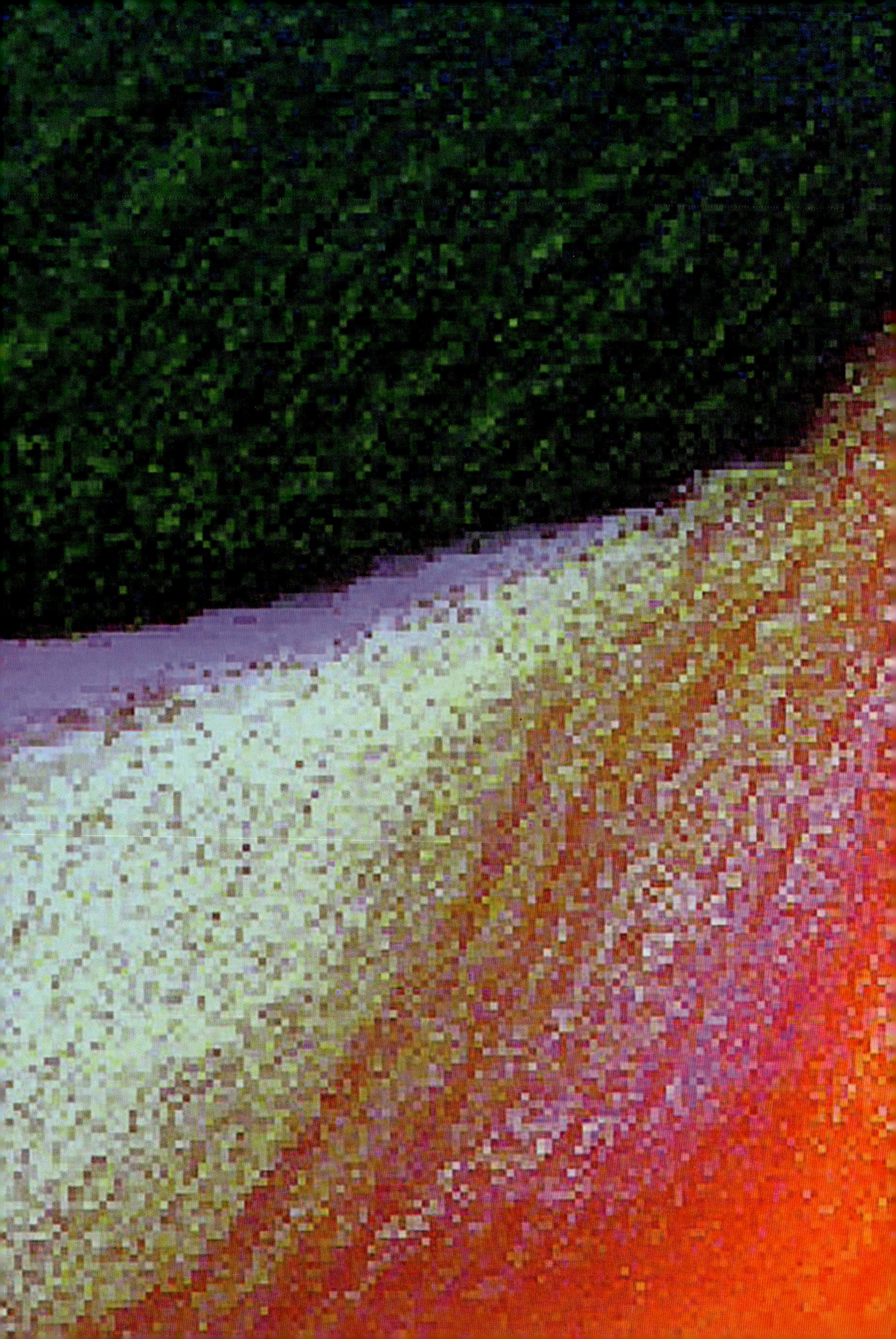

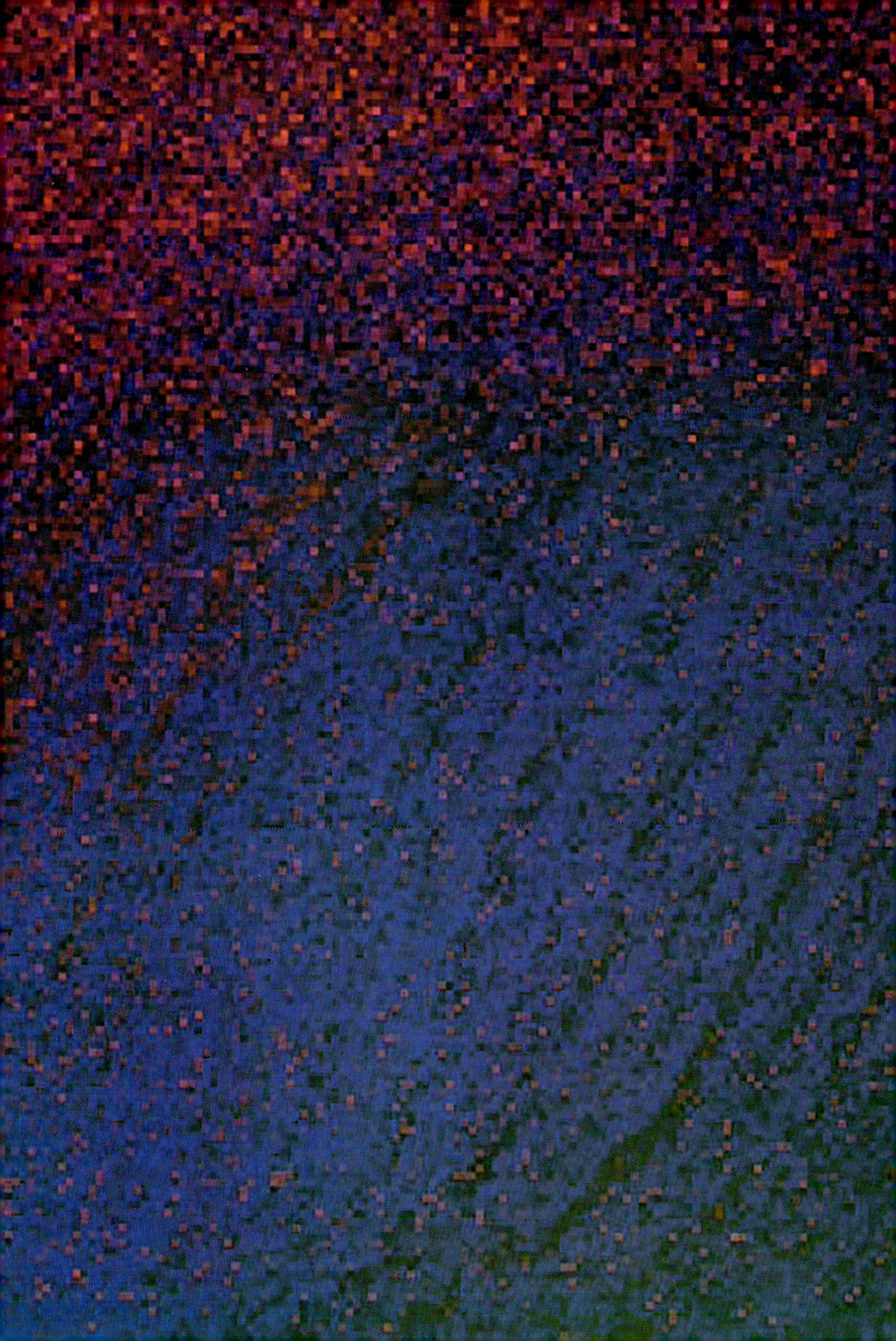

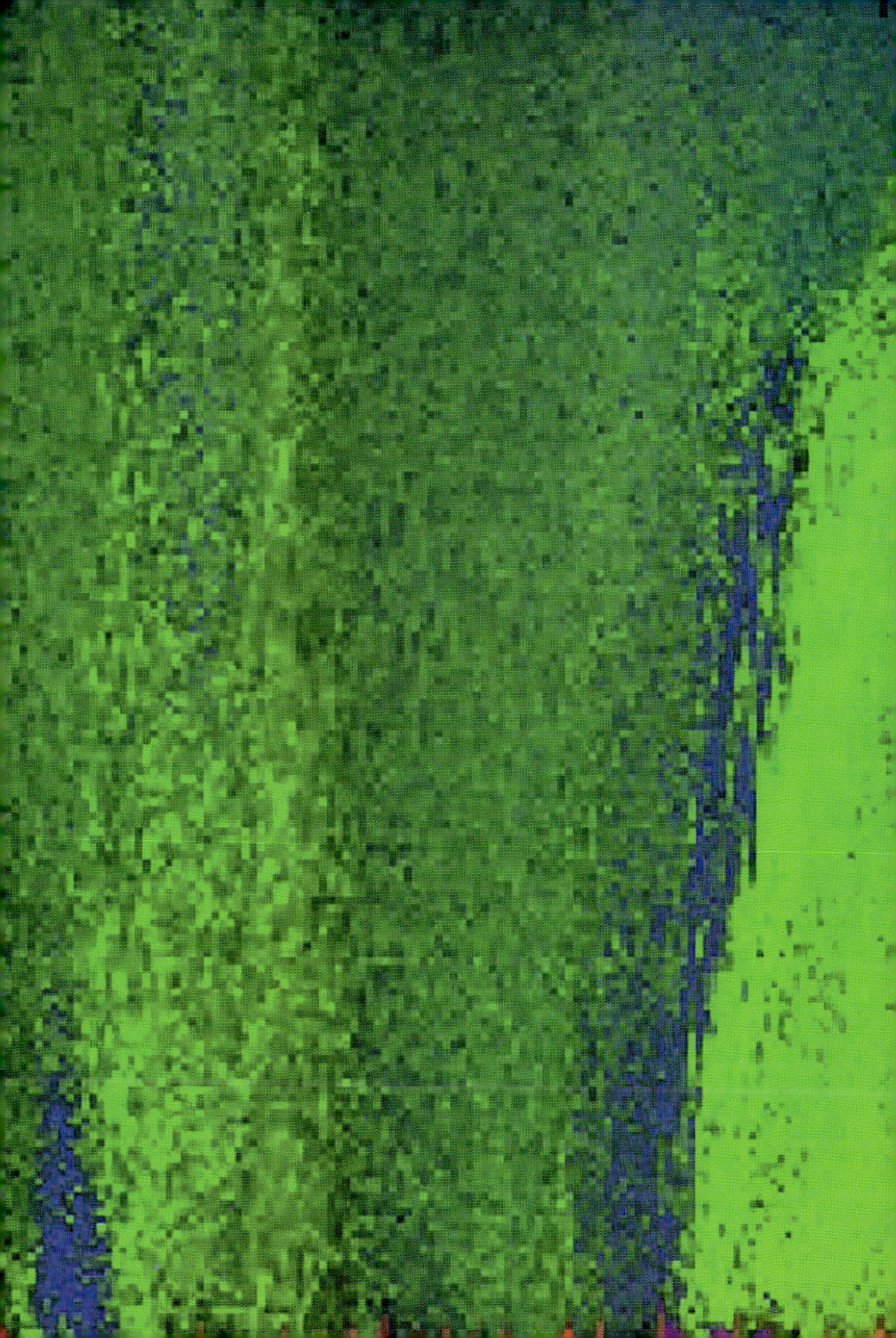

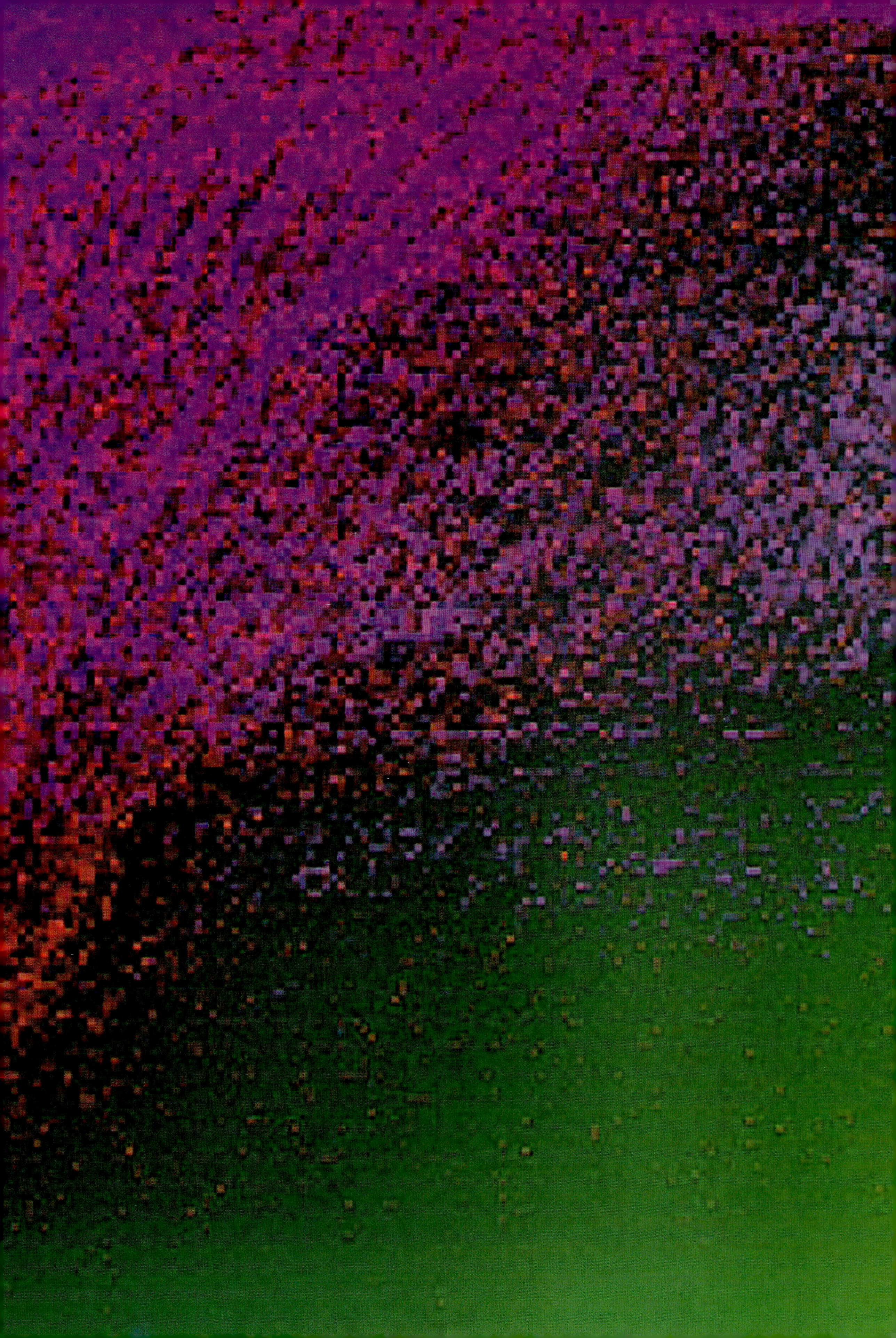

Essays

What's in an Image, Marisa Olson

Artist, Detective, Accomplice, Lucas Wrench

Citizen Selfie, David A. Banks

Photography in the Age of Communicative Capitalism, Ben Burbridge

Wired! Expanding!, Dan Bustillo

Watching Murder Online, Sarah Tuck

Keeping Up with the Cartesians: On the Culture of the Selfie with Continual Reference to Kim Kardashian, Daniel Rubinstein

ESSAY: WHAT'S IN AN IMAGE, MARISA OLSON

In the fall of 2016, two American pop cultural icons became unwitting touchstones in the discourse surrounding the contemporary relevance of data. Naturally, I'm speaking of Kim Kardashian and Donald Trump, both reality-TV celebrities and entrepreneurs. Kardashian was the victim of a horrific gunpoint robbery in her Paris hotel room, only to be brutally victim-blamed in the media for her constant sharing of selfies containing metadata that might lead criminals to her whereabouts. Trump arguably stole the US presidential election by not only bucking the odds—as they had been laid out in predictive national-poll results leading up to Election Day—but also by carrying out essentially civilian psy-ops through contracts with big data firms like Palantir and Cambridge Analytica, whose official tagline is "Uses data to change audience behavior," and who were also behind the recent buyer's remorse–laden Brexit vote. While Kardashian's photosharing practices—a staple of her brand—came under heavy scrutiny, Trump's big-data battle was armed by info. The firms gleaned from millions of social-media users' online posts, from photos to text posts to likes.

In fact, today we are seeing a simultaneous and paradoxical blurring of the boundaries between photographs and their associated (formerly meta-)data, and between a media user/consumer's clinging to a right to privacy versus a tendency to rampantly overshare. This blurring—whether in the name of branding, neoliberal critique, perceived activism, social/familial bonding, or a desire to be validated, i.e., "seen" (given the Pew Trust's designation of the Millennial generation as that of "Look at Me")—somehow persists in aligning recognition with the scopic apparatus.

Make no mistake: The fact that I describe these simultaneous developments (one social, one formal/technological) briefly and in the same breath should not discount the fact that they are both epic in their ramifications and wholly different, even if their coincidence is worth exploring. After all, as artist and writer Trevor Paglen said in a "1,000 Words" feature in *Artforum*, the intervention of AI and algorithms into photography over the last decade has displaced the human eye in the act of seeing, and has become, in his estimation, "more significant than the invention of photography" itself.[1]

1 Trevor Paglen, "1,000 Words," *Artforum*, March 2009.

When I think of a photograph today, I think of the actual image floating askew, like some intergalactic curtain, aimless over the liminal threshold between public and private. A steganographic decoy, the site of cathexisquadata for the photographer's or poster's (who's who again?) attendant fears and fantasies, mirror images of twin drives etched into the photo like a watermark in invisible ink.

We began to hear horror stories about this right after 9/11. Terrorists swapping JPEGs that were literal fronts for the cryptic messages buried inside the files. Meanwhile, the "if you see something, say something" administration was erecting a theater of security in which airport lines, public transportation, teenage bedrooms, online profiles, and selfie phones were all players in the newfangled Globe Theatre. Soon millennials and Gen Z social-media users were born, many after 9/11 or too young to remember a time before such visibly increased state surveillance in the name of "homeland security," for whom a "photo" was almost exclusively a digital object. This is the era in which reality-TV shows like *Big Brother* are no longer shocking outliers, but as my colleague Gene McHugh once said succinctly of post-internet art, the medium has shifted from novelty to everyday banality.

I would argue that we're in an era of photography marked by data ennui. Consider a morning in the life of my own media consumption: Yesterday I checked my email only to find a shockingly prescient promotional message with the subject line, "Is being online fun anymore?" Then I read an article about Roomba vacuum cleaners autonomously collecting data about their owners' home layouts and lifestyle. After this, I came across a well-received tweet by someone proposing that blood-alcohol levels and their GPS coordinates be collected on people's social-media posts. Finally, I read Paglen's article, which points out the politically repressive implications of machines attempting to "recognize" photographic subjects (their race, gender, and age, for instance) according to normative criteria. Somewhere in these scattered scenes, the concept of consent melts away in the hazy playtime of convenience and fooling around online.

Earlier this year, a study out of the Max Planck Institute quantified this data ennui in regard to the privacy risks that users take in posting photos, which are often at odds with their own stated privacy preferences or policies.[2] They were able to identify sixty-eight categories of risk (far more than I think many of us typically realize—part of the point) in the form of information that machines are able to glean in photos. This includes details like recognizable geographic features in the background, a wedding ring suggesting relationship status, objects in the image that might indicate medical history, a child's hand holding an object that might indicate parental status, and many more elements to which people might not give a second thought. The study's authors were advocating for what

2 Tribhuvanesh Orekondy, Bernt Schiele, and Mario Fritz, "Towards a Visual Privacy Advisor: Understanding and Predicting Privacy Risks in Images," https://arXiv: 1703.10660 (August 7, 2017).

they called a "Visual Privacy Advisor," distinct from general, categoric text descriptors that could algorithmically recognize and warn users that images posed privacy risks. The machines could see better than humans or could be trained to care more.

Negotiating participation in image culture in an era of constant state surveillance and self-broadcasting is not easy. For the last fifteen years, there's been increasing pressure to participate in both arenas, to some extent. One is compelled to submit to surveillance "for the greater good," if not to participate in various layers of sousveillance—*sous* being the French counterpart to *sur*, a looking from below rather than above. Citizens' countersurveillance has thus only amped up in the six decades since the phrase "the whole world is watching" has been in circulation, following the rapid proliferation of cameras under the doctrine of media convergence.

It's not just the word *photo* that is up for redefinition today. There is a casual slippage between many of the terms we previously used to ground ourselves—in the art world, the sphere of computing, and in digital culture writ large. For instance, I've written previously about how one of the primary symptoms of network culture, in the post-internet era, is a slippage between the definition of transparency-as-visible in surveillance contexts to transparency-as-invisible in computing parlance.[3] We also tend to conflate participatory art and participatory media, assuming equal levels of informed consent on the part of participants.

And that is the ultimate question raised above: to what extent are people informed participants in the sphere of photography today, and subsequently, in the world of image-embedded data? The participation question might be the easier half to address: there is a tug of war between a desire to expose and a desire to be protected. But to be informed feels nigh on impossible in the undertow of the theoretical singularity invoked by rapidly advanced encryption, AI, and surveillance technologies and their deployment.

Regardless of the everydayness or banality of the photos at stake (or perhaps because of this uncanny-ness), the more one thinks about it, the more one feels like the subject of a Hollywood virtual-reality production. The piece of paper, the screen, the pixel, the contact lens, or the neural implant stands in for the representation that is perceived to be not-there/ previously-there/ there-not-there—whether it is ultra-high-resolution or the kind of "lossy-copy" Hito Steryl has called the "poor image" (a digital artifact accelerating toward a thing of the past; an accidental fallacy). No matter how generous one is in theorizing the materiality of conceptual or digital or performative or time-based or otherwise "ephemeral" media, we have to remember that it is not only image quality that distinguishes digital from analog; it is *data*, the code itself.

3 Marisa Olson, "On the Internet, No One Knows You're a Doghouse," *Post-Internet Cities*, July 31, 2017, http://www.e-flux.com/architecture/post-internet-cities/140712/on-the-internet-no-one-knows-you-re-a-doghouse/.

The digital is always already a medium of doubles, if not duplicity—not necessarily because it is simple to forge, as we easily assume when we swap the term "Photoshop" for "digital," or forget how long predigital cinema carried out special effects—but because alphanumeric code is one language now capable of telling a story altogether different or adjacent to the images that overlay it.

Those of us interested in photography and new media have spent much of the last fifteen years theorizing and aestheticizing digital archives, but we would be remiss not to recognize that *individual photos are now archives*. That is, not just indices of their immediate metonymic namesake (the light that winked them into being, or the space/time event to which the photo bears an immediate, proximate, and consummate relationship) but also carriers (carrions) of whole libraries of information. Consider this in context of a society with ubiquitous image-making devices, where taking and sharing images is de rigueur. People are walking around with databases of databases of databases, ready to post them to public databases that will be hosted on other civic or corporate databases, for analysis by other unforeseen data firms, with unknown aims. The disparity of access to public and private information, the corporate colonization of the net that seeks to monopolize the space, and the looming legislative threats to net neutrality that hover over the landscape of cloud computing only compound this vista. Suddenly the once-novel concept of "database aesthetics" sounds not only trite but Pollyanna.

Artists and other supporters of the photographic arts (by which I mean good old-fashioned point-and-shoot, then print-on-paper photography) who are, at this point, still reading might feel that their practice has been sidestepped in this essay. On the contrary: One of the reasons I so related to the email that asked, "Is being online fun anymore?" is that I once made internet art, cofounded a "pro-surfer" net art community, and curated new-media art at a time when the internet felt like a more utopian, adventurous, less litigious, more neutral place in which the art we were all making had neither become co-opted by corporate channels nor was up for comparison (by us or anyone else) with social media. Likewise, I do not mean to cast "fine art" photography as a fledgling outlier kicked to the curb by the evil internet. In fact, I would invoke the French dramatist Antonin Artaud in arguing that in this era of questionable "truthiness" and threatened arts funding, the nation is in greater need than ever of the arts, if not art therapy.

Few people realize that it was Artaud who coined the term "virtual reality" in 1933, when articulating the concept of the theater and its double in his initial manifesto on the Theatre of Cruelty. Artaud wanted artists to show everyday viewers what was at stake; to create a moment in the middle of all the other moments of buzzing from here to there, one that virtually re-creates or doubles the everyday, but allows us to bifurcate and peel off our consciousness from the imitation—not unlike a nightmare that allows us to wake up from a worst-case scenario and be relieved it didn't happen, a sort of reverse wish-fulfillment.

I am not one of those who believe that civilization has to change in order for theater to change; but I do believe that theater, utilized in the highest and most difficult sense possible, has the power to influence the aspect and formation of things.

That is why I am proposing a theater of cruelty ... Not the cruelty we can exercise upon each other by hacking at each other's bodies, carving up our personal anatomies, or, like Assyrian emperors, sending parcels of human ears, noses, or neatly severed nostrils through the mail; but the much more terrible and necessary cruelty which things can exercise against us. We are not free. And the sky can still fall on our heads. And theater has been created to teach us that first of all ... But it should not be forgotten that if a theatrical gesture is violent, it is also disinterested; and that theater teaches precisely the uselessness of the action which, once accomplished, is never to be done again.[4]

"Never to be done again" would be nice, but this, too, may be Pollyanna and reaching for the stars. Nonetheless, I like Artaud's idea of deploying the creative work to split use from uselessness and violence from healing.

4 Antonin Artaud, *The Theater and Its Double*, trans. Mary C. Richard (New York: Grove Press, 1994), pp. 78–80.

Marisa Olson is an artist, writer, and curator. Her work has been shown at the Venice Biennale; Tate Modern, London, and Tate Liverpool, UK; Whitney Museum, New Museum, and PERFORMA Biennial, New York; Sundance Film Festival, Park City, Utah; and the Nam June Paik Art Center, Yongin, South Korea, among others, and in solo shows at the Bard CSS/Hessel Museum, Annandale-on-Hudson, New York; Samek Museum, Lewisburg, Pennsylvania; PS122, New York; and Vox Populi, Philadephia. She's written for Artforum, e-flux, Aperture, Flash Art, *the* Guardian, Wired, *and numerous books in multiple languages. She is the former editor and curator of Rhizome and associate director and editor at SF Camerawork. She has curated projects at the New Museum, Guggenheim Museum, White Columns, and Artists Space, New York; and SFMOMA, San Francisco. She was artist in residence at Eyebeam, master artist in residence at the Atlantic Center for the Arts, and has been a visiting artist at Yale, Brown, Virginia Commonwealth University, School of the Art Institute of Chicago, Oberlin College, and elsewhere, in addition to serving on the faculty at Rhode Island School of Design and New York University.*

ESSAY: ARTIST, DETECTIVE, ACCOMPLICE, LUCAS WRENCH

Across the US, art spaces have found themselves under increasing criticism over their role in the gentrification of surrounding neighborhoods. However, few places have reached the level of intensity as Los Angeles's Boyle Heights neighborhood. There, the friction between art, security, and housing has seen residents locked in a stand-off with contemporary art galleries and nonprofits over their role in the gentrification of this mostly working-class, Mexican American neighborhood. As art spaces across the political spectrum have come under criticism—from the conventionally blue-chip Maccarone to the self-proclaimed queer and POC-focused nonprofit PSSST—one of the central issues has become to what extent the infrastructural changes caused by art institutions overshadow even the most progressive visions of art programming. In other words, the real estate a gallery inhabits, the security presence it brings along, and the cultural capital it wields all impact the surrounding community in ways that the institutions themselves have difficulty accounting for.

In light of the pressure that anti-gentrification activist groups in Los Angeles, such as Defend Boyle Heights and the Boyle Heights Alliance Against Artwashing and Displacement (BHAAAD), waged against institutions to account for their presence (at times with threats of violence), artists and curators are finding that even after decades of institutional critique, they have few good models to draw from, other than to simply close up shop, as PSSST chose to do. Bearing in mind these questions of art and gentrification—or, more specifically, of how artists participate in the security state, and how their presence impacts their surrounding communities—it is valuable to look at a moment around 150 years ago, when a very different group of artists and intellectuals were transitioning from a position of intense attention and involvement within security practices to the more modern stance of artistic autonomy and critical distance from said practices. In examining the circumstances of this shift, I hope to call attention to what amounts to an absence of discourse around creative infrastructure and policing, and find ways to reintroduce this debate, particularly in the context of creative placemaking and the ongoing conflict between precariously housed communities and art institutions.

Walter Benjamin's unfinished essay, "Charles Baudelaire: A Lyric Poet in an Era of High Capitalism," is a twentieth-century analysis of nineteenth-century France, as Paris transitioned from medieval city to modern capitalist metropolis, largely through the top-down renovation of the cityscape known as the Haussmannization of Paris.[1] Like contemporary gentrification, the process resulted in the displacement of tens of thousands of mostly working-class Parisians to the outskirts of the city, and radically altered the perception of public safety and security. Of primary interest is Benjamin's exploration of the creative practitioners involved in this transformation—the writers of the so-called *physiologies*; the detective; and later, the flâneur—and what the shift in their ideologies reveals about how artists engage with the broader forces of state security.

The narrative begins in Paris in the first half of the nineteenth century, following the Industrial and French revolutions. The promise of new occupations, particularly in textiles, metalworking, and the sex industry, funneled rural farmers and sharecroppers from the countryside into Paris's still-medieval city center, aided by the latest in public transport technology—most notably the steam engine. Accordingly, the increasingly overcrowded Parisians were experiencing a new kind of social friction, specifically an anxiety of physical proximity without conversation. Benjamin quotes sociologist George Simmel: "Before the development of buses, railroads, and trams in the nineteenth century, people had never been in a position of having to look at one another for long minutes or even hours without speaking to one another."[2] This was particularly unsettling for the Parisian bourgeoisie, whom insular manor life had left ill prepared to navigate the newly dynamic cityscape. One such aristocrat, Edmond Goncourt, lamented, "My Paris, the Paris where I was born ... is passing away.... The interior is going to die. Life threatens to become public."[3]

An initial response to this aristocratic class anxiety was to manage it through intellectual means, particularly through physiologies, paperback fictions characterized by Walter Benjamin as a "basically petty-bourgeois genre."[4] Within the stories, readers were presented with characters that corresponded to the various types one might encounter in the city—a sort of nineteenth-century starter-pack meme—articulating superficial patterns and signifiers to create the illusion of a consistent set of personalities and character-types.

"Quiet enjoyment is almost exhausting for a workingman," reads one physiology.[5] "The smoke from the tall factory chimney, the booming blows on the anvil, make him tremble with joy," reads another.[6] Far from any kind of serious sociological analysis, the physiologies were a means of asserting the centrality of bourgeois existence, reducing the city's cohabitants to nonthreatening, easily identifiable casts of characters. Benjamin again notes,

1 Walter Benjamin, "Paris: Capital of the Nineteenth Century," in *Charles Baudelaire: A Lyric Poet in the Era of High Capitalism* (London and New York: Verso, 1997), p. 86.
2 Ibid., p. 38.
3 T. J. Clark, *The Painting of Modern Life: Paris in the Art of Manet and His Followers* (Princeton, NJ: Princeton University Press, 1999), p. 34.
4 Benjamin, "The Paris of the Second Empire in Baudelaire," in *Charles Baudelaire,* p. 52.
5 Ibid., p. 38.
6 Ibid.

"An entrepreneur who read this description may have gone to bed more relaxed than was his wont."[7]

But this "uneasiness of a special sort," as Benjamin euphemistically terms it, was too readily revived for these physiologies to have much longevity. The short works were too rigid in their descriptions, and too easily contradicted by lived experience. The next generation of writers sought a more long-term approach, emphasizing procedure and empiricism as the tools for a more truthful form of social observation, pulling from the rhetorical strategies of the by then mostly discredited physiognomists. Honoré de Balzac, characterized by Benjamin as "more than anyone else ... in his element," writes that "accuracy of detail, to be properly appreciated, demands the critical attention of an expert flâneur," presumably to know that a "smug expression about the mouth" could indicate either a "merchant who's just done a good stroke of business, or a bachelor emerging from a boudoir." It was both a good excuse for the laymen's inability to deduce their neighbors' inner workings, and a direct endorsement of the intellectual or expert observer's ability to render "the masses" intelligible.

During the physiologies' heyday, Charles Baudelaire was at work translating Edgar Allan Poe's detective novels, a new genre of the era characterized by Benjamin as concerned with "the obliteration of the individual's traces in the big city crowd."[8] Through Poe's detective story, the form of close social observation popularized by the physiologies explicitly merges with criminology and law enforcement. For example, in "The Mystery of Marie Roget," Poe's follow-up to "The Murders in the Rue Morgue," detective Auguste Dupin deploys a mixture of scientific analysis—"the specific gravity of the human body, in its natural condition, is about equal to the bulk of fresh water which it displaces"—with notably less objective commentary —"He is a busy-body, with much of romance and little of wit. Any one so constituted will readily so conduct himself, upon occasion of real excitement, as to render himself liable to suspicion..."[9] The empiricism and procedure deployed by the *physiologistes* to classify and categorize their social spheres was now being deployed at the service of solving actual (if fictional) crimes.

From the twenty-first-century perspective of "if you see something, say something," the detective novel represents a benchmark in the normalization of social observation as a vehicle for "public safety." In the context of the bourgeoisie's anxiety around shifting city demographics, detective Dupin offered reassurance as to the intellectual's supremacy among the crowd. By the mid-nineteenth century, however, the calmative capacities of these literary forms were being called into question. The economic boom of the early century had ended in a financial crisis, high unemployment, overstretched city services, and a potato famine. Faced with an unresponsive

7 Ibid.
8 Ibid., p. 43.
9 Edgar Allan Poe, "The Mystery of Marie Roget," in *The Ladies Companion* (New York: William W. Snowden, 1842), p. 20.

and obstructionist government, in 1848 middle-class reformers—inspired by new Marxist ideology, including the right to work and "property as theft"—revolted, barricading themselves within the narrow city streets in a series of bloody skirmishes against the Parisian municipal guard known as the February Revolution, or the 1848 Revolution. While conservative backlash was swift, the barricades left a lasting impression: Paris's physical infrastructure was vulnerable. If the aristocracy was to retain power, it would need a city that was conducive to the centralized control its culture and politics demanded.

Haussmann's urbanization project followed this revolt. According to Benjamin,

> *The true goal of Haussmann's projects was to secure the city against civil war. He wanted to make the erection of barricades in Paris impossible for all time ... Widening the streets is designed to make the erection of barricades impossible, and new streets are to furnish the shortest route between the barracks and the workers' districts.*[10]

Independent of actual strategic gains for the Empire's defenses, Haussmannization, like post-9/11 airport security practices, succeeded in aligning the state behind a particular vision of public-safety Pre-Haussmannian *physiologistes*, and detectives gained public lighting, nightly police presence, and the displacement of tens of thousands of lower income citizens to the outskirts of the city.

Baudelaire's flâneur, wanderer among crowds, "a prince enjoying his incognito wherever he goes," was a witness to the urbanization process, and, as such, the first of these bourgeois figures to benefit from the new expansion of the security state.[11] Benjamin distinguishes the flâneur as an unwilling, or idle detective, or as a detective turned prince, possessing the faculties of the detective but lacking in objective. In 1863, over a decade into Haussmann's renovations, Baudelaire writes, "For the perfect flâneur, the passionate spectator, it is an immense joy to set up house in the heart of the multitude ... in the midst of the fugitive and the infinite."[12] The fugitive is still present, but as a supporting character rather than a person of interest—occupying an emotional extreme of what the city can offer. The crowd shifts from "the refuge of a criminal" to "that of love which eludes a poet."[13]

The initial impulse behind this essay was to examine the incognito observations of the flâneur as an origin point of social surveillance, an early moment when a sort of "see something, say something" culture was normalized and popularized. But Benjamin's analysis of nineteenth-century Paris describes a society where fear and suspicion grew as naturally as the population, occupying the creative energies of some of the most celebrated thinkers of the era. In the context of the *physiologistes* and Poe's detective, Baudelaire's flâneur is less a forefather of suspicion than of nonchalance. Rather than further catalyze suspicion, Haussmann's interventions allowed

10 Benjamin, "Paris: Capital of the Nineteenth Century," p. 87.

11 Charles Baudelaire, *The Painter of Modern Life* (London: Phaidon Press, 1964), p. 9.

12 Ibid.

13 Benjamin, "The Paris of the Second Empire in Baudelaire," p. 43.

a certain Parisian social class to finally relax on the train, making room for new creative practitioners who, following in the flâneurs' footsteps, could take their mobility in the city for granted. A few years later, the Impressionists' seemingly benign practice of plein-air painting can be read as a product of police intervention, securing the parks on behalf of the artists.

Within the current, ongoing controversy over art and gentrification in Los Angeles, the paranoid, security-centric musings of the *physiologiste* would come off as deeply regressive. Indeed, a common refrain by artists is that they are on the same side as the activists—politically left, anti-establishment, opposed to police intervention, in support of affordable housing. However, this perceived autonomy is part of the problem. Whether you're a commercial, blue-chip gallery or a nonprofit that aspires to correct structural art-world inequality, both derive autonomy from a system that privileges creative and geographic freedom over the long-term security of their less affluent neighbors. Art may be endlessly expansive and full of exciting possibilities for critique and resistance, but in order to access those possibilities we need to acknowledge the infrastructure that makes this critique possible, and begin to find ways to undo it.

Lucas Wrench is an artist and events curator. From 2014 to 2017, Wrench served as associate curator and operations manager of Machine Project, a nonprofit art space in Los Angeles, curating their weekly events program; running the unofficial, subterranean performance incubator Mystery Theater Productions Presents!; and organizing institutional collaborations, including Off Road Expo *with High Desert Test Sites, and* Mystery Theater Sports Bar *with* Cabinet. *Outside of Machine Project, Wrench leads performances, role-plays, discussions, and workshops around issues of digital rights and the politics of visibility under ambient surveillance. Wrench's event programming has been regularly featured in* Art in America*'s "The Agenda,"* Hyperallergic*'s "ArtRx," and the* LA Weekly, *and his work has been presented by ForYourArt, Los Angeles; the Museum of Contemporary Art Denver; and the Museum of Contemporary Art on the Moon, among others. Wrench currently works as the Kress Interpretive Fellow at the Philbrook Museum of Art in Tulsa, Oklahoma. He holds a BA from Pomona College.*

ESSAY: CITIZEN SELFIE, DAVID A. BANKS

At a crowded rope line a candidate leans in, inserting arms into the crowd like a child picking berries from a bush. Handshakes follow thank-yous and then a smartphone appears. The candidate grabs the phone—a deeply intimate act given all the secrets and germs we collect on our devices—and takes a selfie with a supporter. In that moment there's a connection that transcends bumper stickers or even a knock at the door. Now there is a one-of-a-kind but infinitely reproducible image of a candidate and a supporter, begging to be shared. Selfies with presidential candidates are American electoral politics in a microcosm: at once intensely personal and inconceivably vast, a personalized memento manufactured at the speed of a news cycle.

Considering the popular perception of selfies, it is a wonder that politicians even take them. Taking a selfie and running for public office often receive the same criticisms: they are both irredeemably contrived and inauthentic acts of vanity. Given the record-low approval ratings of most public institutions, it seems equally unlikely that the average citizen would seek out a photo with a political candidate. What is there to gain for either the supporter or the candidate to be seen with each other?

The answer lies in peoples' ongoing struggles with their visibility to others. Privacy and publicity are often confronted in dangerously extreme terms. The word *publicity* conjures images of corporate public relations and celebrity gossip. Privacy is, for moments at a time, shared with our closest companions, or our own thoughts. Most of human life, however, is spent between these extremes, and taking photos with politicians highlights the complicated nature of visibility. For every potential audience, both real and imagined, there is a self to be shared. This is neither deception nor vanity. Privacy, publicity, audiences, and the self are deeply intertwined; one exists only in relation to one or the other. The self, sociologists Jaber F. Gubrium and James Holstein have argued, is not so much a static identity as a story—a story made out of our past experiences, future hopes, and immediate surroundings. We change it and abbreviate it depending on context and audience, but it is in the telling that we find anything approaching a "true" self.

That self is not a given; it is made and learned like language. Or, as the prominent nineteenth-century sociologist George Herbert Mead put it, "The self is something which has a development; it is not initially there, at birth, but arises in the process of social experience and activity."[1] Just as with languages, some of us are fluent in multiple means of communication while others struggle to make a connection with a single person. When we take a photo with a political candidate—or of our food, a scenic background carefully included—we are not only stating an allegiance but also saying something about who we are. Theresa M. Senft and Nancy K. Baym, in their introduction to a special issue on selfies of the *International Journal of Communication*, note that: "First and foremost, a selfie is a photographic object that initiates the transmission of human feeling in the form of a relationship."[2] That relationship might be intimate—a photograph meant for a single recipient—or very public, as when politicians post photos on their own accounts to share with their supporters.

Selfies, then, are aptly named because just about every part of the photo contributes to the story of the self. Senft and Baym go on to say that "selfies function both as a practice of everyday life and as the object of politicizing discourses about how people ought to represent, document, and share their behaviors." It is this process of constructing one's identity that is crucial to understanding why selfies with political candidates happen at all. Rather than two photographic subjects, there is a single political object: a candidate-supporter dyad that is mutually beneficial to its constituent characters. It must be mutually beneficial or candidates would not spend precious time pausing to take them, and supporters would not clamor to ask for them.

Donald Trump's authoritarian populism and Hillary Clinton's historical status as the first woman to become general-election candidate of a major political party served as powerful rhetorical tools, but they both run counter to something equally important: the idea that the candidates are likable and approachable people. Narendra Modi, the prime minister of India, had a similar problem in his 2014 election. His popularity was monumental and his campaign wanted potential voters to feel as though they could peer behind the curtain. Communications scholar Anirban K. Baishya observed that the tactical deployment of selfies helped Modi convey "the sense of a more believable person rather than an inaccessible icon."[3] Selfies let politicians have it both ways: icon-celebrity status and accessible, expressive authenticity.

And yet, media accounts filled with selfies as exercises in vanity pose a danger to some candidates' likeability. Men, especially Trump, can bask and even revel in their vainglorious posturing, but everyone else has to be a modest, almost begrudging, selfie taker. The Clinton campaign went out of its way to not only clear time for the candidate to take photos with her supporters, but to use the selfie as a starting point for a flurry of headlines about her relationship with supporters and close confidants. In the month of February 2016, *Esquire*, *People*, *Time*, the BBC, and the *Hill* all ran stories

1 George Herbert Mead, *Mind, Self, and Society: From the Standpoint of a Social Behaviorist*, ed. Charles W. Morris (Chicago: University of Chicago Press, 1934), p. 135.

2 Theresa M. Senft and Nancy K. Baym, "What Does the Selfie Say? Investigating a Global Phenomenon," *International Journal of Communication* 9 (2015): pp. 19, 1589.

3 Anirban K. Baishya, "#NaMo: The Political Work of the Selfie in the 2014 Indian General Elections," *International Journal of Communication* 9 (2015): pp. 15, 1589.

about Clinton's relationship to the selfie, including the people she took them with, how she learned to master the form, and her concerns that the selfie was replacing other forms of interaction at the rope line. In her interview with *Esquire*, Clinton went so far as to bemoan the "tyranny of the selfie" and its supposed consequence of supplanting conversation.

The supporter who takes a selfie is at once a micro-surrogate for the candidate and the potential recipient of an influx of likes and other popularity metrics. Your selfie with Bernie Sanders could stand as a prominent but passive form of protest against the Democratic primary election. Every time you commented on a political story there you were, standing with giddy excitement next to the Vermont senator. More generally though, a photo with nearly any presidential candidate could distinguish you as engaged in mainstream politics: you were someone who participated in the political process.

While the supporter may draw some social capital, the candidate gains an air of authenticity. A selfie with a candidate reveals that, in spite of all the professional messaging and the relatively small chance that a candidate will deliver on their promise, elections are still about deeply held sentiments. They are about seeing one's future nestled in the warm words of a soaring speech or in the hot anger that may further propel our security state.

Through what sociologist Nathan Jurgenson has called our "documentary vision," we now see the world as a series of potential social-media posts.[4] In this way, selfies with politicians also demonstrate the complicated interactions between publicity and privacy: intentionally public displays of allegiance have a way of illuminating deeper, more private aspects of our selves. When we go to a rally we are not only looking to engage in politics in that moment but we are also in search of a photo, video, or some other media artifact that will communicate to others that we were there.

Humans have always done something like this, looking for stories and anecdotes to tell our friends at the water cooler or bar, but social media asks that we make specific decisions in the moment about what to capture. A popular interpretation of this sort of behavior is that our documentary practices are self-centered and take us out of the moment and into a device, but even this short discussion about the self makes such a claim seem shortsighted. If the self is a story we tell others, then even as we are thinking about ourselves we are thinking of others—not only of their judgments but also of our relationships with them. Moments are *made* as much as they are experienced and our documentary vision provides a wide palette to play with. For a politician, this is the most precious prize of all: to carve out some space on that palette and be part of an intimate story about our relationship with others.

From campaign lapel buttons to bumper stickers, political candidates have always sought out ways to

4 Nathan Jurgenson, "The Faux-Vintage Photo: Full Essay (Parts I, II and III)," *Cyborgology* (May 14, 2011), http://thesocietypages.org/cyborgology/2011/05/14/the-faux-vintage-photo-full-essay-parts-i-ii-and-iii/.

incorporate their brand into our presentations of self. The selfie provides an opportunity to do so even more directly: it allows us to inject a political message into our stories. Posing with power makes us surrogates and deliverers of authenticity. Unlike a lapel button, however, a single digital photo has the ability to travel great distances almost instantaneously. The political selfie requires our participation and opens the door for satire, resistance, and a host of new political messages—which will either dovetail with or run against the political choices on offer. It is in this affordance that the selfie demonstrates its greatest liberatory potentials and its gravest dangers.

David A. Banks is an interdisciplinary researcher, a cochair of the Theorizing the Web conference, an editor of the Society Pages' technology and society blog Cyborgology, *and editor-at-large of* Real Life *magazine.*

ESSAY: PHOTOGRAPHY IN THE AGE OF COMMUNICATIVE CAPITALISM, BEN BURBRIDGE

Self-Fashioning

The culture of online photographic showing/sharing answers the socioeconomic imperatives of neoliberalism in at least two ways. For sociologists Luc Boltanski and Eve Chiapello, networked capitalism is a response to the "artistic critique" leveled against mid-twentieth-century Fordism.[1] This demanded greater autonomy, authentic experience, freedom from the monotony of mass-produced consumer culture and the drudgery of nine-to-five working. Capitalism responded by "liberating" the workforce; fragmenting cultural and commodity production to meet the minutiae of personal preference; creating a flexi-time world where success is gauged not through movement up definable hierarchies but by a capacity to move between projects and across global networks. *So this is what it feels like to be free?*

The shift has had a fundamental impact on subjectivity, on the processes through which we understand who we are. As citizens of what Boltanski and Chiapello call the "projective city"—a social space "founded on the mediating activity employed in the creation of networks"—we are unbound by traditional structures of family, church, and profession.[2] So we have to construct our selves through the micro-identities we consume. Work today is based on the relationships we develop and the connections we forge: on the extensiveness and effectiveness of our networks. As the distinction between labor and leisure becomes unclear, the identities we fashion play an integral role in what would once have been called our professional lives.

Across the twentieth century, photography, in the guise of fashion shoots and advertising, provided templates for self-presentation. As "prosumers," we take on much of that work ourselves, reproducing lifestyle as image. Lives are broadcast to friends, friends-of-friends, colleagues, employers, potential employers. And to anyone else who's looking. *Check out my outfit, my baby, my book; the party I'm at; the protest I've joined; the private viewing I'm attending.* "I" has become the commodity we spend most of our lives producing. In real time. Around the clock. We fashion a self that we peddle to others in

1 Luc Boltanski and Eve Chiapello, *The New Spirit of Capitalism* (London and New York: Verso, 2005), pp. 103–67.

2 Ibid.

search of the next job, the next contact, the next "like." *I do exist. This is really happening. See?*

Digital Labor

Advertisements for photography used to tell us that good parents and good friends preserved precious memories to look back on, nostalgically, from a future yet to happen. Remember those Kodak moments? Today we are told to show others how much we care across social-media platforms. When photography answered the demands of the Fordist economy, profits were generated through sales: of cameras, film, developing services. Now its main economic value lies in rendering lives visible to multinational corporations.

Most of us are aware of, if not particularly concerned about, the economic machinations that power this brave new world. Every time a photograph is uploaded, tagged, shared, viewed, liked, geotagged, and commented on, our preferences, relationships, and social networks become clearer. Visibility in this context refers less to what is traditionally thought of as the content of a photograph, and more to the web of data we create through the interactions that our photographic sharing allows. When algorithms know what we do, what we like, who we like to do it with, they get better at knowing what to sell us.

Like personal conversations, sharing photographs was once an activity outside the reach of the market. Today it represents an important part of our unwaged digital work-lives: what media theorist Trebor Scholz describes as "the activation of behavior on the social web as monetized labor."[3] Photography is a vital component in the (un)virtuous cycle at the heart of what the political theorist Jodi Dean has termed "communicative capitalism": a regime in which "[r]hetorics of access, participation and democracy work ideologically to secure the technological infrastructure of neoliberalism, an invidious and predatory politico-economic project that concentrates assets and power in the hands of the very, very rich."[4]

We enact our lives as though they are a public image-stream—a desperate response to a system that has cast us adrift. By surveying our efforts to achieve selfhood, corporations sell our preferences to advertisers, who sell them back to us in the form of commodities, through which the process of self-fashioning is enacted again. And again. And again. And again.

Art/Work

The effects of this exhibitionism can be felt within the field of photography-as-art, as it jostles with mass culture to maintain some sense of distinction. The work of Nan Goldin was once discussed in terms of a personal compulsion to record, along with the voyeurism it potentially sanctioned. Photographs documented the world and were looked at by others. Today, writers frame her work in terms of the public sharing of a private life—

3 Trebor Scholz, "Introduction: Why Does Digital Labor Matter Now?" in *Digital Labor: The Internet as Playground and Factory* (New York and London: Routledge, 2013), p. 2.

4 Jodi Dean, *Democracy and Other Neoliberal Fantasies: Communicative Capitalism and Left Politics* (Durham, NC, and London: Duke University Press, 2009), p. 23.

a matter of showing and being seen. For curator Martina Weinhart, Goldin's imagery marks a "step on the path towards post-privacy."[5] Her public display of highly personal photographs willfully transgressed social norms: part of the countercultural assault on suburban normalcy so effectively absorbed as justification for the freedoms of precarious workings and kaleidoscopic consumer choice that we enjoy today. Against the backdrop of our relentless photo sharing, along with the general corrosion of the distinction between public and private, what once appeared to flaunt good taste no longer looks so different from what everyone else is doing.[6]

As for diaristic art photography after Goldin? The work of Ryan McGinley soon gave up the claim to authenticity: the artist and his friends went on road trips funded by art buyers, stripping naked and taking drugs in order to be photographed. "Reality" entertainment for the high-end cultural market? The ugly phenomenon of Terry Richardson belongs here, too—in a space where the bohemian idealism of Goldin and her friends is reduced to a grotesque celebrity pantomime. Richardson poses, dick in one hand, camera in the other; celebrities vomit, take off their clothes; models feel compelled to do what they're told.[7] The need-to-be-seen as ironic metanarrative. Performance and reality blur. *There is no choice. And certainly no outside*. Capitalist realism finds the "artist" it deserves?[8]

Appropriation 2.0

Exhibitionist image culture has provided rich pickings for appropriation art. Here, says photo historian Geoffrey Batchen, is a "surrealist ethnography of global photography today."[9] But what does it mean when rich middle-aged men take to trawling the net to show gallery-going elites what the photo-sharing classes are up to? When Joachim Schmid makes a whole book of other people's cleavage shots, a whole book of other people's selfies? When Martin Parr puts those books in his great big "book of books," causing prices to soar? When Richard Prince sells blow-ups of micro-celebrities' Instagram shots to his gallerist's rich clients? Views of appropriation art as an affront to private property have always relied on a disavowal of art as an activity embedded in, and dependent on, capitalist markets. But it was easier to turn the other way when imagery was being taken from cigarette companies, not young women working hard to maintain their own precarious visibility.[10]

5 Martina Weinhart, "Truth or Dare—Intimate Images on the Path to Postprivacy," in *Privacy*, ed. Martina Weinhart and Max Hollein, (Frankfurt: Schirn Kunsthalle, 2012), p. 52.

6 I develop this point in an earlier essay: Ben Burbridge, "Paradise Lost: Exhibitionism and the Work of Nan Goldin," *Either/And*, 2013, http://eitherand.org/exhibitionism/paradise-lost-exhibitionism-and-work-nan-goldin/.

7 Jamie Peck, "Take It from Someone He Abused: Terry Richardson Is a Predator with a Camera," *Guardian*, June 17, 2014, https://www.theguardian.com/commentisfree/2014/jun/17terry-richardson-new-york-magazine-model.

8 On "capitalist realism" see Mark Fisher, *Capitalist Realism: Is There No Alternative?* (Winchester, UK, and Washington, DC: Zero Books, 2009).

9 Geoffrey Batchen, "Observing by Watching: Joachim Schmid and the Art of Exchange," *Aperture* no. 210 (Spring 2013), p. 47.

Others have chosen to enter the fray: Amalia Ulman spoofs online female stereotypes; Arvida Byström and Molly Soda transgress the idealized norms enforced by Instagram's Community Guidelines. The paradoxical bind of their participatory performance lies in the remove that is eventually required if it is to undertake its critical work in terms recognizable to art discourse. The trolling masses and policing of obscenity regulations are replaced by text panels and folio essays as appropriate modes of interpretation and response. The shift is economic, as well as discursive, of course—and here an interesting reversal occurs. Now it's Instagram that gains ubiquity through its presence in unfamiliar cultural spaces; the art world that reaps profits through spin-offs and sales. *There's no such thing as bad visibility.*

The Work of Being Watched

The art world focuses too much of its attention on the behavior of internet users. But the fragility of the neoliberal self, the compulsion to be seen, the norms that our photographic sharing reproduce and subvert, remain just one side of the (bit)coin. This limited view loses sight of the processes through which money is being made, both in and outside the art world. Exhibitionism is big business—for Mark Zuckerberg and for Larry Gagosian. Which means that photography is labor; the art world, like the internet, a factory, not just a playground.[11]

Ben Burbridge is senior lecturer in art history and codirector of the Centre for Photography and Visual Culture at University of Sussex. His writing on photography, contemporary art, and politics has been published widely. He has curated the exhibitions Revelations: Experiments in Photography *(Media Space/National Media Museum, 2015) and the 2012 Brighton Photo Biennial,* Agents of Change: Photography and the Politics of Space, *among others. Burbridge is cofounder of Ph: The Photography Research Network. He is currently working on a book about photography, contemporary art, and neoliberalism.*

10 Hannah Jane Parkinson, "Instagram, an Artist and the $100,000 Selfies—Appropriation in the Digital Age," *Guardian*, July 18, 2015, https://www.theguardian.com/technology/2015/jul/18/instagram-artist-richard-prince-selfies.

11 Hito Steyerl, "Politics of Art: Contemporary Art and the Transition to Post-Democracy," in *The Wretched of the Screen* (Berlin: Sternberg Press, 2012), pp. 92–101; Mark Andrejevic, "Estrangement 2.0," *World Picture*, no. 6 (Winter 2011), http://www.worldpicturejournal.com/WP_6/PDFs/Andrejevic.pdf.

> *i created my interior thoughts as a means of production for the corporation that owned the board i was posting to, and that commodity was being sold to other commodity/ consumer entities as entertainment. that means that i sold my soul like a tennis shoe and i derived no profit from the sale of my soul.*
> —Carmen Hermosillo, aka humdog[1]

On August 16, 1858, the first message sent via the transatlantic cable read: "Europe and America are united by telegraphy. Glory to God in the highest; on earth, peace, and good will toward men."[2] From his residence in Pennsylvania, President James Buchanan responded to Queen Victoria's telegraphed excitement by lauding the transatlantic cable as "an instrument destined by Divine Providence to diffuse religion, civilization, liberty, and law throughout the world."[3] As nineteenth-century European and US technological advancements precipitated global communications, they also brought about an imperial geopolitical remapping that collapsed territorial and teletechnological expansions. The following overview proposes that the social, political, and economic conditions for the development of submarine telegraphic networks primed current information channels to become technologies for control and management.

The electric telegraph offered a much faster way to send and receive information than by carrier pigeon, horse, or ship. Building up from the optical telegraph and earlier models that used static electricity, long-distance electric telegraphic transmissions emerged in the 1830s in Russia,

1 Carmen Hermosillo aka humdog, "*Introducing Humdog: Pandora's Vox Redux*" (1994). The original essay was published online in 1994 as "Pandora's Vox: On Community in Cyber-space." The most-cited online source is http://folksonomy.co/?permalink=2299. It has also been cited in other volumes such as Fred Turner, *From Counterculture to Cyberculture: Stewart Brand, the Whole Earth Network, and the Rise of Digital Utopianism* (Chicago: University of Chicago Press, 2010).

2 Bill Burns, "History of the Atlantic Cable and Undersea Communications from the First Submarine Cable of 1850 to the Worldwide Fiber Optic Network, The Curious Story of the Tiffany Cables," http://atlantic-cable.com/Article/Lanello/index.htm.

3 Simone M. Müller, *Wiring the World: The Social and Cultural Creation of Global Telegraph Networks* (New York: Columbia University Press, 2016), p. 5.

Germany, and the United States. After decades of technical flops, telegraph lines were finally set up in England by William Cooke and Charles Wheatstone, and in the US by Samuel Morse, which prodded the engineering of a transatlantic cable. Though largely unsuccessful, the fledging attempts at transatlantic, cabled communications amassed substantial funding from British and US entrepreneurs and industrialist investors. In their respective struggles to ensure subsidies for the telegraph, both Morse and Cooke boosted its commercial value. The first commercial, electric telegraph of 1837—the Cooke and Wheatstone telegraph—gave rise to what Tom Standage has called the "Victorian internet," a telecommunications agora from which a highly complex information economy would evolve in subsequent centuries.[4] In 1870, the Eastern Telegraph Company connected London to Bombay, and by 1872, British imperial bandwidth reached as far as Australia, Singapore, China, Japan, and New Zealand. The Western and Brazilian Telegraph Company linked the US, England, and Bermuda, leading to a South American cabled expansion, and, in 1889, cables lined the coast of West Africa, reaching Cape Town. Finally, in the early 1900s, the United States connected its own territories: Hawaii, Guam, and the Philippines. While this list overlooks many cities, towns, and countries, my intention is to point out the speed and breadth of a colonial power-led global telecommunications industry. In addition to quickening transnational communication between trading, news, and shipping agencies, routing these networks through their colonies and territories helped guarantee the British and US empires' social, economic, and political monopoly over them.

In the 2016 essay "From Cabling the Atlantic to Wiring the World," historian Simone M. Müller recounts the moment in which the transatlantic cable arrived at the thriving city of Aberdeen, in the Scottish Highlands. The event was described in the *Aberdeen Weekly* as an "example of commercial heroism, which deserve[d] a wide and hearty recognition in every part of the world" given that it was "not England and America alone that benefit[ed] by it but almost every quarter of the globe."[5] As is the case today, access haunts all technological developments. According to Müller, even though the vast majority of Europeans and Americans could not afford to transmit a telegraphic message through the newly laid cable, it claimed the imaginations of users and nonusers alike. Müller, then, asks us to consider whose globalism was championed by the success of the "the wire that changed the world." Applying this to today's infrastructure, dominated mainly by US companies, design-research studio Metahaven refers to all transactions made

4 Tom Standage, *The Victorian Internet: The Remarkable Story of the Telegraph and the Nineteenth Century's On-line Pioneers* (New York: Walker Publishing Company, 2007), p. 101.

5 Gillian Cookson, *The Cable: The Wire that Changed the World* (Strout, Gloucestershire: Tempus, 2003), quoted in Simone M. Müller, "From Cabling the Atlantic to Wiring the World: A Review Essay on the 150th Anniversary of the Atlantic Telegraph Cable of 1866," *Technology and Culture* 57, no. 3 (July 2016): https://doi.org/10.1353/tech.2016.0069.

on a Google server as events under American jurisdiction: "The United States' global communication standards have network power. Yet, the territorial bases of these standards bind global subjects to key aspects of US hard power—predominantly, its judicial regime and its pervasive surveillance, by which the United States can effectively seek to control events on foreign soil."[6] This affords the US judicial protection over extralegal activities, such as surveillance, through the very telecommunications networks it owns.

Some argue that the postal institution provided the first blueprint for monopoly over a networked communications market that served both state and corporate actors alike. When Italian radical nationalist Giuseppe Mazzini's fight for a unified and independent Italy in the early 1800s landed him in exile in Geneva, Marseille, and London, he organized riots and uprisings remotely, primarily via mail correspondence. Following the failure of one of his plans, Mazzini accused the British government of "post-office espionage" and went so far as to lace his wax-sealed envelopes with poppy seeds and strands of hair to prove that the government was opening his mail. In response to his petition to the House of Commons, a Committee of Secrecy investigated and released a report confirming the post office's interception. The Mazzini affair speaks to a particular relationship between governance and information. Historian Daniel R. Headrick ascribes the state's need for gathering information on its subjects to a shift in power that took place in Europe at the time of its Enlightenment, when political systems moved from absolutism to enlightened despotism.[7] Reconnaissance would be considered essential if monarchs were to make their rule beneficial to their subjects. Driven by interests in territorial expansion and control, the spread of global telecommunications networks and information collection technologies might have been seen as a similar response to a perceived political benevolence.

If in the past security was deemed a matter of the state, today, left to surveillance technologies, it caters to the private, industrial, and corporate sectors. With networked ecosystems as far-reaching and intricately connected as social-media platforms owned by corporations, overseeing the activities of their users unites state and corporate interests. One of the benefits of private communication technologies is that they can presumably expedite customers' privacy over the expectation to comply with state-issued gag orders or subpoenas. But the commercial information sector also has a vested interest in mobilizing the data it vows to protect, which means corporate-state complicity ensures the survival of a live information market.

To solely attribute what privacy expert Bruce Schneier calls "the

6 Metahaven, *Black Transparency: The Right to Know in the Age of Mass Surveillance* (Berlin: Sternberg Press, 2015), p. 126.

7 Daniel R. Headrick, *When Information Came of Age: Technologies of Knowledge in the Age of Reason and Revolution, 1700–1850* (New York: Oxford University Press, 2000), p. 10.

business model of the internet" to the entrepreneurial patronage of the telegraphic cables and to the political demands of the Age of Reason and Revolution as a way of claiming that "dataveillance" is as old as telecommunications networks overlooks a crucial point.[8] Not only does the data siphoned from users function as currency to fuel corporate interests in building consumer profiles, it also assists the government in targeting subjects for surveillance. Together, surveillance and security practices extend latent criminality beyond justifiable authorization, as evidenced by the broad and discriminatory National Security Entry-Exit Registration System (NSEERS), an entry-exit registration used by the Department of Homeland Security to observe and regulate all movements by Muslims and Arabs at the US border. Much like routing telegraph cables throughout their colonial empires granted overseers the ability to assert and maintain order in their territories through telecommunications systems, watch-list databases often unjustly parse subjects into those who warrant protection and those who require surveillance. While it may seem like dataveillance has little to do with the optic regime of surveillance, it is important to remember that bodies are digitized, catalogued, and qualified based on their digital patterns and behaviors, which is the very information companies with stakes in a corporate-run cabled communications system are experts at mining. How, then, do we negotiate our relationship within these infrastructures? It might be precisely because the minority or colonized body is perpetually reconstructed as a threat by discriminatory channels of veillances that we are in fact superbly equipped to dismantle their biases. Disrupting the directionality of power inscribed in the potentate's gaze requires a critical relooking at designs of compliance. Fittingly, in the expanded version of her 1989 CBC Massey Lectures, "The Real World of Technology," the late activist, physicist, and researcher Ursula M. Franklin tasked us with the investigation of technology on the basis of its "organization, procedures, symbols, new words, equations, and most of all, mindset."[9] Such excavations are necessary if we are to find just uses for our tools.

Dan Bustillo is an artist and writer based in Los Angeles. They investigate power dynamics and surveillance culture through research, letter writing, workshops, experimental lectures, and collaborative and organizational work.

8 Fahmida Y. Rashid, "Surveillance Is the Business Model of the Internet: Bruce Schneier," *Security Week*, April 9, 2014, http://www.securityweek.com/surveillance-business-model-internet-bruce-schneier.

9 Ursula M. Franklin, *The Real World of Technology*, CBC Massey Lectures, Revised Edition (Toronto: House of Anansi Press Inc., 2004), p. 3.

ESSAY: WATCHING MURDER ONLINE, SARAH TUCK

The website of the US television network CNN hosts numerous visual testimonies of US police officers killing black Americans.[1] Moving beyond an evidentiary function that lays bare and makes explicit police brutality, the chronicle of public executions of black Americans shared and monetized across multiple platforms repeats the vulnerability of the black body.

Viewing the visual records of dash cams, police body cams, and mobile-phone footage of black lives killed by the police has a cumulative consequence, with each event assuming a familiar format that explicitly demonstrates how racial difference operates as a determinant of whose lives count as a "livable life and a grievable death."[2]

In the introduction to the exhibition and publication *Without Sanctuary: Lynching Photography in America*, Leon Litwack describes a public lynching in Georgia on April 23, 1899:

> *No member of the crowd wore a mask, nor did anyone attempt to conceal the names of the perpetrators; indeed newspaper reports noted the active participation of some of the region's most prominent citizens. And as in most lynchings, the public expressed its solidarity and ignored any information that contradicted the peoples' verdict.*[3]

As Paul Gilroy notes in a discussion of 1970s black Britain, "crime came to occupy the place which sexuality, miscegenation, and disease had held as central themes and images in the discourse of 'race.'"[4] His observation that the discourse and image of black criminality replaced earlier definitions of the "black problem" when transposed to the US, links the present of extrajudicial killing of black Americans to the history of lynching. Fundamental to this resemblance is the persistence of injustice, which at its most basic level demonstrates the continued vulnerability of black life. Suggesting continuity between the postcards of lynching and the footage of extrajudicial killings is not to project contemporary conditions backward, but instead to recognize how the postcards and the footage both circulate as evidence of murder and as spectacle of white terror. It thus necessitates a more thorough and critical account of the political effects of the display of the violated black body in order to curtail the images' power.

On February 26, 2012, George Zimmerman, a neighborhood-watch volunteer in Sanford, Florida, fatally shot Trayvon Martin, seventy yards from the rear door of the townhouse

1 Madison Park, "Police Shootings: Trials, Convictions Are Rare for Officers," CNN, June 25, 2017, http://edition.cnn.com/2017/05/18/us/police-involved-shooting-cases/index.html.

2 Judith Butler, *Precarious Life: The Powers of Mourning and Violence*, repr. ed. (2004; repr., London; New York: Verso, 2006) p. xv.

3 James Allen, *Without Sanctuary: Lynching Photography in America* (Santa Fe, NM: Twin Palms Publishers, 2000), p. 9.

4 Paul Gilroy, *There Ain't No Black in the Union Jack* (London: Routledge, 2002), p. 140.

where he was staying. Zimmerman claimed that Trayvon Martin had attacked him, invoking Florida's controversial "stand your ground" self-defense law.[5] Two days prior to being charged on April 11, Zimmerman launched a website to raise funds for his legal defense. It raised $200,000 in two weeks before the site was shut down.[6]

On July 13, Zimmerman was acquitted of all charges in the death of Trayvon Martin by a jury of six women. The "not guilty" verdict prompted national protest and catalyzed #BlackLivesMatter as a political, social, and virtual demand for justice and as an act of mourning. In the original Facebook status in response to Zimmerman's acquittal, which contains the phrase "black lives matter" posted by Alicia Garza, she imagines "a section of America who is cheering and celebrating right now." Her post, a love letter to black people, registered the dehumanizing effects of racism that makes "whiteness" a prerequisite for recognition and justice.

Following the conclusion of the trial, Zimmerman began selling signed 3-D lithographs of the gun he used at a Florida gun shop[7] and paintings on eBay. The first painting, a blue-toned American flag featuring the words "God One Nation with Liberty and Justice For All" sold to an anonymous online bidder for $100,099.99.[8] On the same day that Zimmerman's auction closed, eBay withdrew the painting *A Tale of Two Hoodies* by the artist Michael D'Antuono. The painting depicts a police officer as a hooded Klansman pointing a gun at a child holding a pack of Skittle-like sweets; in the background, a torn American flag reveals the Confederate flag beneath. Ebay pulled the painting on the grounds that it violated their Hateful or Discriminatory policy.[9]

In September 2015, seven months after the Justice Department officially closed its investigation into the death of Trayvon Martin, Zimmerman retweeted to his eleven thousand followers a photograph of Trayvon Martin's corpse. The photograph, with

5 The Stand Your Ground statute was signed into law by Florida Governor Jeb Bush on April 26, 2005. Stand Your Ground provides legal protection for a person who believes they are facing an imminent physical threat and uses lethal force.

6 Sean Hannity at Fox News actively encouraged viewers to donate to the website. See: Amber Robb, "George Zimmerman, Darren Wilson and the Kickstarted Defense: You Call This Justice?," the *Guardian*, October 1, 2014, https://www.theguardian.com/commentisfree/2014/oct/01/george-zimmerman-darren-wilson-crowdsourced-legal-fees.

7 In partnership with the Florida Gun Supply Shop, Zimmerman sold prints of the Confederate flag with the caption "THE 2ND PROTECTS OUR 1ST" for $50. Proceeds from the sale were shared between Zimmerman and the gun shop owner Andy Hallinan, who was facing a federal lawsuit from the Council on American-Islamic Relations after declaring the gun shop a "Muslim-free zone." Peter Holley, "'Muslim Free' Gun Shop Owner Takes Aim After Judge Tosses Lawsuit against Him," *Washington Post*, November 30, 2015, https://www.washingtonpost.com/news/acts-of-faith/wp/2015/11/30/muslim-free-gun-shop-owner-takes-aim-after-judge-tosses-lawsuit-against-him/.

8 See: http://abcnews.go.com/blogs/headlines/2013/12/george-zimmerman-painting-sells-for-100000/.

9 Russell Goldman, "George Zimmerman Painting Sells for $100,000," ABC News, December 23, 2013, https://abcnews.go.com/blogs/headlines/2013/12/george-zimmerman-painting-sells-for-100000/ (link no longer active).

police forensic marker numbers 5 and 6 on the ground next to the teenager's body, was captioned "Z-man is a one man army." The caption reframes "neighborhood watch" as a proxy for a racist vigilantism and rebukes the legal commentary of "self-defense" used during Zimmerman's trial. The following year, Zimmerman listed the 9mm handgun he used to kill Trayvon Martin on the United Gun Group auction site as "an American firearm icon" and "collectible." It was sold through the online public auction for $250,000.[10] In this repurposing of criminal evidence as souvenirs, the structural connection and continuity to lynching is made explicit, with simply a shift in the mode of distribution of images of racist violence and murder.

Just over one year after Zimmerman's acquittal, on August 9, 2014, the eighteen-year-old, unarmed black American Michael Brown was killed by Officer Darren Wilson in Ferguson, Missouri. According to the autopsy report, Officer Darren Wilson had shot Michael Brown at least six times, including twice in the head. At 7:05 p.m., Thee Pharoah uploaded a mobile-phone image of Michael Brown face down in the road, his right arm raised in the signal position of surrender.[11] From the time stamp of the live tweets, Michael Brown's body remained on the road for several hours. At 9:36 p.m., Thee Pharoah tweeted, "Homie still on the ground, tho."[12]

In the wake of Michael Brown's death, a GoFundMe page was set up to support police officer Darren Wilson. It raised $225,000 in eleven hours before it was closed down as a result of the scale of protests in Ferguson. A second GoFundMe site was then created, raising the total to $433,000, collected to cover legal fees incurred by the trial.

On November 24, 2014, the grand jury elected "not to indict Wilson," a verdict stating as a matter of historical record that Darren Wilson was justified in the use of force and had "reasonable" fear for his life. Following the acquittal, donations raised through a social-media campaign increased Police Officer Wilson's total to $1 million, with the Facebook pages "We Are Darren Wilson"[13] and "We Support Officer Darren Wilson"[14] gaining over fifty thousand likes.

Announcing the verdict, Bob McCulloch, the prosecuting attorney for St. Louis County, Missouri, criticized media coverage: "The most significant challenge encountered in this investigation has been the twenty-four-hour news cycle and its insatiable appetite for something, for anything, to talk about, followed closely behind with the nonstop rumors on social media."[15]

10 "Gun that Killed Trayvon Martin 'Makes $250,000 for Zimmerman,'" BBC, May 22, 2016, http://www.bbc.com/news/world-us-canada-36354206.

11 The dispute over whether Michael Brown raised his arms to signal surrender was crucial to the trial. See: Nicholas Mirzoeff, "The Murder of Michael Brown," *Social Text*, vol. 34, no. 1 126 (2016): pp. 49–71.

12 For Thee Pharoah Twitter feed on August 9, 2014, see: https://storify.com/mashable/this-kid-live-tweeted-michael-brown-s-shooting.

13 "WE ARE DARREN WILSON," Facebook, https://www.facebook.com/wearedarrenwilsonofficial/.

14 "We Support Officer Darren Wilson," Facebook, https://www.facebook.com/isupportofficerdarrenwilson/.

15 For a comprehensive analysis of the grand jury trial based on transcripts, see Nicholas Mirzoeff, "The Murder of Michael Brown," *Social Text* 34, no. 1, 126 (2016): pp. 49–71.

McCulloch's claim that "nonstop rumors" were hindering the trial makes clear that the campaign to achieve an acquittal was fought across media platforms. In the immediate aftermath, reports stressed Michael Brown's physical build—six-foot five-inch height, and 289 pounds—and CCTV footage from a local shop, released to the media by the police, was repeatedly screened across television networks. The CCTV allegedly showed Michael Brown stealing fifteen dollars' worth of cigarillos. Made integral to the account of the events in Ferguson, the footage was used to define Michael Brown and influence public opinion to secure an acquittal on all charges. Its use as a material alibi to validate shooting an unarmed man six times exposed both the corrosive power and durability of racist stereotypes in shaping how black lives are imagined, made visible, and not seen.

Transferred to keyword-linked algorithms online and reused across news networks, the images and footage of extrajudicial killings of black Americans set an explicit challenge: to create an account that engages with the toll of racism and its consequences, but doesn't reduce the lives of the victims simply to the status of victim. From there on, the challenge is also to reject the violence of misrepresentation in the media, which the Twitter feed #IfIWasGunnedDown terribly anticipates. Initiated in 2014 by criminal-defense lawyer C. J. Lawrence, in response to the image chosen by the media to represent Michael Brown, the Twitter account invites those subject to predatory policing to dissect the politics of representation with the prompt: if I was gunned down, which image would the media use? The two images—one of a professional person dressed in graduation robes, surgical scrubs, or a military uniform; the other, of a person in a tracksuit, drinking beer, or grimacing into the camera—answer the question. The simplicity of this project lies in its questioning of the status of the image that marks recognition as both acknowledgment of and complicity in the visual imaginary of black criminality.

The failed expectations of justice commensurate with watching murder online emphasize how this footage exists without guarantees of its affective meaning. It exposes the devastating effects of racism that connect the histories of lynching to the extrajudicial killings of the present as well as the "hundreds of Kodaks clicked" at the 1915 lynching of Thomas Brooks in Tennessee to the hundreds of online clicks generated by the footage of the present. Just as the photographers "reaped a harvest"[16] selling postcards of the lynched, the footage of extrajudicial killings is monetized across media platforms. The political and ethical challenge is therefore to attend to the images both as visual testimonies of black subjection and as actions in this subjection.

Incapacitated to produce a consequential legal response, the images of extrajudicial killings circulate as signifiers of white supremacy and the necropolitics of racism. Mediated and monetized as news rather than crime, the images and footage form a recursive loop with the postcards of

16 Allen, *Without Sanctuary*, p. 11.

lynching, in a pattern and routinization of violence, where no one image can be treated as an anomaly. It indicates the need to complicate assumptions of shame and empathy while making these very qualities the mainspring of oppositional politics that cut across the Manichean divisions and categorizations of "race." This is a challenge which must simultaneously resist displacing the body of the "victim" from the center of analysis and equally withstand the exaltation of the image of the victim that forecloses the ontological depth of black lives in a repetition of the summary execution of black life. The central purpose of this challenge is therefore twofold: to resignify the visible as evidence of crime and to reclaim the political subjectivity of the victims. This task—of making an account of the images' effects while refusing the image as obituary—is not to suppose that the images should remain unseen. Instead, it is to address the implication of the pictures in the violence they depict, bringing the past more fully into focus in the present circulation of images online, which make murder a public event and its footage a political and economic resource.

Sarah Tuck is a postdoctoral researcher in photography and human rights based at Valand Academy, Gothenburg University, Sweden. Her current research project Drone Vision (2016–18) is a collaborative initiative that explores the effects and implications of drone technologies on warfare, surveillance, and protest. It includes as research partners the Hasselblad Foundation and Valand Academy, Gothenburg, Sweden; the Nicosia Municipal Arts Centre, Nicosia, Cyprus; and Zahoor Ul Akhlaq Gallery, at the National College of Arts in Lahore, Pakistan. Tuck's work has traversed a wide range of situated practice, including community development, post-conflict processes, and institutional networks where questions of agency, knowledge production, and representation have always been central. She is the author of After the Agreement: Contemporary Photography in Northern Ireland *(Black Dog Publishing, 2015).*

ESSAY: KEEPING UP WITH THE CARTESIANS: ON THE CULTURE OF THE SELFIE WITH CONTINUAL REFERENCE TO KIM KARDASHIAN, DANIEL RUBINSTEIN

Is there anyone reading this who did not spend some time online in the last twenty-four hours? The question is: how does it feel? Perhaps it does not feel like the first time, as we are so used to it. But on second thought, it is rather different from most other things. Sitting at my desk, I can say that the book is closer to me than the coffee cup, and that the armchair is further than the phone. But what does it mean to say that online something is closer to me and something is more distant? Online distance is not measured in meters or feet, it is measured in clicks, swipes, flicks, and taps. How many clicks does it take to buy this book on Amazon? How many swipes to get to the news feed? *Pinching* and *dragging*, *flicking* and *swiping* might be words previously used to describe the playground bully, but now these are the coordinates of a new territory and a new economy in which a Twitter bot can run a country and a computer hack can change governments.

The binary conventions of political reality—for instance, Democrats versus Republicans—give way to an ever closer alignment of biological and artificial neural networks, and of social and computer codes, that is nowhere more visible than in the phenomenon of the selfie. Both the analogue and the digital snapshot still belong to the industrial age, in which the greatest threat to humanity was the man-machine hybrid—the Frankenstein monster who turns on his own maker. But as the online philosopher Kim Kardashian teaches—by inviting us to look at her through touching, pinching, and swiping—the man-machine paradigm is now replaced by wo/man-image. This is not only a change in the status of the image, it is also, and for the most part, a change in the status of "man." That is because the gendered language in the previous sentence is another direct consequence of the demand issued by Descartes to maintain clear separation between mind and body, in which the mind always has the upper hand. Since Descartes, the human being has been defined by the ability to think rationally and to doubt everything, which just happens to be the preferred pastime of white men of a certain age. For the Cartesian, the only appropriate way to study the world is by forming an image of it in one's mind's eye. Take, for example, the sculpture *The Thinker* (1904), by Auguste Rodin: the massive head over the immobile body contemplating the world from a distance. In Kardashian's Instagram stream, on the other hand, the image/body opposition is overcome in favor of a new world order that merges looking and touching. Following in the footsteps of Nietzsche who proclaimed "the death of God," the Kardashian selfie makes us take seriously the question of the death of man and ask what new friendships, temporary allegiances, one-night-stands, and battle lines are called for in this mutual interdependence of "post-wo/man" and image.

Before the age of the selfie, vernacular photography was mostly dominated by pictures of past events, operating as an extension of human memory. But selfies eliminate distance and shrink time to an instant because they proliferate both vertically and horizontally, not only propagating on one's Instagram stream, but also spreading via copy, repetition, and self-replication. Just as the image exists only as a transmission of signals shuttling back and forth between nodal points, the selfie also obliterates the distinction between the author and audience, making everyone a participant, and between past and present, as both are equally available, perfectly preserved for eternity as data. Because of this nonlinear notion of time in which future is the recording of the past, selfies draw attention not so much to past events and human memory but to the fluctuating forces that connect human bodies to machines, algorithms, and networks.

Selfies remind us that we have the duty not only to record and represent the world, but also to actively engage with it by connecting and sharing with other human beings. When Martin Heidegger attended to the question of sharing he considered a jug. Like the selfie, the jug has the ability to share its contents, and for Heidegger in the outpouring of the wine from the jug the essence of being human *as sharing* is disclosed: "In the gift of the pour, the earth and sky abide. In the gift of the pour there abides at the same time earth and sky, divinities and mortals. These four, united in themselves, belong together." For Heidegger, the materiality of the jug is expressive of all the essential components of human life: earth, water, fire, ritual, culture, and art combine in the simple gesture of pouring from the jug. The gesture of the selfie is equally telling of life as intersubjective feedback loop, for it is making visible the essential components of the network, which are not earth and water, but bits of data. These bits of data are organized not according to Descartes's mind/body dualism, but according to code, and therefore the pictures formed by these bits of data are descriptive of the new categories of thought, art, play, and action that these codes make possible.

It is even possible that by looking carefully at the selfie we can discern the future shape of our own species—not as individuals connected to each other via social fabric, governed by self-interest and competition, but as nodal points formed from the cross-fertilization between human and artificial intelligence. The question is not whether this picture of ourselves as immaterial and imperishable is terrifying or comforting.

The selfie fractured the shell of modern individuality that is founded on the false certainty of the body-image dualism: an image is not a body, and a body is not an image. The selfie is not only a picture of someone's body, it is also a fragment of the second-order body, the synthetic trans-subjective entity that is formed through interchange between electric currents passing through synapses in the brain and microchips in motherboards. Kardashian's selfie stream shapes clear and lucid pictures out of this trans-subjective experience, offering a key-hole view of a post-individual existence that is dedicated to calculated creativity that consists of processing and combining data derived from human and nonhuman sources.

This strange cross-species connectivity is establishing a new collectivity that is sending shock waves through a society that insists on thinking in fixed, binary categories. The selfie might be seen as the first expression of a new political grammar, one that is not structured on a binary axis of rich and poor, black and white, or progressive and conservative, but instead offers specific insights into the nature of reality that speculative reason, logic, and rationality alone cannot grasp. This is not because the selfie can have multiple meanings, but because the selfie shows what happens to meaning when it is detached from the structure of the sign (signifier/signified) and aligned instead with the contemporary experience of post-truth, in other words, of digital-born images created and served via feedback loops that recombine visuals, texts, and sounds into malleable mashups that flow through the screens of smartphones, laptops, and tablets.

Selfie is defined by the Oxford Dictionary as "a photograph that one has taken of oneself ... and shared via social media," which suggests that unlike an ordinary photograph, it is not aimed at recording the past but at creating a different future by recombining recorded data to produce new and previously unimaginable mashups. The selfie is subversive because the distinction between life and image is being erased: sharing is not something that happens as an afterthought, but almost the other way around: it is the desire to share and to be shared that manifests itself in the production of the image. This reversal calls for a new, reinvented conception of a community—not as a collection of individuals united by a shared goal, but as a scrollable feedback loop that does not seek to obtain objective mastery over nature, but to attain a more-than-ordinary state of being. In this new community, neither the image nor the person making it are known in advance, instead they are formed by bio-digital processes that create the worlds and the lives of all the participants in the network. Two logics that have been kept separate for millennia are brought together and form an image that allows us to experience an inconvenient truth, namely that every rational act is also a sensual act, because here the representational logic states, "This is I" precisely at the same time (and within the same space) that the logic of sharing, of intimacy, and of ecstatic desire screams, "This is now!"

But what—one might ask—is being shared in the sharing of the selfie? Are we talking about pixels, packets of data, algorithms, or information? Not at all. Once we cease to try to understand the selfie in terms of representation we are free to explore its condition of self-replication without any metaphysical baggage. The right question to ask is not, "What does the selfie represent?" but "Where is it?" as it is the latter question that opens up the possibility of conceiving the selfie as a field of synchronized appearances impervious to the laws of space, time, and history. The selfie is not only similar to itself in all its iterations on various screens and devices, it is also self-similar to and different from all other selfies. Type "selfie" into your favorite image-search engine and you will be looking at a wall of pictures, an on-the-fly archive of poses, postures, identities—but this is not all. Something else is there, something less visible than the pictures, but not less real or tangible. This something is the difference between the selfies, a difference that can only become manifest due to their self-similarity. This, finally, is what is being shared: not the picture of a face, a six-pack, or a protruding arm, but the difference that emerges from an archive of self-similar selfies. The real purpose of Kardashian's Instagram stream might be not to preserve memories and construct identities, but to produce in the viewer the experience of difference. Wikipedia says that the universe is 84.5 percent dark matter, yet it cannot be directly observed. Like dark matter, difference cannot be directly observed, but its existence can be inferred from the effects produced by images online.

It is this difference between selves that overcomes identity as the ideological linchpin of society, and allows for a prolific multiplicity of assemblages, and for the creation of new communities to which the old political categories of "left" and "right" do not apply. What is being shared in the act of the selfie is the possibility of detaching the image from its foundations in Platonic metaphysical unity and the chance of overcoming the representational force of photography. The selfie opens up a possibility of a future that is not bound to traditions of representation and memory, but instead proliferates via the network expressed through the plurality of its fragments. What we see in the selfie stream is not Kardashian's self-portrait, but how the future present is being created. When dreams and fantasies are made of pixels and controlled by algorithms, it might be time to ask what new forms of fight, creativity, and resistance are called for.

Daniel Rubinstein is a reader in philosophy and the image at Central Saint Martins, University of the Arts, London. He has written extensively on contemporary visual culture, photography, and digital art. His current work investigates the radically fractal nature of images with a specific link to desire and memory. He is the editor of the journal Philosophy of Photography, *codirector of the Centre for the Study of the Networked Image (CSNI), and course leader of MA Contemporary Photography, Practices and Philosophies. His recent publications include* On the Verge of Photography *(ARTicle Press, 2013), "Digital Image in Photographic Culture: Algorithmic Photography and the Crisis of Representation" in* The Photographic Image in Digital Culture *(Routledge, 2013), and "Life More Photographic: Mapping the Networked Image" in* photographies *(Routledge, 2008).*

GALLERY 01

Public, Private, Secret, ICP Museum, 250 Bowery, NY, June 2016–January 2017

This exhibition explored the roles that photography and video play in the crafting of identity and in the reconfiguration of the social conventions that define our public and private selves, embedded and implicated in a wider matrix of online behavior and social codes. For better and for worse, this network culture provides us all a platform for direct address, an unmediated outlet for image creation and distribution. We adopt different behaviors within these networked systems, whose built-in mechanisms ensure that any notion of privacy is surrendered. This status quo of exposure without recourse is militated further by the pressure to participate in and labor for the culture of public visibility, now an established form of social currency and a prime demonstration of "being social."

Gallery 01 was given over to Natalie Bookchin, Jon Rafman, Doug Rickard, and Martine Syms, four artists whose articulations and observations are drawn from aggregations of visual material. Each artist reconfigures and recontextualizes existing video imagery—most of it native to online platforms—to create highly subjectivized and alternate readings of visual culture. They ask that we pay attention to the profound and deeply social urges that underpin our collective creation and how these enable different readings of our image world, ever a proxy for the actual world.

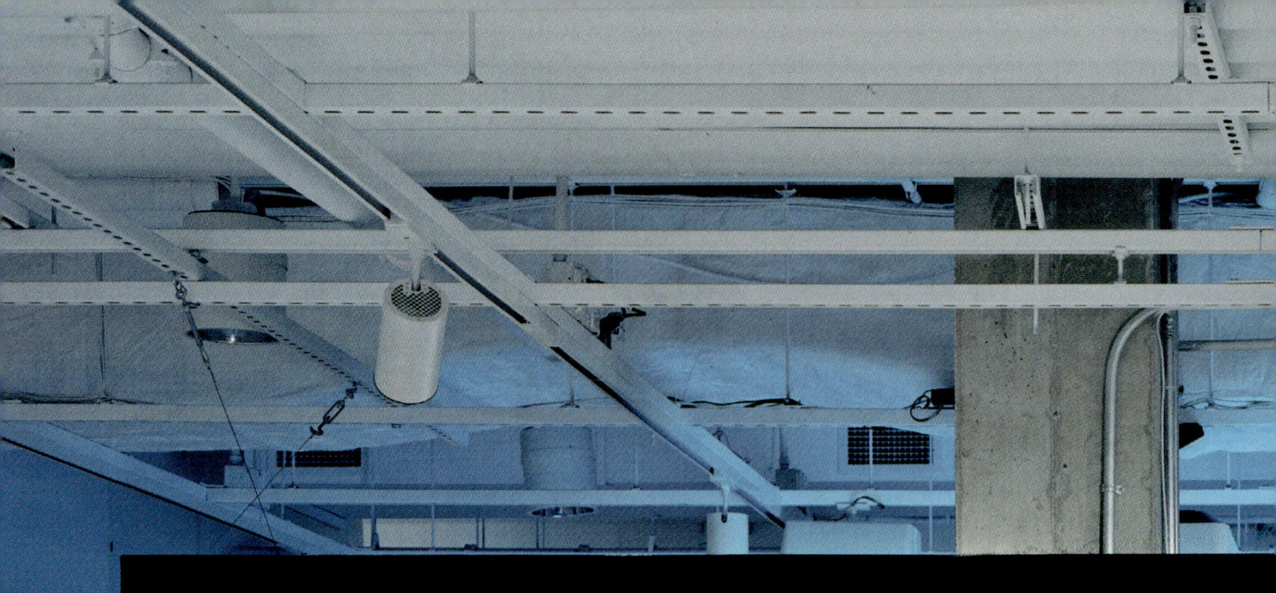

PUBLIC, PRIVATE, SECRET
JUN 23, 2016–JAN 8, 2017

CURATED BY
CHARLOTTE COTTON

This exhibition explores the roles that photography and video play in the crafting of identity and in the reconfiguration of the social conventions that define our public an private selves. Consciously framed by our present era, the works on view signal how our image-making and consumption patterns are embedded and implicated in a wider matrix of online behaviors and social codes which in turn give images a life of their own. For better and for worse this network culture provides us all a platform for direct address, an unmediated outlet for image productio and distribution. Within this context, our visual creations and online activities blur and remove conventional delineations between public and private—and sometimes secret—expression; in fact, they multiply and expand the number of potential selves.

In turn, we adopt different behavio within these networked systems, whose built-in mechanisms ensure that any notion of privacy is surrendered. Any behavior within th system thus becomes fair play to be mined for data by for-profit and stat organizations. This status quo of exposure without recourse is militatec

Photo © Bertrand Cavalier

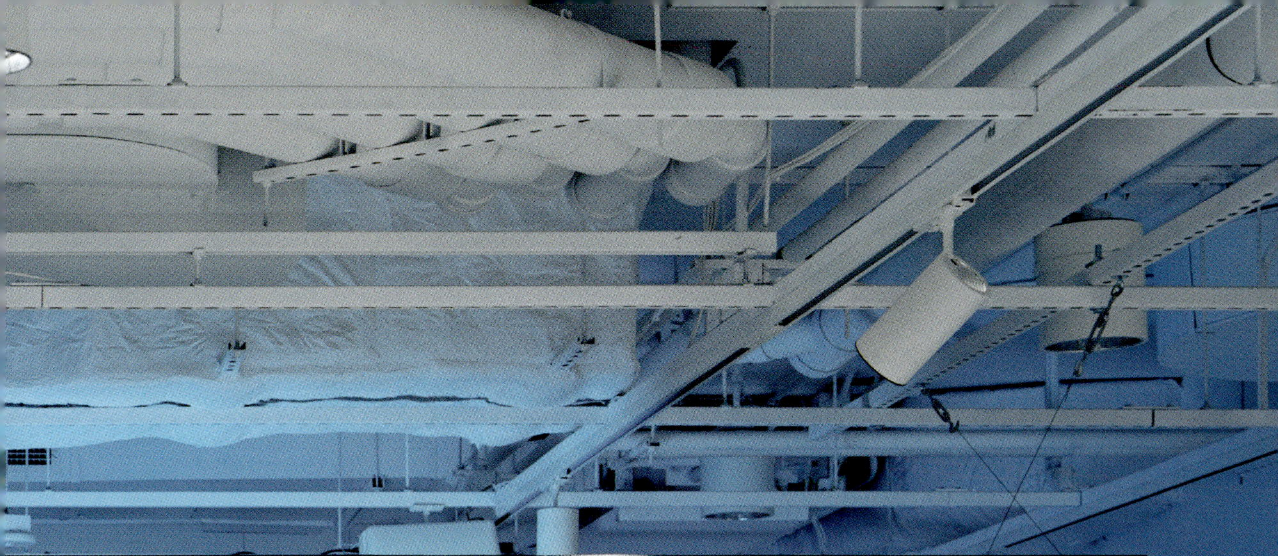

rther by the pressure to participate and labor for the culture of public sibility, now an established rm of social currency and a prime emonstration of "being social."

This gallery is given over to Natalie ookchin, Jon Rafman, Doug Rickard, nd Martine Syms, four artists whose ticulations and observations are rawn from aggregations of visual aterial. Each artist reconfigures nd recontextualizes existing video nagery—most of it native to nline platforms—to create highly ubjectivized and alternate readings f visual culture. Through their works ney ask that we pay attention to ne profound and deeply social urges nat underpin our collective reation and how these enable different eadings of our image world.

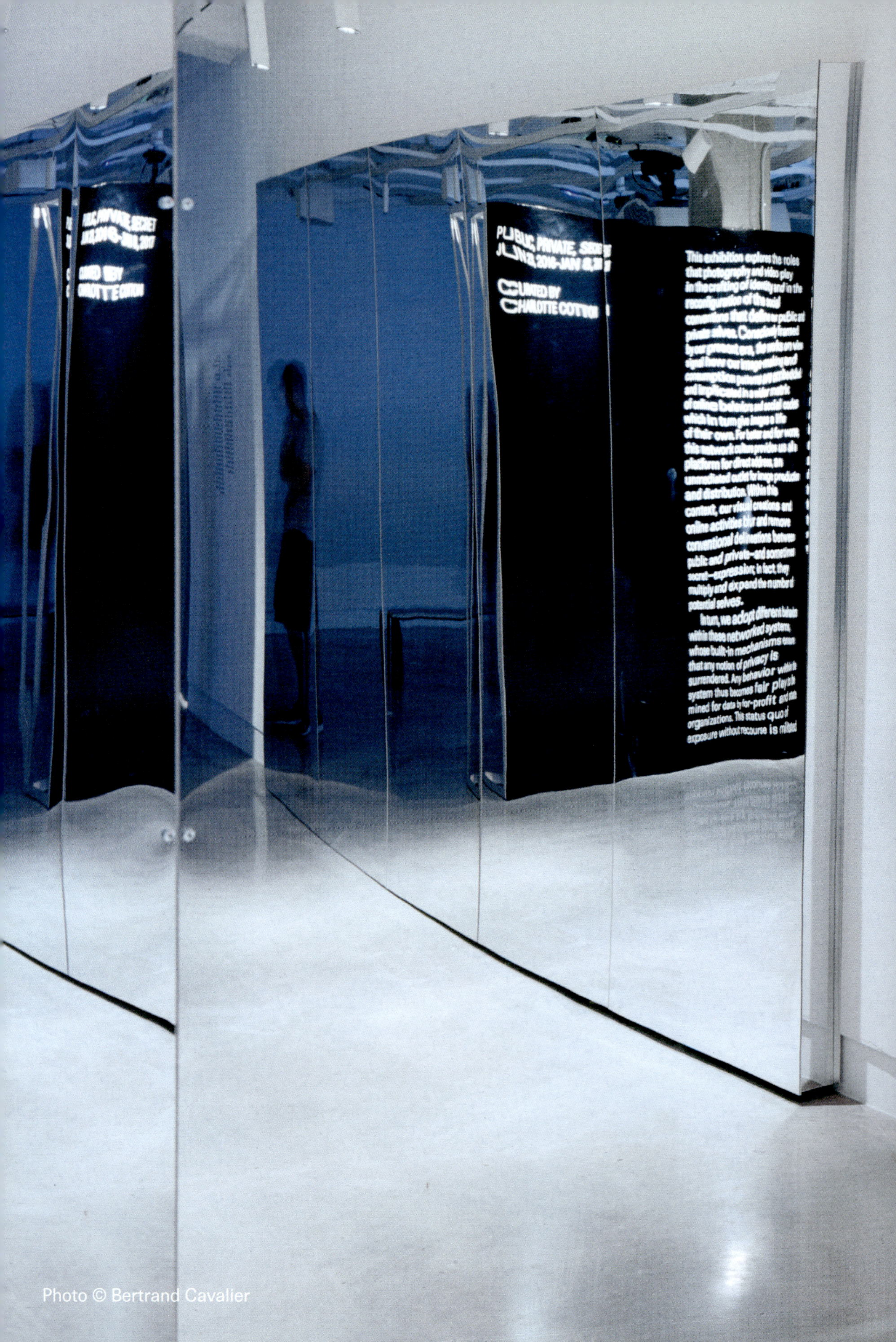

Photo © Bertrand Cavalier

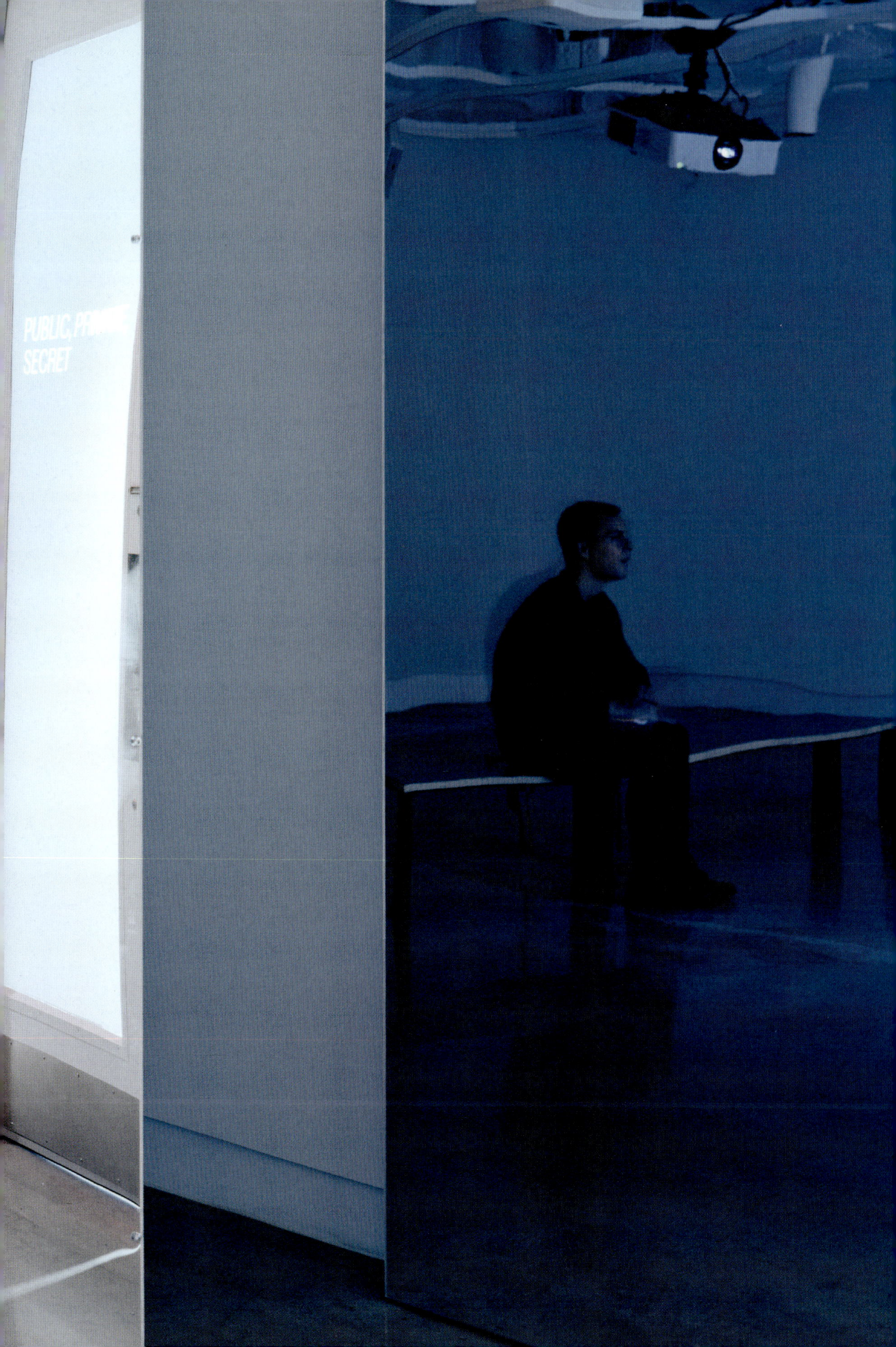
PUBLIC, PR
SECRET

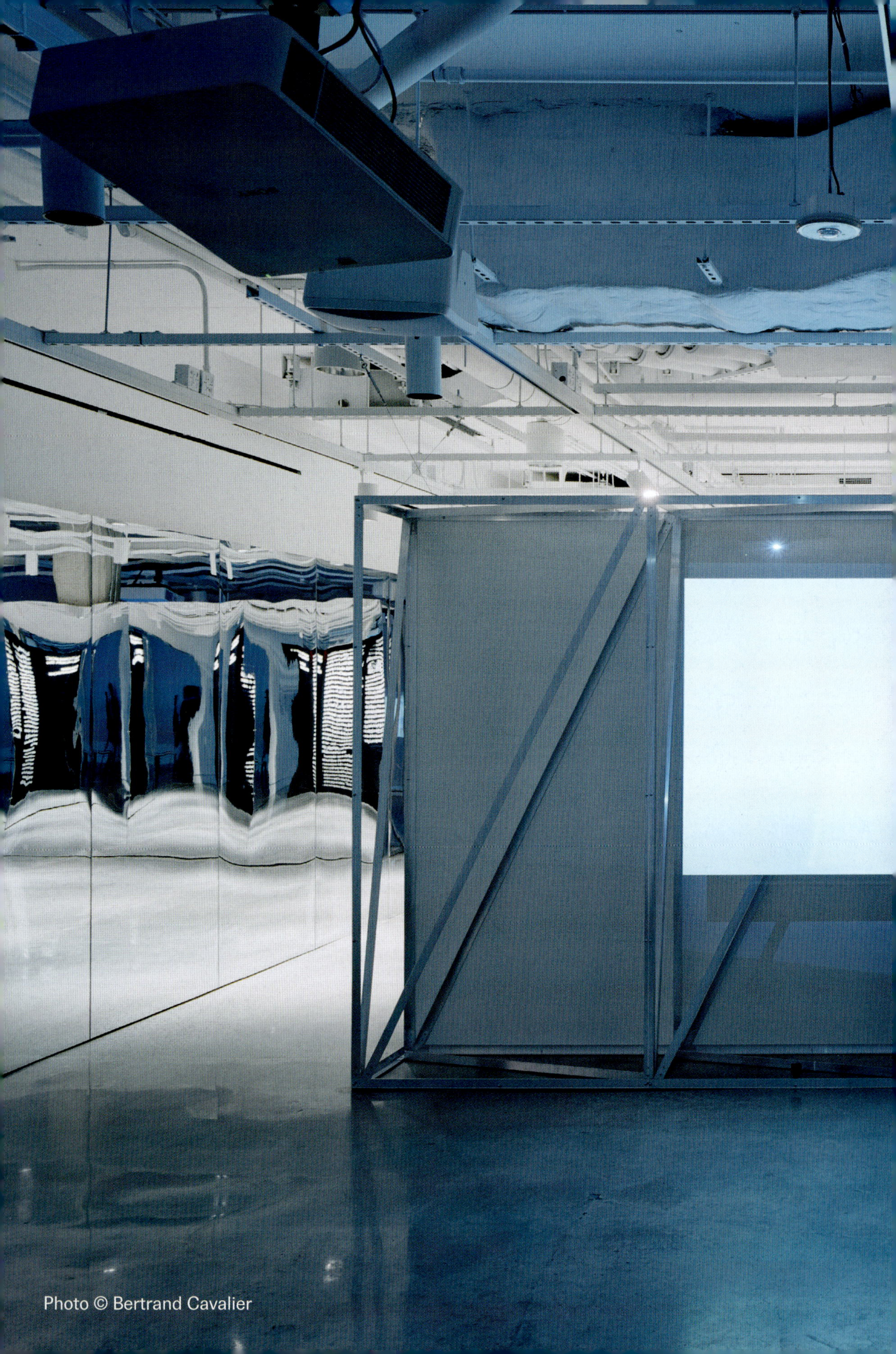

Photo © Bertrand Cavalier

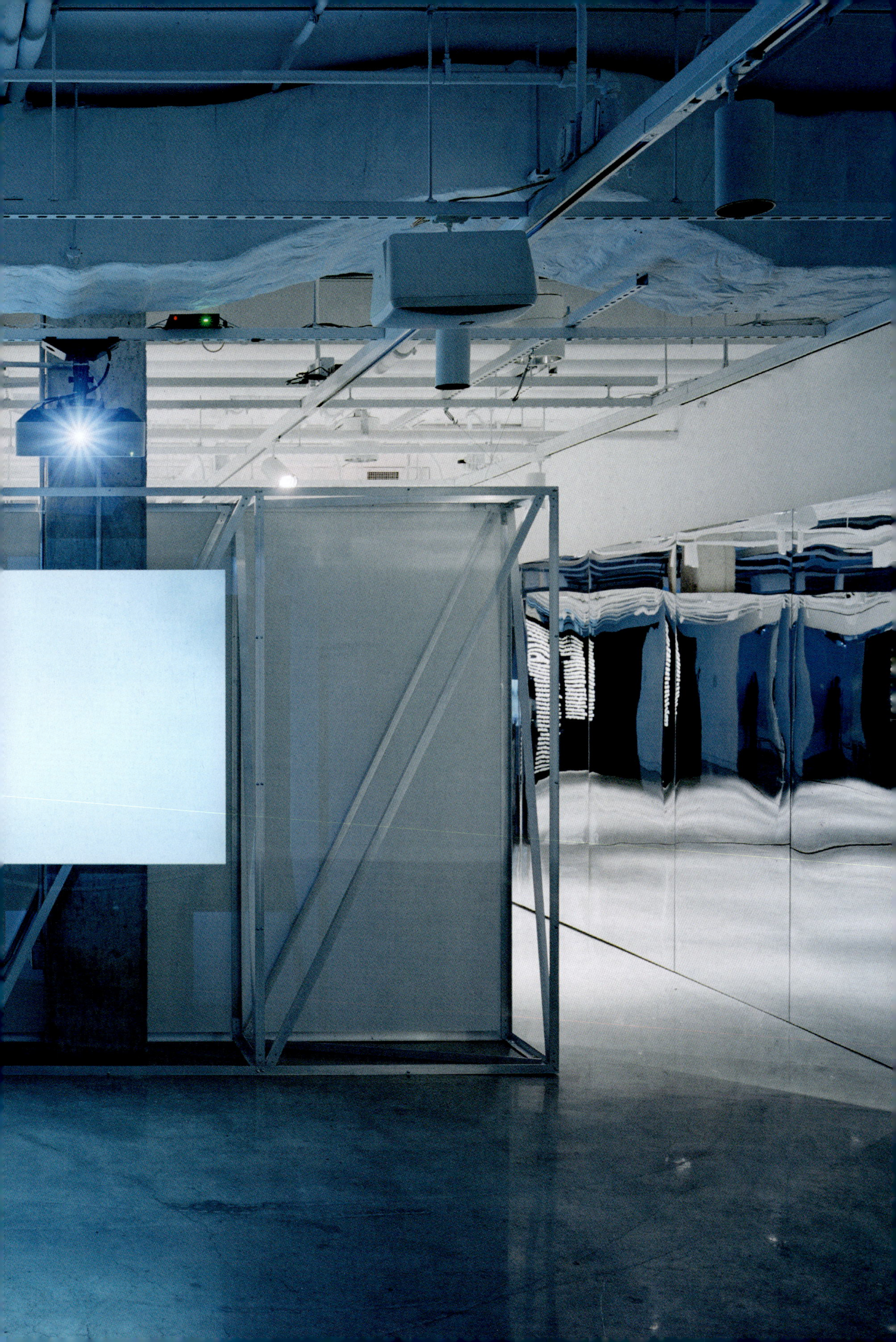

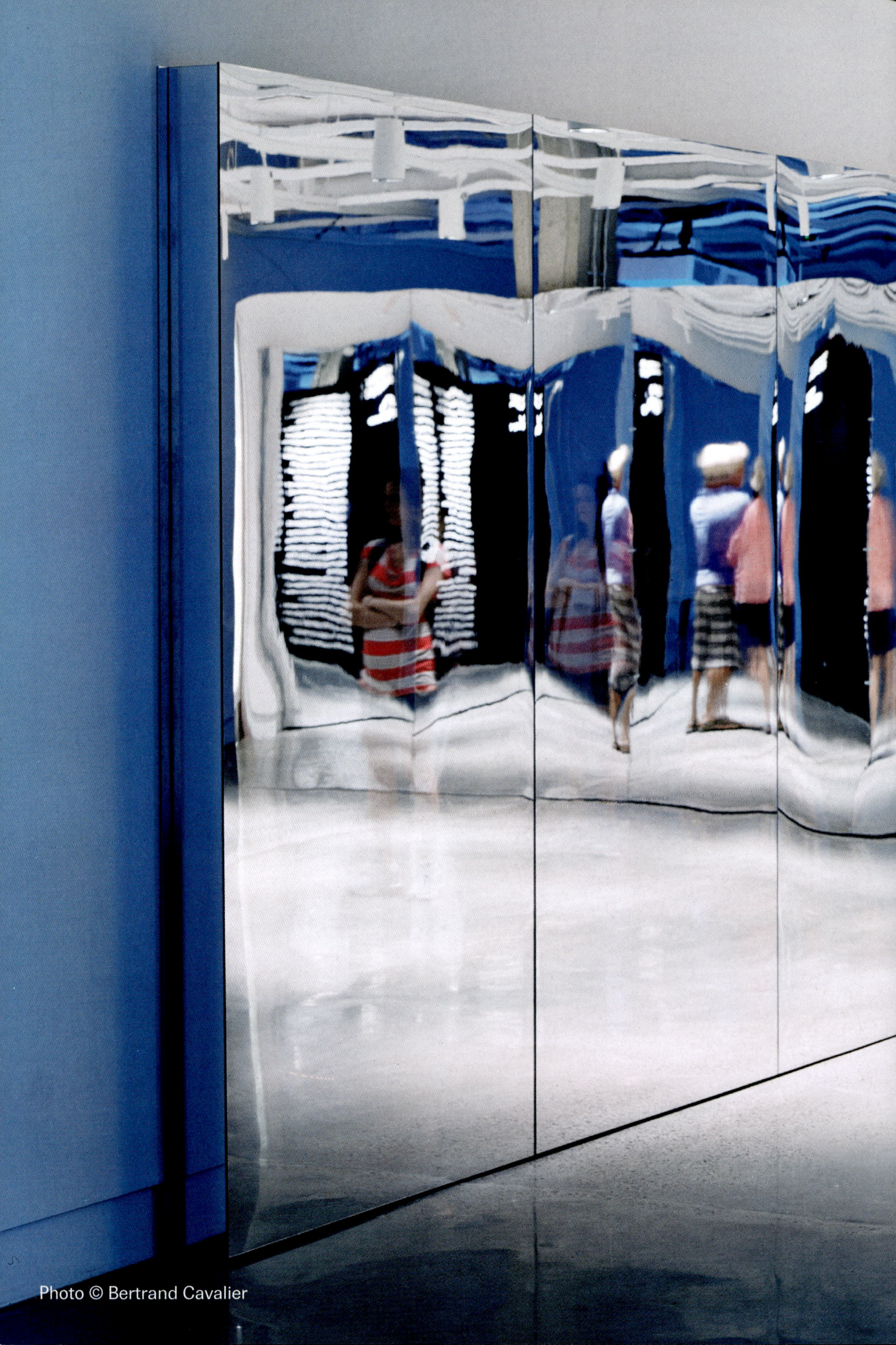

Photo © Bertrand Cavalier

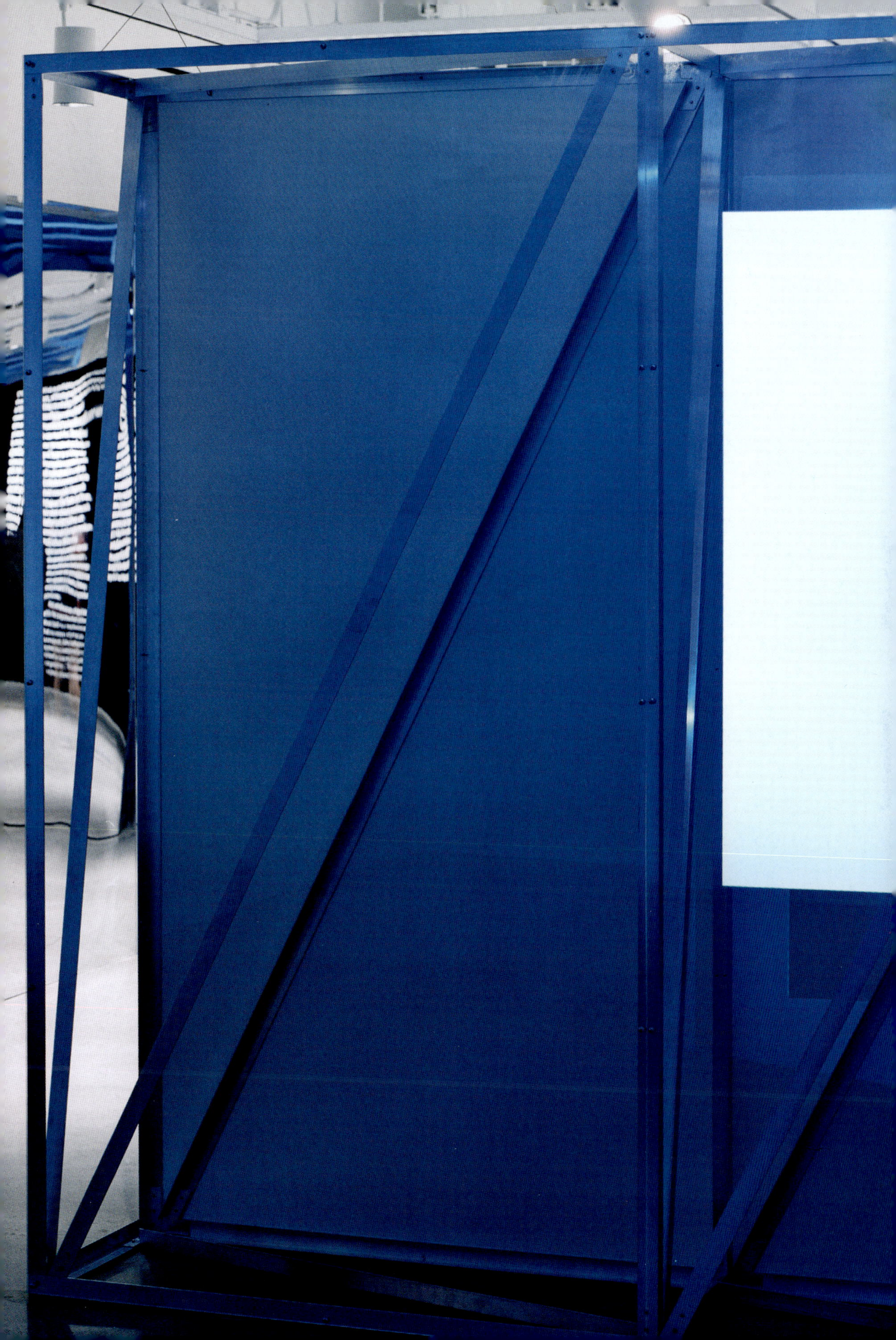

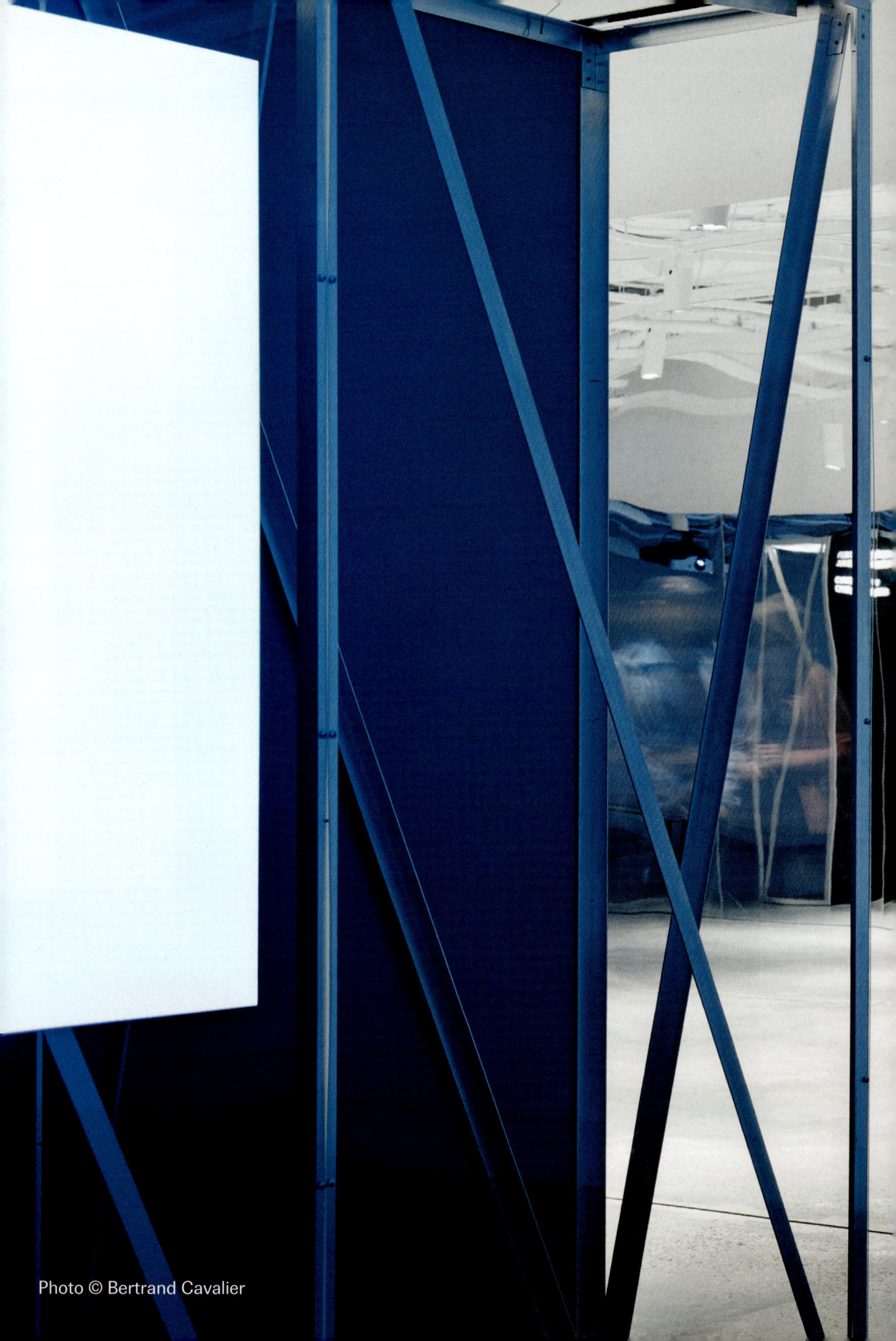
Photo © Bertrand Cavalier

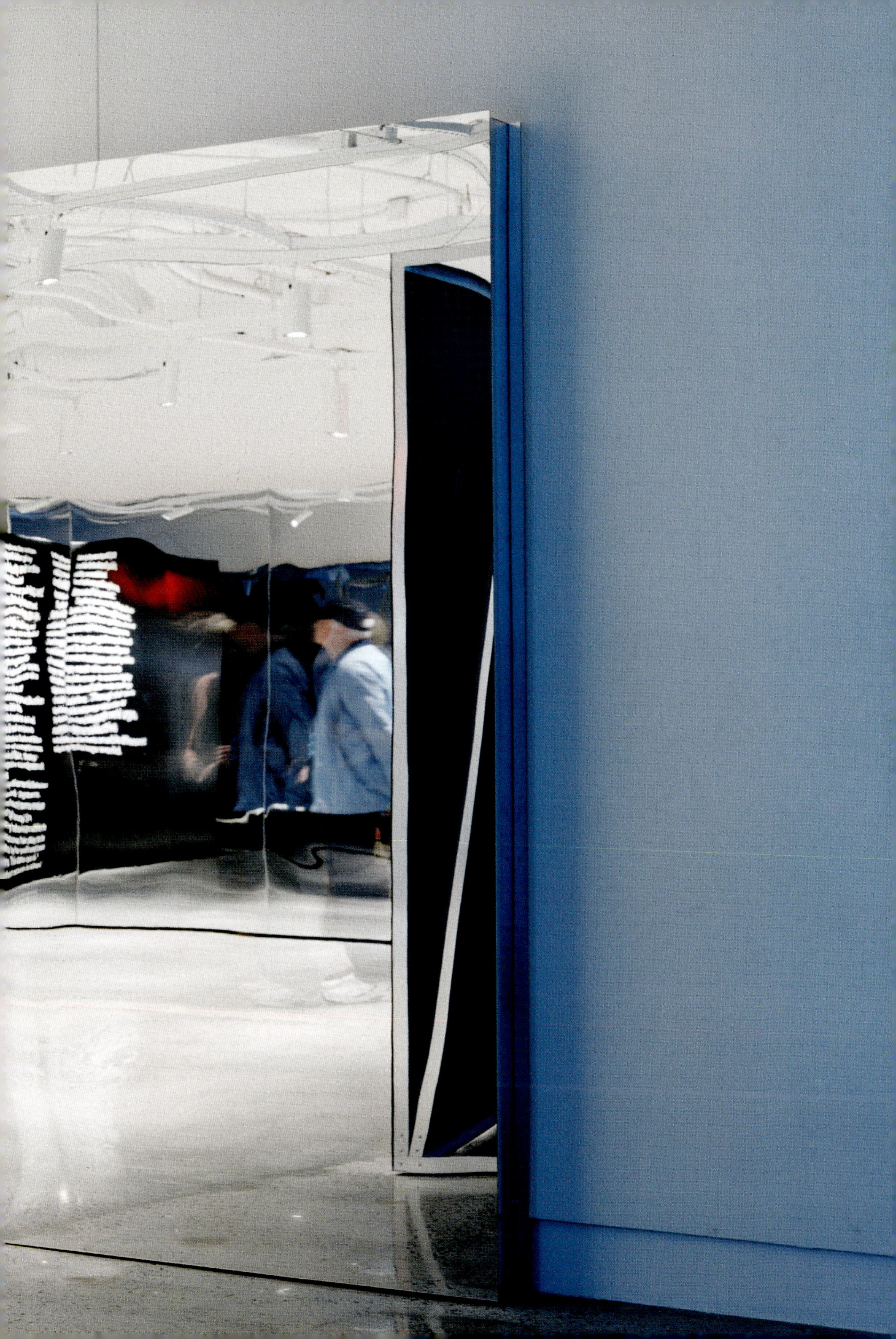

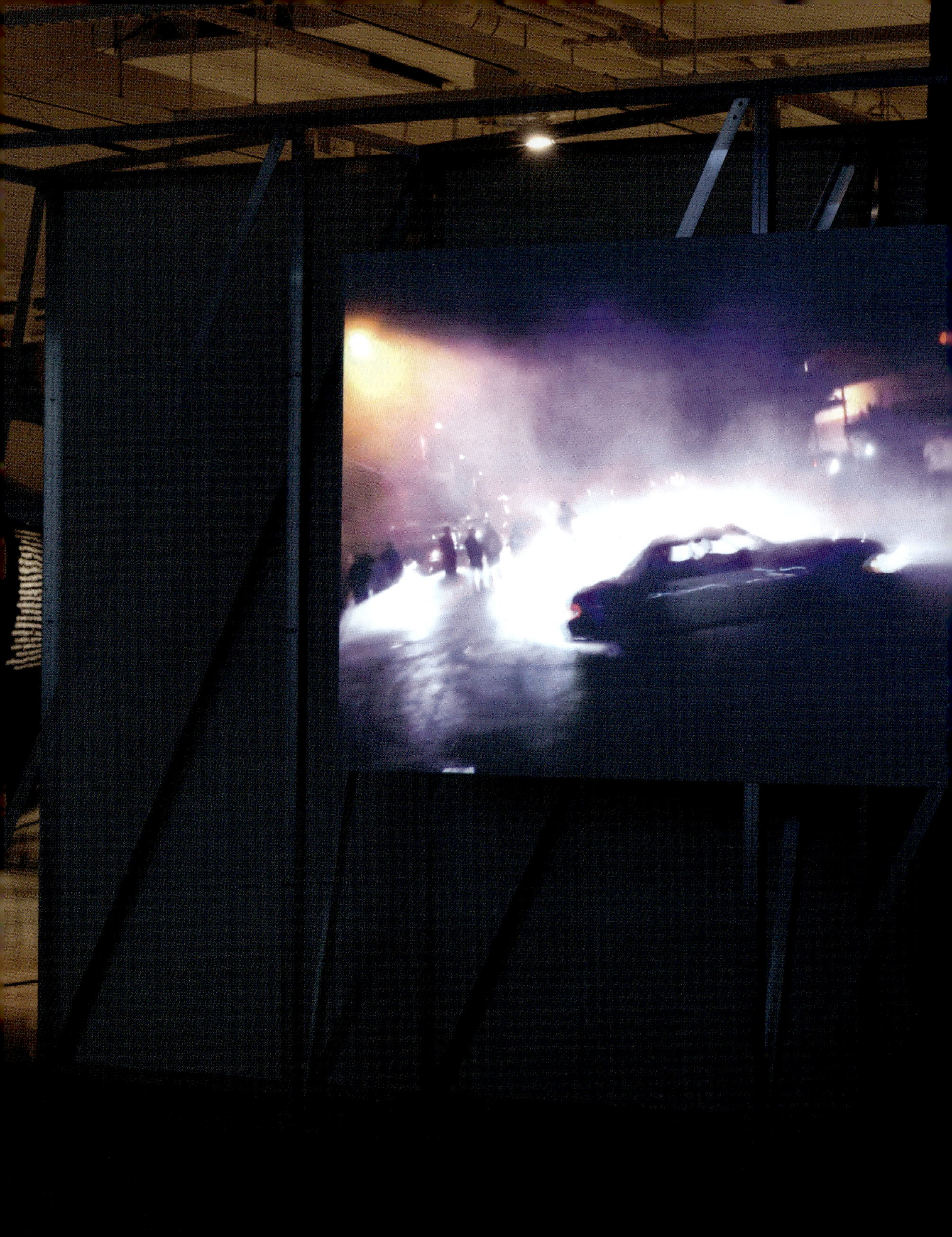

Photo © John Berens

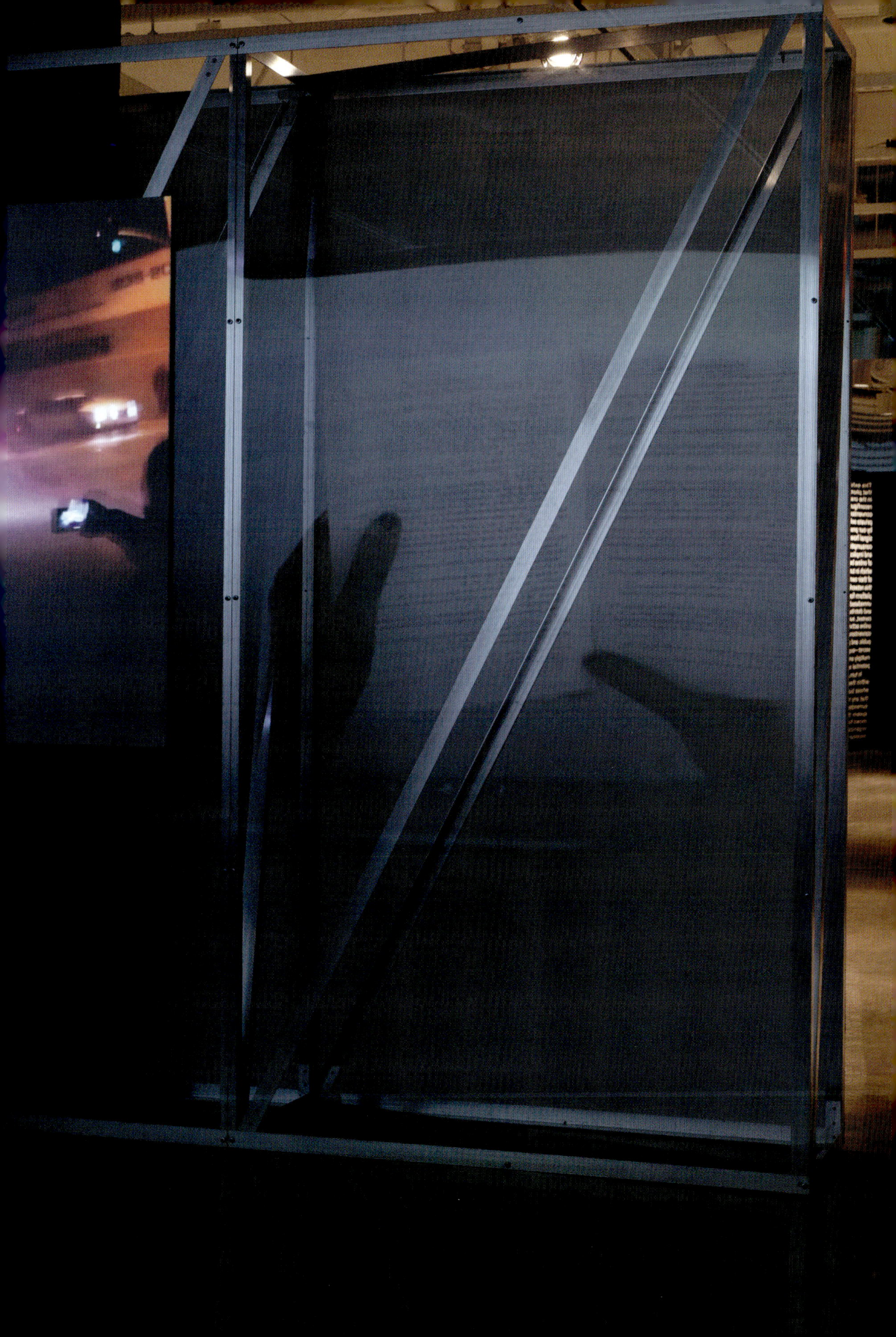

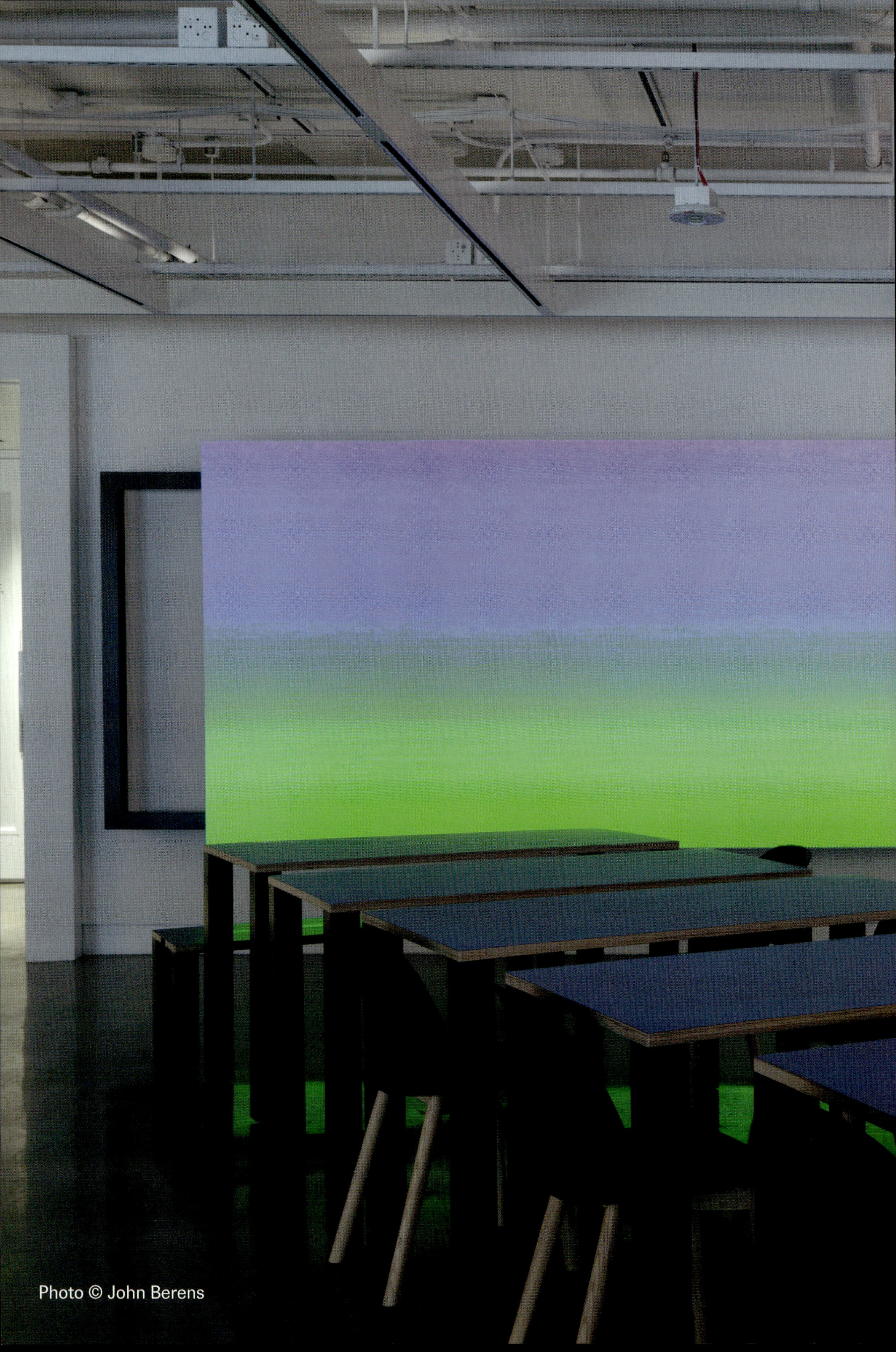

Photo © John Berens

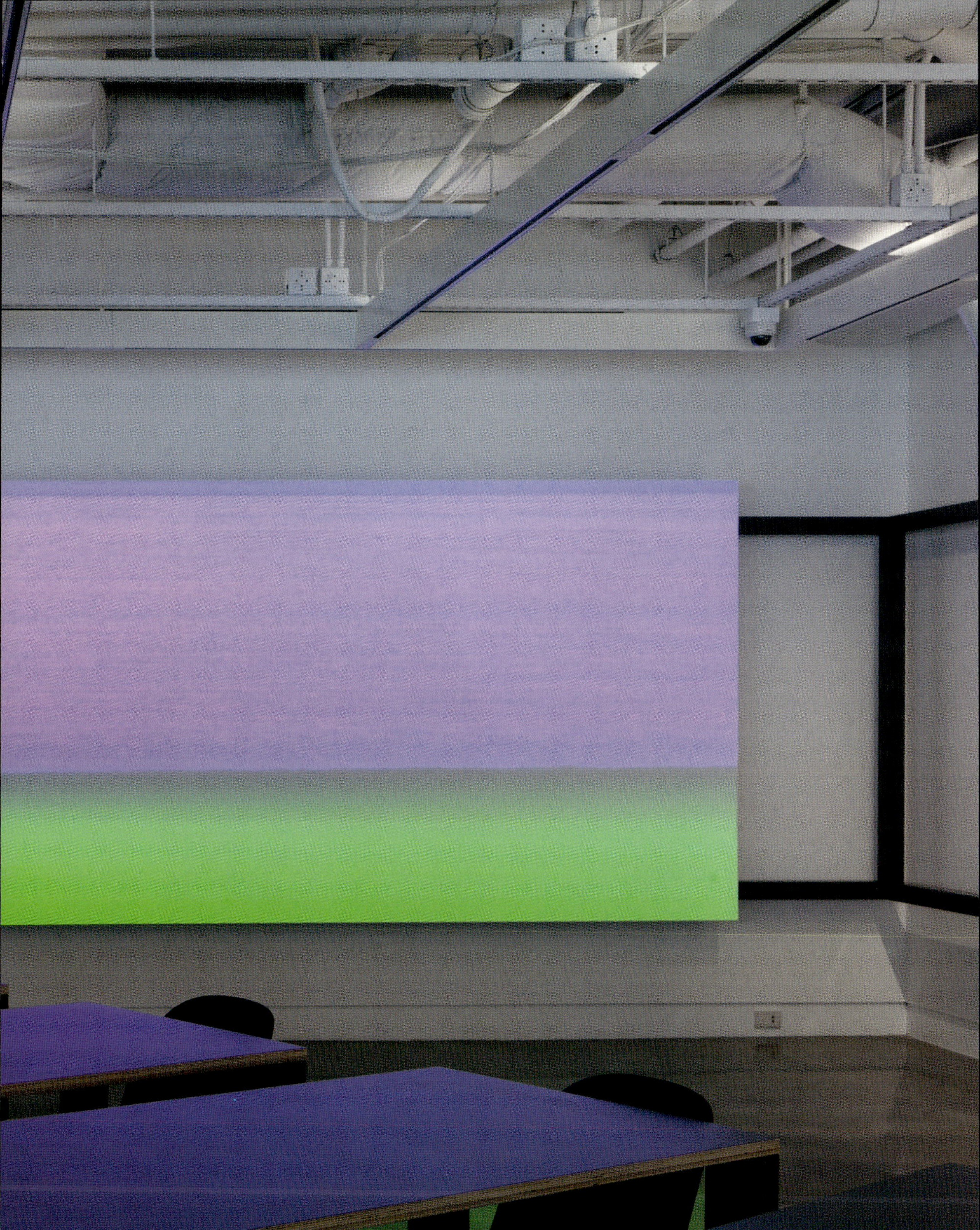

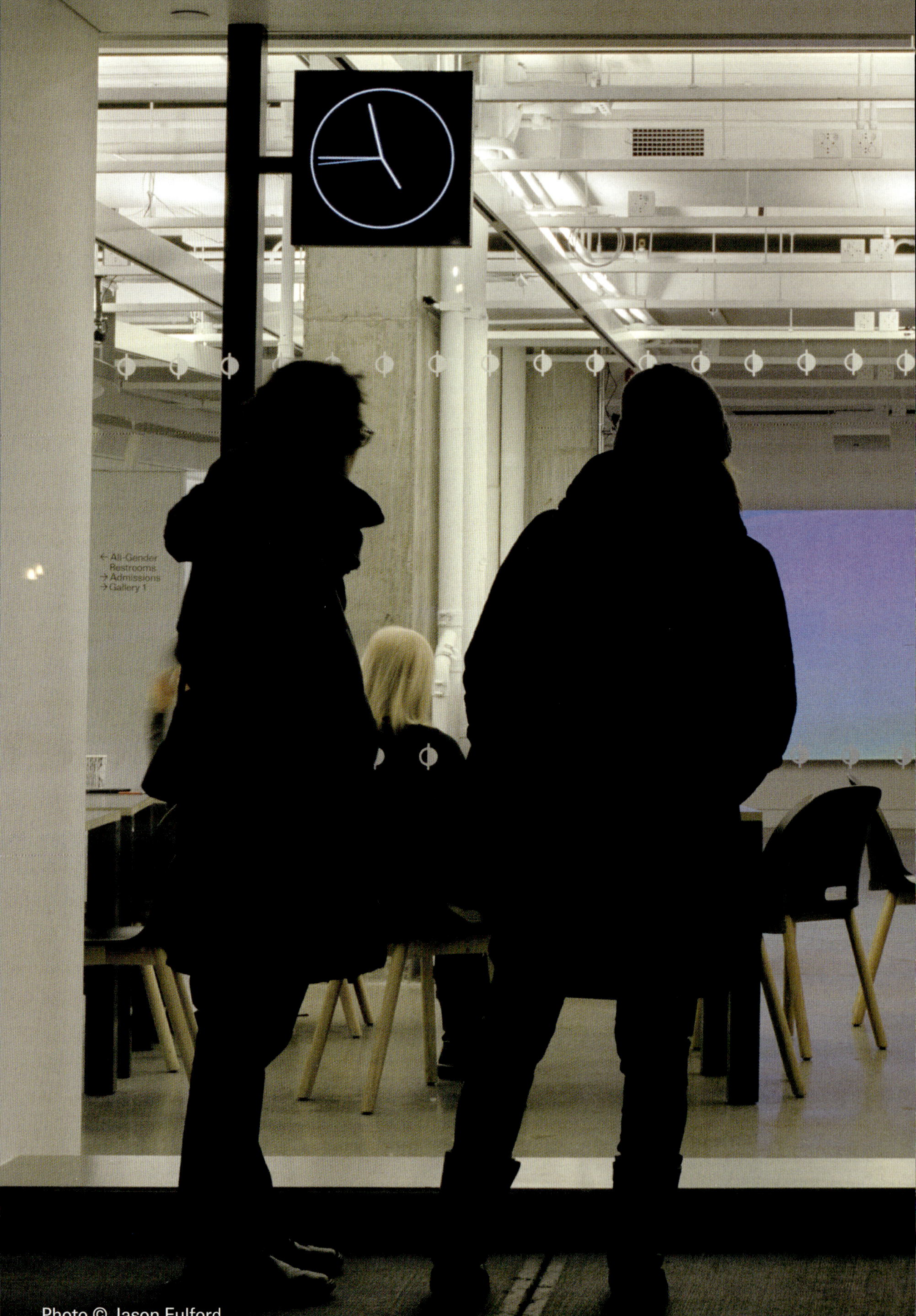

Photo © Jason Fulford

Interviews

Zach Blas with Lucas Wrench
Ann Hirsch with Marina Chao
Martine Syms with Lucas Wrench
Shelly Silver with Marina Chao
Nancy Burson with Pauline Vermare
John Houck with Pauline Vermare
Kate Cooper with Marina Chao
Stefan Ruiz with Pauline Vermare
Merry Alpern with Pauline Vermare
Trevor Paglen with Paula Kupfer
Doug Rickard with Paula Kupfer
Jon Rafman with Marina Chao
Natalie Bookchin with Paula Kupfer
Lyle Ashton Harris (as told by Parissah Lin) with Marina Chao

INTERVIEW: ZACH BLAS WITH LUCAS WRENCH

The practice of artist and writer Zach Blas confronts technologies of capture, security, and control. His recent work responds to biometric governmentality and network hegemony. His Facial Weaponization Suite (2011–14), of which several works were included in *Public, Private, Secret*, consists of masks that can be worn as a protection against biometric facial recognition software. Blas's work has been exhibited internationally, including at Gasworks, London; Institute of Modern Art, Brisbane, Australia; Van Abbemuseum, Eindhoven, the Netherlands; Institute of Contemporary Arts Singapore; e-flux, New York; Whitechapel Gallery, London; and Museo Universitario Arte Contemporáneo, Mexico City. His writing has appeared in *Documentary Across Disciplines* (MIT Press and Haus der Kulturen der Welt, 2016), *Queer: Documents of Contemporary Art* (MIT Press and Whitechapel Gallery, 2016), and *e-flux journal*.

Lucas Wrench: Something I appreciate in your work is the way you've provided new frameworks or lenses: from introducing the notion of opacity to how we talk about biometrics, to applying the idea of the "contrasexual" to how we talk about internet infrastructure, which have, at least for me, dramatically expanded the set of issues I think about when I think about security and surveillance. Could you start by talking about why something more expansive might be needed?

Zach Blas: When I began work on the biometrics artworks, surveillance and privacy were not the core focal points. I was much more interested in biometrics for a very particular reason: the quantification of identification. What are the implications for living in a world where biometrics emerges as a mode of global governance, where identity becomes something that is fully quantifiable, disembodied, and extracted from the surface of our bodies?

Of course, this evokes pressing concerns around security and surveillance, but I wanted to look precisely at capture. Capture is about developing computational grammars or algorithms for extracting and interpreting information. In part, capture works by quantifying and standardizing identity, behavior, and gesture. Capture presents a really different kind of question than the more common idea of a surveillant state watching you. Notice the emphasis on "watching."

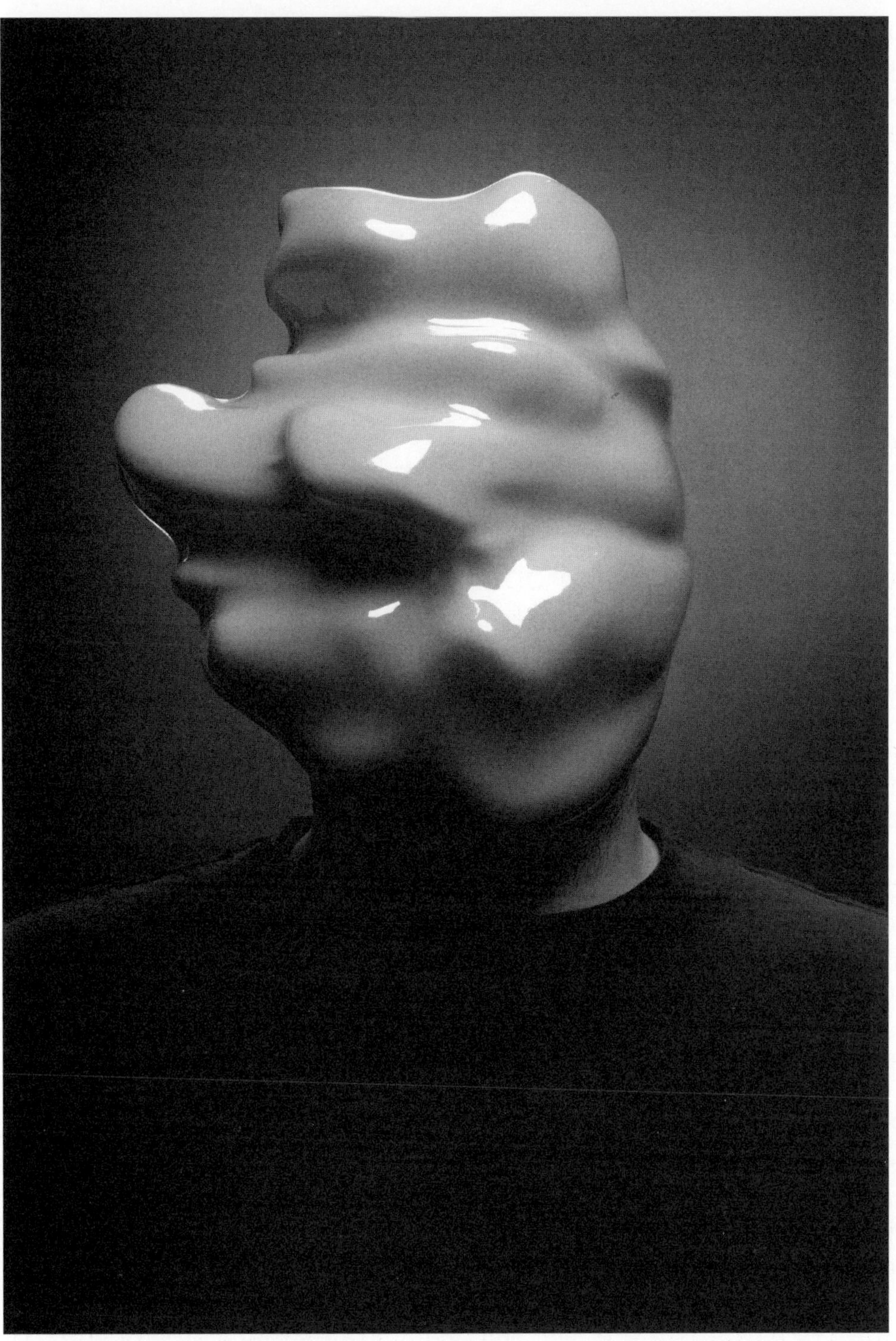

Zach Blas, *Facial Weaponization Suite: Fag Face Mask—October 20, 2012, Los Angeles, CA*

I'm not that fond of the term "surveillance" because it's sort of an empty catchall that says everything and nothing at the same time. Alternately, researching capture is a way to be more precise with the political problematics around biometrics. Interestingly, I think capture doesn't automatically lead to the common knee-jerk anti-surveillance goal of privacy. I wanted another horizon to move toward, as privacy just falls a bit flat. I do not want to invalidate the work that others do around privacy, but I think in my works Facial Weaponization Suite [2011–14] and Face Cages [2013–16] I wanted to shift the location of the political goal or horizon.

In this sense, the political vision can avoid becoming limited to policy change, or simply to politics as we know it. Which is a more transformative and collective possibility, beyond privacy. Privacy can easily remain at the level of the individual, and of private property. I'm not saying opacity takes us all the way to the horizon, but it articulates something that exceeds privacy, for sure.

Can you expand on this idea of opacity that you borrow from Édouard Glissant, and how it's informed your thinking around the idea of capture?

What if community was established through a shared understanding of opacity as an ethics, rather than an individualist practice of privacy? I gravitated toward opacity instead of queerness because I found Glissant's writings more expansive. For instance, opacity is something ontological for him. Glissant writes of opacity as "the ontological relation of the world," so the point is not to become opaque—we already are. Problems emerge when certain things—apparatuses—in the world violate opacity. This could be in the name of security, colonialism, or a mode of conquest or oppression. The violation of opacity, for Glissant, is imperialist, a form of barbarism. He doesn't provide us the tactics to resist, necessarily, but he does the philosophical work of articulating opacity as an ethical mandate. For Glissant, it's political but also aesthetic. It's a quite robust concept, which is very appealing to me. I find it a more powerful and convincing conception of an anti-identity politics than queerness. These days, I find myself on the fence about wielding queerness. I wonder if it does the theoretical or political work one might think it's doing? *Queer* gets used so often as a shorthand for LGBT. I think opacity takes us somewhat past identity—to materiality, to relations, to things beyond the human. Making work around biometrics and opacity draws one's attention to a provocation around queer, feminist, and other minoritarian politics, around the question of what it means today to have an identity, to become visible, to become legible. Biometric governance illustrates that visibility and identification are core modes of control today. These are complicated minoritarian political vectors because if you think to various histories of political struggles throughout the twentieth century—whether gay rights, women's rights, or civil rights—the goal is often toward gaining representation, gaining recognition from the state. Biometric control throws a wrench into this move toward visibility. Of course, more radicalized politics often have their critiques of this—consider older, queer critiques of gay marriage in the US as an example.

Dildotectonics?

The dildo is kind of an analogy for me, or a method. Paul B. Preciado's contra-sexual manifesto is really a philosophy of the dildo, and one of the main arguments is that the dildo is not the same thing as a penis, that the dildo can never be fully reduced to a symbol of phallocentrism or patriarchy. A contest point, to be sure. But Preciado shows that the dildo is a form—I even like to think of this as an abstract, diagrammatic form—that fractures any assumed totality or naturalization of heterosexual/heteronormative sex. That's the contra-sexual power of the dildo! As something unnatural, it undoes assumptions about sex being this way or that way. In the manifesto, Preciado develops a set of experimental practices with the dildo form, as a way for us to get in touch with our contra-sexuality. These are called "dildotectonics." So my question is: what are the dildotectonics of the internet? If the dildo gives access to contra-sexuality, what does that do for the contra-internet? The point here is that the default—or naturalized—form that is used to describe or understand the internet is always the network form. So, the dildo for the contra-internet is definitely not a network! Besides, networks are the prized forms of power and control today. So I'm interested in a formal question: if dildo = contra-sexual, then X = contra-internet. We're solving for X. We can say that X is definitely not a network, because that would be like cishet sex.

INTERVIEW: ANN HIRSCH WITH MARINA CHAO

The video and new-media projects of Los Angeles–based artist Ann Hirsch explore gender, sexuality, and the intersection of self-representation and performance in online spaces. She has created the much-followed, often-trolled YouTube persona Caroline; competed on a reality-television dating show as the good-natured girl-next-door Annie; and subverted pornographic tropes as Ann Hirsch, the "horny lil' feminist." Her video *Here for You (Or My Brief Love Affair with Frank Maresca)* (2010) and the sound piece *YouTube Whispers* (2013) were both included in *Public, Private, Secret*.

Marina Chao: *Here for You* documents your appearance as a contestant on the VH1 reality-dating show *Frank the Entertainer in a Basement Affair*. *YouTube Whispers* is a sound piece in which a woman and a man read fan responses to a series of YouTube videos that feature you as Caroline, a college student and "hipster artist." You frame both of these experiences as larger research projects from which discrete artworks emerged. How do you approach your projects?

Ann Hirsch: I work intuitively and gravitate toward things that naturally interest me, even if I'm not always sure why. I've always been someone who gets caught up in fantasies of herself, or of things that could be. When I was younger and the internet was too, I saw it as an escape, an ultimate fantasy space where I could watch others and project a vision of myself that maybe I couldn't offline. When YouTube came along, I wanted to be a part of it. I had always loved reality television, ever since the first season of *Survivor* in 2000. I wanted to be on it, see what it was like to live the fantasy. Once I became a part of these worlds—YouTube, TV, etcetera—I realized, of course, the fantasy is different than I imagined. I live the roles as research. I make art pieces from the research so other people can understand what it means to experience these situations. They are increasingly commonplace, but sometimes I feel the art world is slow to catch on.

Did you have any assumptions going into these experiences—being on a reality show and performing for the camera online—that were completely disproven? What surprised you?

Before I went on reality TV I was nervous that the other girls on the show would be crazy and scary—because that is how I had seen them portrayed! But (almost) all of them ended up being very normal, kind, regular people. I was surprised by the way producers manipulated us. There wasn't much in the media at the time about manipulation of reality-TV contestants so I walked in blindly. I felt caught off guard by their lies and manipulation, which they employed to create sort of a stereotypical narrative that they thought viewers wanted to see.

With YouTube, in 2008, I was initially surprised by the dark corners of the web. Today, 4chan and Reddit are mainstream. Following the election of Donald Trump, people now understand how internet forums foster micro-communities of people with dystopian worldviews. But back then, we were naïve to that. So when I was being trolled by 4chan, it was very scary. It makes me sad to think that today maybe half the women I know have been heavily trolled online. In 2008, it was unusual and I didn't know how to handle it so I had a meltdown at one point, when it got really bad.

I spent a lot of time listening to the whisper piece in the museum and thinking about what motivates people to respond to complete strangers. Many comments were intimate and earnest, people telling you about their days, their families; others were of the more expected, lecherous variety. What did the responses teach you about our impulse to connect with others online?

Just that people were curious, and very open online in ways they maybe couldn't be offline. Even if someone was fabricating their identity in some way, they were probably telling me things they felt they couldn't tell anyone else, and the fake identity was just a shield. But I think a lot has changed since I did that project, and I wouldn't say people on social media now are there necessarily because they're open and curious. Maybe that time is over. Also, it's much harder now to hide your identity online or to hide any of your online activities from people you know offline.

Are you an active commenter online? If so, what do you get out of it? If not, why not?

No. My Twitter is active but that's about it. I try to avoid confrontation on the internet. It's ugly and I don't think you can have a reasonable argument online. Offline is better. I like to keep a separation between my art and my social-media presence. Some artists consider their social media their art but sometimes people mistakenly think someone's social media is their art. I want to avoid that. It's important for me that people can distinguish between the two. My social media is for me and my friends. My art, I hope, speaks to a wider audience.

Did women and men respond to the Caroline character differently? A signature of Caroline's was dancing to pop songs in a humorously seductive way. I assume male followers would react positively to the performance. What kind of feedback did you get from women?

At the time, there were two groups of women experiencing the project. There were the young girls on YouTube who were "fans" of Caroline, and there were female art peers who knew the project was an art piece. I think the young female YouTube fans really understood the playfulness and the fun of the project in the way male YouTube fans did not. I think they also understood I was just trying on an identity to see how it stuck, and it made them want to try that, too. In terms of my female art peers, I think at the beginning anyone my age [about 23] or older didn't really understand what I was doing and they were worried for my mental well-being. At the time, putting yourself out there online like that was unusual. As the project went on, I started to have younger female artists looking at the project and they really understood it because such experiences were increasingly becoming part of their lives. So I think there was a bit of a generational divide.

I've read that there were a lot of young, female fans that looked up to Caroline. How did you feel about that? And what was their read on her—did they appreciate the nuances of the project, or did they just want to be YouTube stars?

At first I felt bad about the young, teen-girl fans. I thought "No, don't be like me! I'm a slut!" But then I had to reevaluate why I felt that way and realized it was because my thinking was entrenched in this patriarchal tendency to shield young girls from sex. But young girls are sexual. And I think we should let them be sexual. It's when we don't let them be sexual that they end up getting exploited. So I ended up happy that they wanted to imitate me, and that they were beginning to express their sexual selves. I don't think any of them were trying to become famous, they were just experiencing life and experimenting.

Public, Private, Secret was in part about visibility and power. We looked at two sides of a coin: the influence held by those who are seen—or, who actively put themselves on display—and the control that comes with anonymity and obfuscation. In your work, you're an open book, and quite sincere, even as you're being critical. This puts you in both a powerful and extremely vulnerable position. What do you think about the relationship between authority and vulnerability as you make your work?

I dislike the art of artists who try to take an objective position, or try to be moralistic about something they are merely observing, something they haven't experienced. Artists are people. Artists are fallible. I like art that shows humanity. The best art opens up humanity, and allows it to be seen in ways we maybe haven't considered before. I think you can only do that as an artist if you allow yourself to be seen as human. That often means I must be very vulnerable. I don't think of myself as an authority, I only see myself as one voice in a sea of many. But as an artist it is my goal to show experiences that not enough people are paying attention to.

You wrote a play called *Playground* [a Rhizome commission that debuted at the New Museum in 2013], based on your first sexual experience in an online chat room as a preteen. Your recent gallery exhibitions at American Medium in Brooklyn—*Muffy* in 2014 and *A Formidable Daughter* in 2016—both draw from your childhood. Can you talk about the relationship between these projects and describe the role of nostalgia in your work?

I think a lot about childhood sexuality—the ways in which I was sexual as a child, the ways society represses children's sexual tendencies yet simultaneously encourages them through what I call soft-sexual violence in children's media programming. When you're a kid, sexuality feels like a dream, which you can sort of piece together through random things but is ultimately out of your grasp as a concrete idea. The two shows at American Medium, particularly *Muffy*, explored those ideas. *Playground* was, again, about fantasy, but the fantasy of a twelve-year-old living out what she believed to be adult sexual experiences. And ultimately how that fantasy became a sort of fucked-up reality.

I'm not interested in nostalgia per se, but rather in how our childhood experiences affect our adult selves. I'm a big Freudian so I'm interested in the subconscious. I think a lot of people thought *Playground* was an exercise in nostalgia, because it was so much about the late-nineties AOL chatrooms, but really, I wanted to create a clear picture of that time, so people could more fully understand the motivations of the characters.

After all of your research, how would you articulate what it means to be a woman making yourself visible in online space? I'm thinking about a quote of yours that appears in the online exhibition project *Body Anxiety* [2015]: "Whenever you put your body online, in some way you are in conversation with porn."

I would say it sucks. There's no winning. There's no empowerment. You just open yourself up to the worst of the worst. Does that mean we shouldn't do it? Absolutely not. The internet is a public space, and we

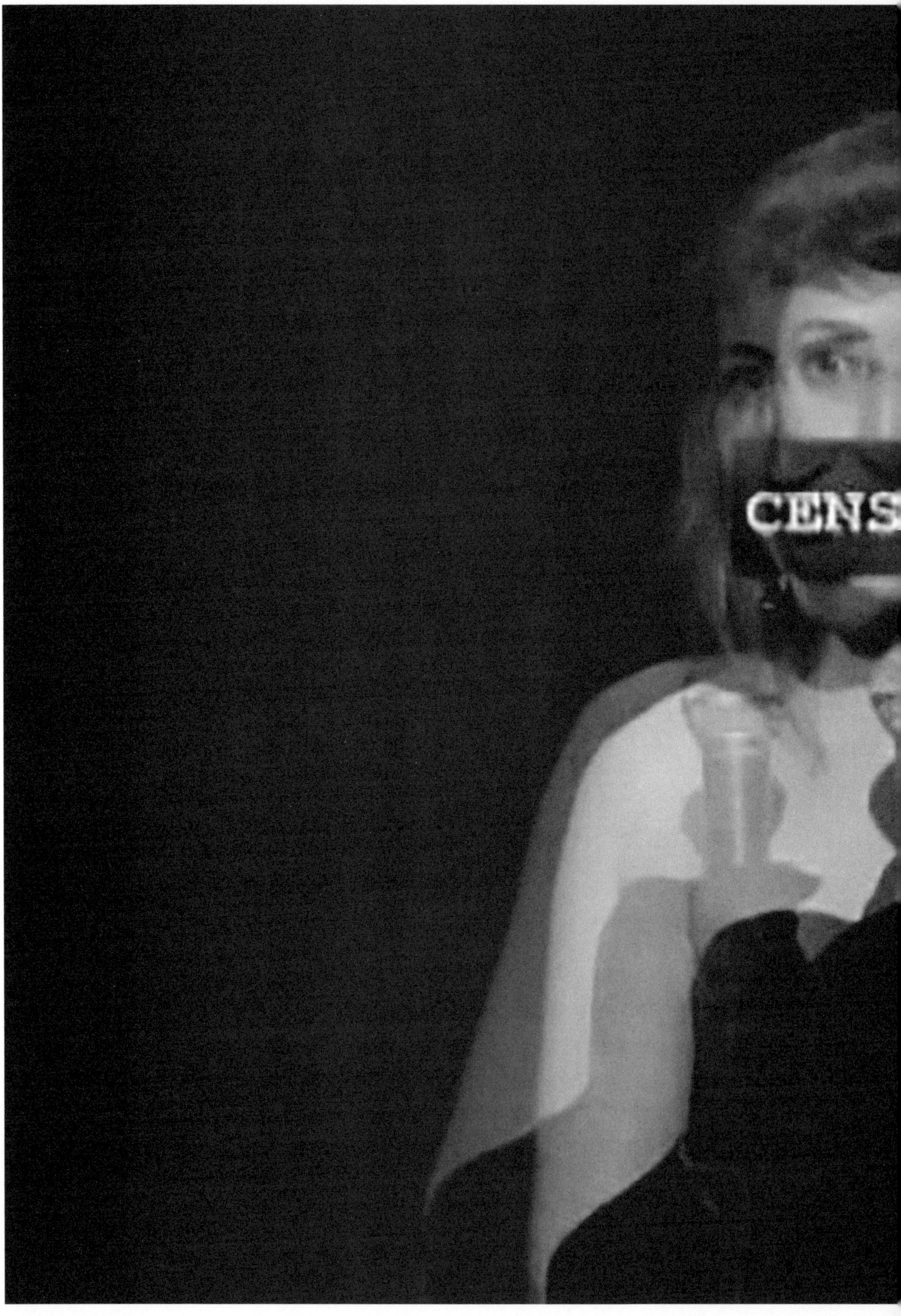

CENS

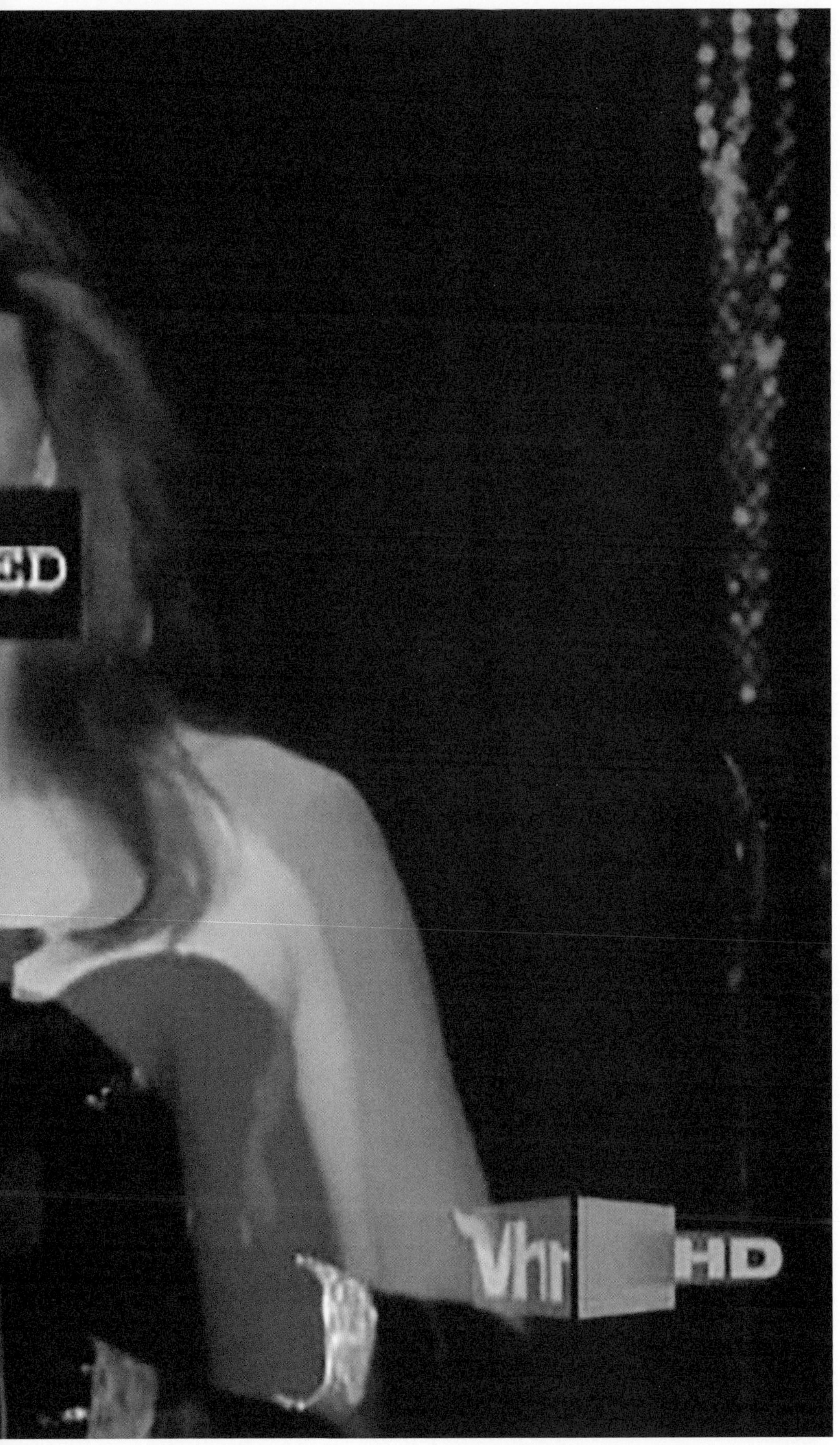

Ann Hirsch, *Here for You (Or My Brief Love Affair with Frank Maresca)*, 2010

can't let ourselves be scared out of it. But it is a really hard space to occupy as a woman or POC.

What I meant by that quote is that a woman's presence online becomes "pornified," which essentially means a woman is viewed as an object, or a nonhuman. In the same way porn compounds gender stereotypes with racial ones, this happens as well with women of color who are visible online.

Thinking about it differently, do you see the internet as a potentially empowering platform for women? There's the idealistic rhetoric about the democratic nature of the internet, and within the discussion of empowered representations of women, the idea that since we're in control of a significant part of the media machine we can diversify the kinds of women—in both appearance and behavior—we see on our screens. Is it playing out that way?

In some ways, sure. I've seen a lot of positive changes in the last ten years, in the way women are viewed and the conversation around feminism. But capitalism is a strong force, and it loves finding ways to co-opt empowering platforms. Let's say we fight a stereotype, and through our actions, people come to understand that stereotype. We've won a battle. But, as a result, new stereotypes pop up that maybe didn't even exist before. It's a never-ending battle. But one I think is worth fighting and does ultimately lead to a greater good.

What are you working on now, and what are you looking forward to getting to work on?

Nothing, I'm retiring from art for the foreseeable future.

INTERVIEW: MARTINE SYMS WITH LUCAS WRENCH

Martine Syms is a conceptual entrepreneur based in Los Angeles. Her artwork has been exhibited and screened extensively, including presentations at Karma International, the New Museum, the Studio Museum in Harlem, Index Stockholm, and MOCA Los Angeles. Syms has lectured at Yale University, SXSW, California Institute of the Arts, University of Chicago, Johns Hopkins University, and MoMA PS1, among other venues. From 2007 to 2011, she directed Golden Age, a project space focused on printed matter, and she recently founded the small press Dominica. Her ongoing work *Lessons* (2014–16), made from found online and personal videos that collectively meditate on black identity and aesthetic traditions, was exhibited in *Public, Private, Secret*.

Lucas Wrench: Thanks for taking the time to talk with me today. I wanted to start by asking about the performance you did at Machine Project back in 2015, *Notes on Gesture*, which was this semi-autobiographical narrative, ranging from memories of your aunt's home in Los Angeles and her home filmmaking, to your encounter with Tyra Banks at her self-esteem-building summer camp (she didn't like her ankles), to Beyoncé and Nicki Minaj's music videos. Could you expand on the idea you presented, about more radical possibilities for empathy, within the potentially more toxic, dominant meme and GIF culture?

Martine Syms: The piece was very much influenced by, or made in contradiction with, Italian philosopher Giorgio Agamben's essay *Notes on Gesture* [1992], in which he half-posits the blocking of movement work as a sort of transference of movement into self, and that's the kind of places they're stored, and that puts them into the political realm.

I was arguing that there was more of a dialectic between the gesture and film. I was focusing on the physical vernacular of black women, and how that was starting to circulate outside of that group, through GIFs or Vines, and meme culture, and these ways that video—you know, slang—as well as actual movement circulate digitally. The GIF was particularly interesting to me because I saw similarities between it and early cinema, in terms of the kinds of images that are used, and they are forms of gesture within digital space. With several friends, we text GIFs to each other, I don't know, shaking my head, giving a high five, sending GIFs of someone

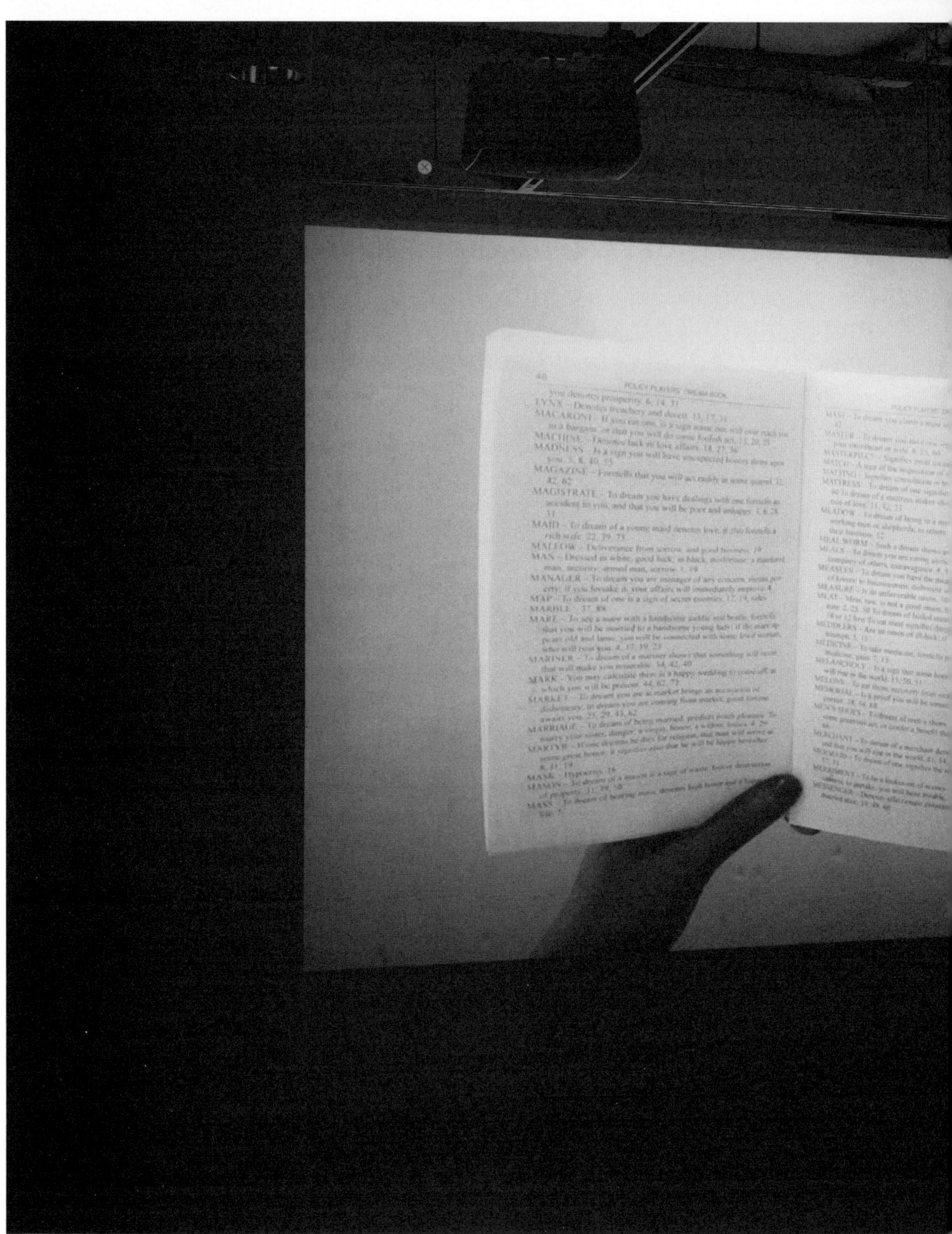

Martine Syms, *Lessons I–LXVIII*, 2014–16. Photo © John Berens

doing that, and so this form of communication is operating in the same way that the gesture would. There is this commodification and marketplace that has existed, but I was thinking about this sort of joy, and fun, and the creative possibilities in being a black woman and communicating with other black women.

The text around your recent show at MoMA, *Projects 106: Martine Syms*, reminded me of *Public, Private, Secret* in that it's using this language of public and private space, but it's not explicitly going into themes such as "surveillance" or "state security." I know for ICP it was a conscious decision to avoid that kind of explicit framing, so I'm curious how you approached that.

The limit between public and private, in my mind, is directly connected to the idea of surveillance. But it also relates to interiority versus some kind of exteriority—interiority as that more psychoanalytic space that speaks to what the self is, an existential space of sorts. I think about this specifically in relationship to performance. That was really what I was thinking about more broadly: the idea of surveillance that I'm calling "ambient cinema," ambient as environmental, ongoing, continued, that there's constantly a filmmaking, or at least image-capture, going on. It could be a film if edited, live or offline. So if those are the conditions that we're living in, where else is production coming into "real life"?

But also in terms of public and private, interior and exterior, there's a micro and macro scale. Gesture is on a micro scale; it's someone's actual body and how their body becomes a document of their experiences. On a macro level, there is, for example, the great migration of African Americans from the South to the North, the large-scale movement of a lot of people. I was looking at function, or utility, on a small scale, on a mundane plane: getting ready for work, getting ready for the day, getting ready to be seen, versus using the language of Motown, of getting ready to perform in front of this huge audience. So there's the question of where they bleed into each other, where the public or the private becomes surveillance. Because, where the bleed is, is that what's private? That's kind of the question right now, or at least it has been, for a long time. There's a kind of self-pastiche, or discussion around surveillance, that talks about it as this contemporary phenomenon, but it's not. From ICE [Immigration and Customs Enforcement] to COINTELPRO [Counter Intelligence Program] to the Middle Passage—this kind of documentation, the watching and tracking of many bodies, and the relationship between that and image technology—is ongoing. It's part of history.

Speaking to this ongoing relationship, the phrase "ambient cinema," ideologically, sounds fuller with possibility than the typical discourse around surveillance. It speaks to a positive potential, or is at least not anxiety inducing in the way, for example, digital-rights advocates speak about privacy. It sounds like you're not pessimistic?

It is all about the conditions. How do you continue to act? How do you continue to have agency? Because for me, thinking about it in terms of autonomy is a dead end. How is anyone going to become autonomous, if that's the goal? You are implicated in every step of the way, implicated in this global system, and the question for me became much more about agency in terms of action, of how to continue to do things, and my own agency. I always think about this line from BARR's album *Beyond Reinforced Jewel Case* [2005]: "How do you start something, you start it." You always have space to act, regardless of what your conditions are, so what action do you take, given the conditions? I'm a filmmaker primarily, so for me the condition of having hours upon hours upon hours of footage means I want to make a film with it, you know what I mean? So I don't know if it's so optimistic or pessimistic, it's just the reality I live in. So I just have a fantasy of like, Damn, if I could get access to PRISM that would be so sick. That's more how I think about it. It's honestly an ethical gray area, but there's this big desire I have to use that stuff.

INTERVIEW: SHELLY SILVER WITH MARINA CHAO

Shelly Silver is a New York–based artist working in film, photography, and video. Through her work, Silver navigates the uncertain and unfixed boundaries between public life and private moments, document and fiction, observation and objectification. Her short film *What I'm Looking For* (2004)—a story of strangers seeking intimacy in public spaces through photography—was part of *Public, Private, Secret*. Silver has screened and exhibited her work widely, including at the Centre Pompidou, Paris; ICA London and Tate Modern, London; the Los Angeles Museum of Contemporary Art; the Museum of Modern Art, New York; and at the Berlin, London, Moscow, New York, and Singapore Film Festivals. She is associate professor and director of the Moving Image in the Visual Arts Program at Columbia University School of the Arts.

Marina Chao: *What I'm Looking For* is currently on view at the ICP Museum. Can you describe the circumstances surrounding the genesis of this work? What made you want to reach out to strangers on an online-dating site with the request, "I'm looking for people who would like to be photographed in public revealing something of themselves...," and document your interactions?

Shelly Silver: I had just finished *Suicide* [2003], a feature film in the form of a personal travel diary cum road movie, about a suicidal filmmaker who travels the globe in an effort to find a reason to go on living. Filmed run-and-gun style in public spaces spanning fourteen countries over four peripatetic years, I was exhausted with inhabiting this woman's persona. I wanted to continue this exploration that one could call "woman with a camera in public space," but to flip the direction of the impulse. I wanted to capture images based on the desires of those in front of the camera.

I wrote in my proposal to the Lower Manhattan Cultural Council [LMCC] Studio Residency that I wanted to capture "moments of intimacy" in Lower Manhattan through traditional street photography and by contacting interested subjects via internet dating sites.

The activity of taking the so-called street photographs wasn't about locating visible examples of intimacy and pressing the shutter; the act of photographing was the intimate act. The experience brought me, for the brief time of framing and taking the photograph, into a one-sided intimate contact with the individual, couple, or crowd. However, photographing the people I met turned out to be a two-sided relationship. Each time I was about to meet a stranger I felt the pressure to perform. It was freezing outside, the winter days were short, and there wasn't much time to pull out the wants, ideas, and desires that would lead to an image. Most often, I think, the pressure to perform was mutual, although I felt I had more at stake.

What questions were you hoping to answer?

The process was more experiential than intellectual; it was grounded in a process of discovery. What could intimacy mean? What is visually revealed in public space, and are these revealed moments meant to be public? Would anyone show up? Now it's pretty typical for people to solicit all sorts of things from these sites, but at the time, I had never heard of this happening.

Were you ever nervous or afraid, going into these encounters? What was your overall experience with the people you met during this project, and how did they handle the vulnerable positions they had opted into?

I was nervous, absolutely. So I made rules. I broke contact with anyone I thought was crazy and I never gave my name or address, just my cellphone number, procured especially for the project. Otherwise I would meet anyone, always in a public space, most often at the Starbucks in the Woolworth building, where my LMCC studio was located.

Otherwise, I used my intuition and hoped for the best. One confrontational gentleman insisted on meeting on a quiet corner in Tribeca at 10 p.m. on an extremely cold night. He pulled up in his car, rolled down his window, and said, "Get in." I had to make a quick assessment. I got into his car and it could have turned out badly, but it didn't. We talked as his heater blasted lukewarm air, he told me what he wanted to do, and then we got out of the car and he did it. Afterward we went for pizza.

It's interesting that you describe the subjects as being vulnerable. Perhaps this man, who later undressed to his socks and underwear, was acknowledging this vulnerability by making me get into his car, putting me in what we both knew was a threatening situation. It was a form of equalization. Of course, in the finished film, the power rests firmly in the hands of the fictional narrator/photographer.

In this work, you play with the documentary form, both in film and photography. There's an immediate sense as you watch the film that it isn't all fiction but the hand of the artist is visible in the narrative style and editing. What, for you, is the value in this slippage between fact and fiction, or documentary and narrative?

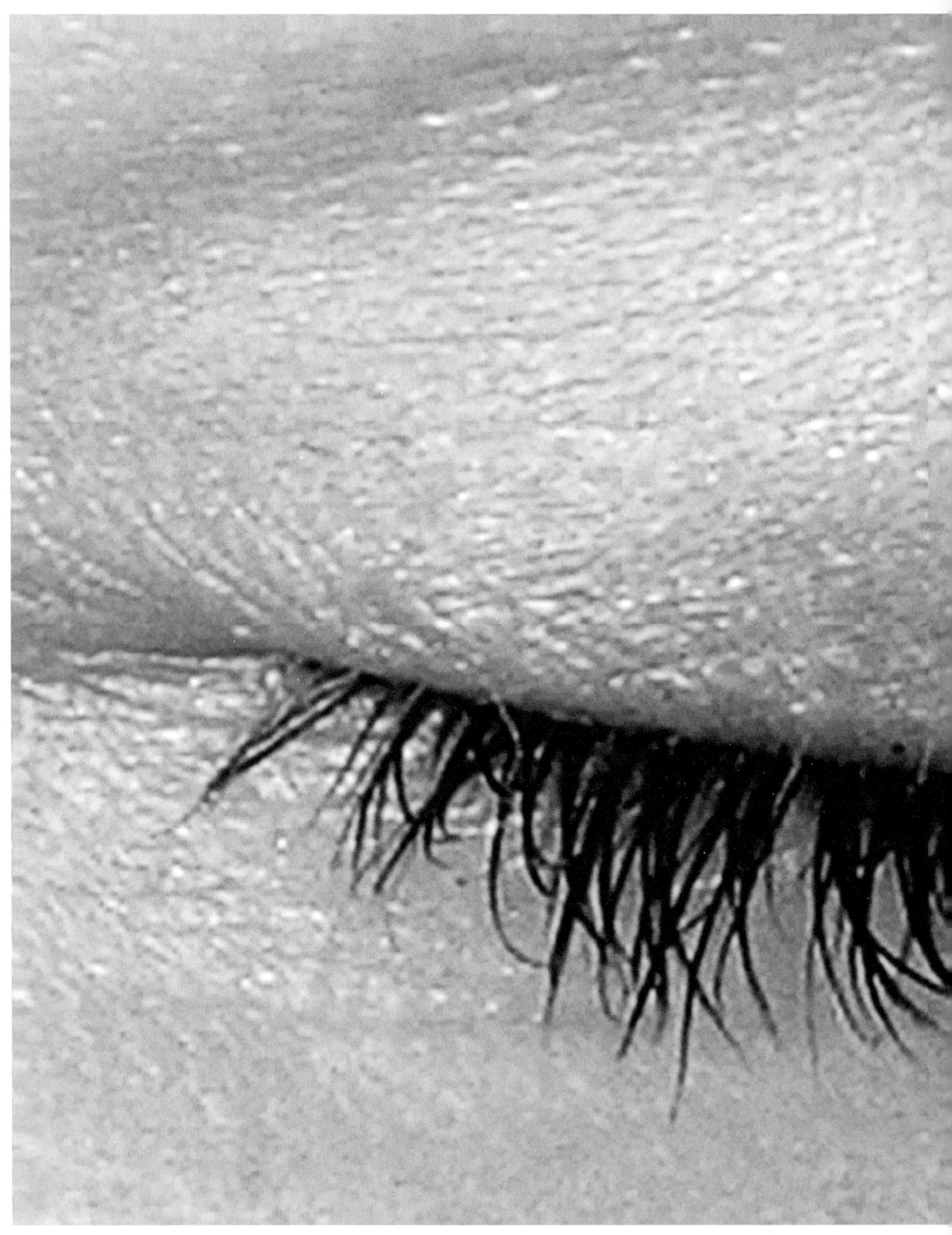

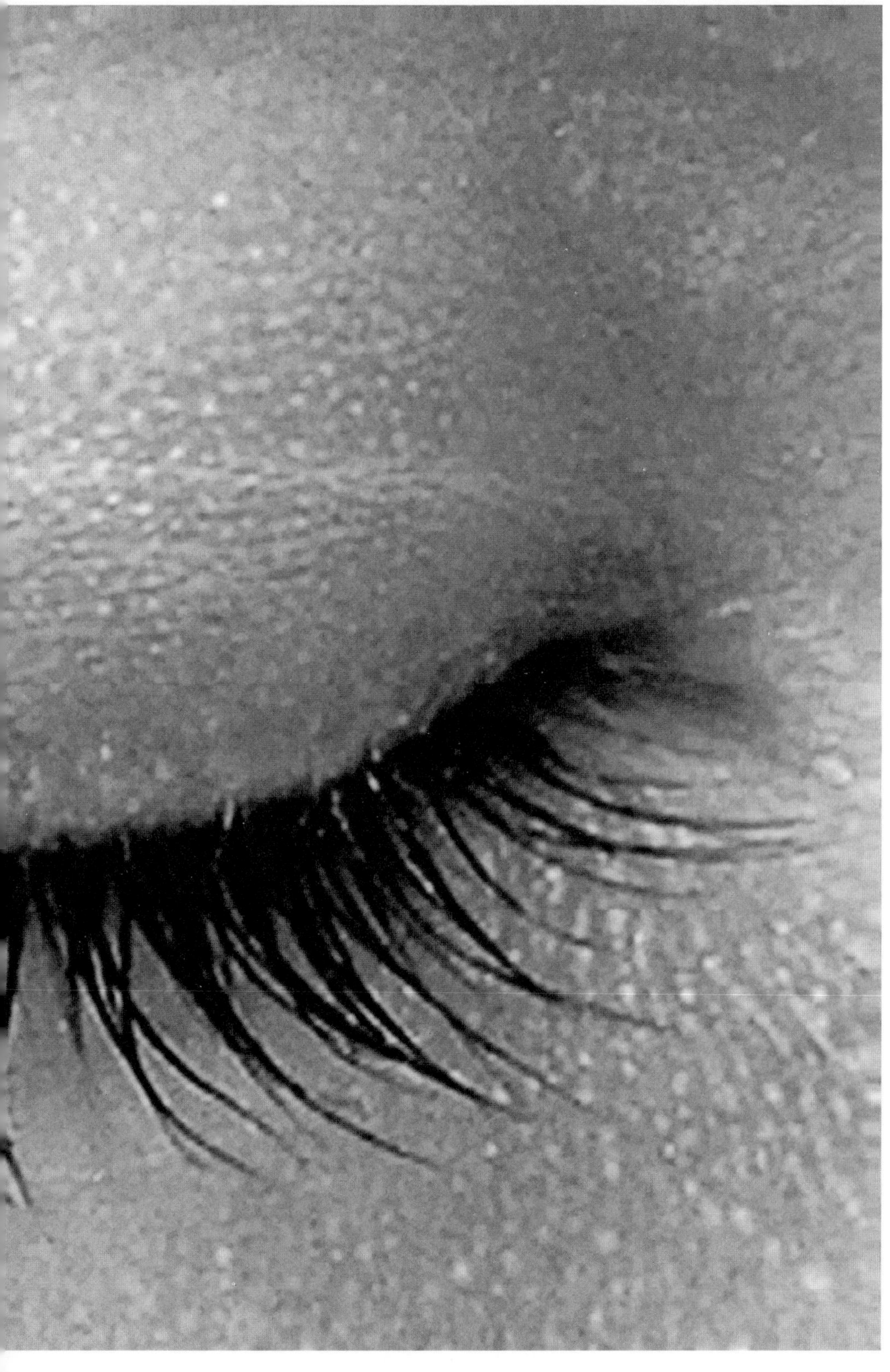

Shelly Silver, *What I'm Looking For*, 2004

I wouldn't call this work a documentary, although I had to confront a standard set of documentarians' ethical issues. Above all, I felt a responsibility toward my collaborators to represent our interaction as accurately as possible. Otherwise, I took great pleasure in shaping the character of the narrator, her tone and use of language, as well as the overall arc of her narrative. She is not me, and for that reason I found her seductive.

The formal decisions I made were, in part, motivated by how best to bring out the different dynamics: between model, photographer, and audience, and between one still frame and the next. The rich space emerged from the play between distance, closeness, and unknowability.

I've been thinking a lot about genre and expectation as we, the public, shift from mainstream media—broadcast television news, magazines, and newspapers, which have moderate controls and accountability—to the Wild West world of social media. This has been in full focus after the recent election. The normalizing of word phrases such as "post-factual" and "post-truth" has frightful implications. The rebranding of the word *alt*—as in "alternative"—on the part of white nationalist groups is a co-opting of a word that has otherwise been used to describe something better. Historically, artistic tropes have often gotten cannibalized. The artist's role is always one of recalibrating, of finding new cracks in the system, new ways of speaking. It's time for new strategies.

Could you speak to the format of *What I'm Looking For*? It is made up entirely of still photographs edited into a continuous film, rather than moving footage. What factors—formal, practical, and conceptual—influenced this decision?

The original project was meant to be a series of photographs. I started out as a photographer, and I wanted to go back to making non-ephemeral objects that did not require additional technology for display. I also wanted to take a break from the relentless editing that my projects require. I was curious to find out how it would feel to capture one image, as opposed to thousands at a time.

And then I photographed the man from Japan, who talked about the destruction of the World Trade Center, the earthquake in Kobe, and the bombing of Hiroshima. I met with him twice, trying my best to photographically tell his story, and I decided I couldn't. The question the narrator asks at the end of his sequence—"Can a photo capture this?"—was also my own. I decided it could not, and at this point thought, Damn, I'm going to have to turn this into a film.

How much was Chris Marker's *La Jetée* [1962]—its form, and the questions it raises about memory, fantasy, and desire—a direct influence?

Chris Marker is someone I've been in a one-sided dialogue with since 1998, when I started to film *Suicide*. I never actually reached out to him, something I now regret. The films share commonalities, overlaps, and disagreements—at times the main character Amanda speaks directly to Marker. *La Jetée* is often referenced in relationship to *What I'm Looking For*; it's true that they share the use of still images.

But when I was writing this work, it's Marker's *Sans Soleil* [1983] that I returned to, which is in part about a man filming and commenting on the people he shoots, many of them women. It is also a fictional essay–film shot in a personal-diary, documentary style, and Marker uses narrative displacement, in the form of a fictional female narrator receiving letters from a cameraman, to tell the story. The film is punctuated by the lovely phrase, "he writes from," which my narrator, twenty years later, echoes when speaking of the many men and women who have sent her messages through the internet. Both films flirt with the confessional and the secretive.

In *Public, Private, Secret* we're exploring, in part, the persistent human impulses that drive us to seek intimacy, which require us to cross emotional and physical boundaries. Were you inspired by the rapid changes in technology in making *What I'm Looking For* in 2004? If so, how would you characterize the landscape now, more than a decade later, and can you imagine the next big paradigm shift?

The landscape has indeed changed and will continue changing: Facebook started in 2004, after this piece was completed, then Twitter began in 2006, Tumblr in 2007, Grindr in 2009, Instagram in 2010, Snapchat in 2011, Tinder in 2012, etcetera. Then there's the way we interact interpersonally, the ubiquitous use of cell phones, and the decline of the mainstream media.... I'm answering this question two weeks after Donald Trump was elected so I still find it hard to give you an entirely rational response, except to say, as an overwhelming understatement, that things have changed. The landscape is not looking good: we are losing the ability as a society to regulate the content of mass communication. There are no longer checks and balances, such as the FCC [Federal Communication Commission], to ensure a modicum of control over information. I'm concerned both about surveillance and information gathering on the internet, as well as threats to net neutrality.

To end, I'll ask the unanswerable question: Do any of us ever find what we're looking for, or is that a fallacy? Is there something eternal about desire?

This question is a complicated one, tied to our culture, to the deeply ingrained way we think about ourselves, but also to the system of advanced capitalism, which runs on a never-ending flow of manufactured desires that must be endlessly fed, that structurally will and can never be satisfied. Without this cycle, neoliberalism, the economic system that we live under, collapses, perhaps in a very ugly way; however, if we maintain this endless addiction to consumption and growth, we will bring about the end of the world.

And then there's the cheery cashier at the big-box store who asks, "Did you find what you were looking for?" which you can answer with a simple "Yes," pointing to the toothpaste and donuts in your cart.

It would be a mistake to say all desire is eternal and unrequited. Perhaps I'll veer slightly from the word *desire*, and bring in the words *time*, *solitude*, *connection*, *finitude*, and *plenitude*. The film has an underlying sense of time and time passing, whether it's the years between a nuclear bomb, an earthquake, and a plane flying into a building, referenced by a visitor from Japan, or a London man's uncanny ability to digitally freeze the precise moment of his ejaculation. There is a sense of physical fragility. It references closeness and death, which is something that Roland Barthes and Marguerite Duras, among others, write so movingly about in relationship to photography. The character of *What I'm Looking For* is susceptible to the open structure of desire, her camera is open to whoever contacts her online. And even if only for a fraction of a second, she is connected.

A person is always a partial being. We are thus always in the throngs of desire, if desire means both reaching out and taking in. The act of looking is a taking in. If our eyes are closed, our ears remain open, our skin—the largest organ in our body—is ever-vibrating with interaction. Desire is not only *for* something or someone; it also functions outward from the body, from the mind, for stimuli, for interconnectivity, for touch, air, sound.
It doesn't mean that we don't find, at any particular moment, what we're looking for.

INTERVIEW: NANCY BURSON WITH PAULINE VERMARE

Since the dawn of the digital age, artist and photographer Nancy Burson has combined art, technology, and innovation to challenge notions of photographic truth. She became well known for her pioneering work with morphing technologies that "aged" the human face and helped law enforcement officials locate missing children and adults. Her public art project *Human Race Machine* (2000–), which allows people to see themselves as a different race, has been used on college and university campuses since 2003. She has collaborated with Creative Time, the Lower Manhattan Cultural Council, and Deutsche Bank in completing several important public art projects in New York. Her work *Big Brother (Stalin, Mussolini, Mao, Hitler, Khomeini)* (1983) was exhibited as part of *Public, Private, Secret*.

Pauline Vermare: Your iconic piece *Big Brother* is currently on view at the International Center of Photography as part of *Public, Private, Secret*. Would you tell us about it and how it came to be?

Nancy Burson: *Big Brother* was a commission for a CBS Walter Cronkite special that drew some interesting parallels about where we were collectively as a society, compared to Orwell's fictional vision in *1984*. They made a poster out of the composite image of Hitler, Stalin, Khomeini, Mao, and Mussolini, and used it as a backdrop for Cronkite, who was standing in front of it on a London street corner. I especially like the end, where Walter rips up the poster and throws it in the gutter.

You were one of the first artists working with morphing, in the 1970s. When and why did you become interested in combining photography and technology?

I was a painter in college and wasn't thinking at all about photography. I was thinking about ideas and how to make things that hadn't been made come to life.

When I moved to New York City in 1968, the first museum exhibition I attended was MoMA's *The Machine as Seen at the End of the Mechanical Age*. I was thrilled by the interactive nature of the art and Nam June Paik's video works. These were new concepts to me.

Shortly after seeing that show, I began to develop the idea of aging people by computer—and I knew

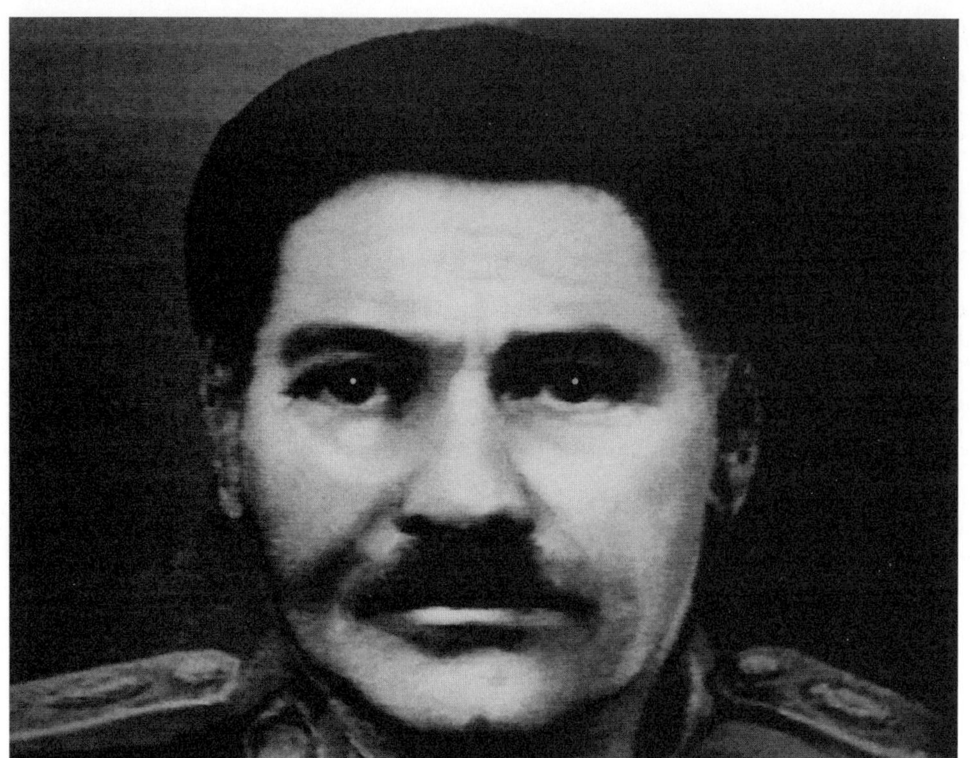

Nancy Burson, *Big Brother (Stalin, Mussolini, Mao, Hitler, Khomeini)*, 1983

nothing about computers. Of course, in those days, relatively few people knew much about computers! I went to Robert Rauschenberg's organization, EAT [Experiments in Art and Technology], and they paired me with an early computer-graphics expert who told me I'd have to wait for the technology to catch up to the idea. Eight years later, I ended up working with what is now MIT's Media Lab and that collaboration resulted in the methodology of what became known as facial morphing.

Would you tell us about the psychological intent of your composite portraits, including the *Human Race Machine* [2000–]?

Actually, the first portraits I made were more about visual experiments that served as answers to things I was thinking about. For example, what would happen if you put an equal number of men and women's faces together? Would the composite look more feminine or more masculine?

It was the later composites, made between 1988 and 1990, that were viewed as confrontational. Many of those images were taken from medical textbooks. However, when I made them, I didn't see them as anything other than beautiful and was rather surprised when viewers found them to be a challenge. I wanted to get pregnant and at forty-one years old, I was thinking a lot about what might happen if I gave birth to a child with a deformity.

The intent of the *Human Race Machine* was to produce an empathetic response in everyone who used it, so it was really about the impact of seeing oneself as something different from who we are.

Can you talk to the social and political nature, and impact, of your work?

The real-life impact of my work was finding several missing children in the mid-1980s, when my former husband and I were working with the FBI and National Center for Missing and Exploited Children. We used either a sibling look-alike or an old picture of one of the parents as a child to provide a second image with which to age-progress the missing child. Several of the missing-kids' updates were aired on national TV and on two occasions, the producers brought in a crew to film the parent's reaction to the composite update being made. Both video and stills were shown in those segments, and the children were found within an hour of the show's airing. There were about four children that were found in 1986 and the FBI located at least one adult who had been age-progressed using our software.

You recently created the series *What If He Were?* [2016], on Donald Trump. Do you feel that photographers—and photographs —can still play an important role in American politics?

What If He Were was a commission by a prominent magazine that ultimately decided not to publish Donald Trump as five different races. My interest in creating this work was the desire to know what his reaction might be if he saw the images. Current research shows that the experience of oneself as another produces an empathetic response within the mirror neurons of the brain. The question in my mind was whether Donald Trump's brain would be affected with an empathetic response upon viewing the work.

I believe that in any given moment and in any situation, there's always the potential for change. And whether or not those changes occur is dependent on what I'd call destiny. And since we never really know what's meant to be until it is, the best we can do is to make every effort to make a difference.

What are you currently working on?

I've been working on what I refer to as "secret stuff" for the past several years. For now, I'd say that my interests are physics and its relationship to metaphysics, and the conjunction of cosmic consciousness to the Higgs boson and dark matter.

INTERVIEW: JOHN HOUCK WITH PAULINE VERMARE

The Brooklyn and Los Angeles–based artist John Houck works with photographic materials and installation to explore photography as a mode of thought, focusing on the relationship between embodied perception and depiction. He received his MFA from UCLA in 2007, and completed the Whitney Independent Study Program in 2010. His most recent solo exhibitions include *Playing and Reality* at On Stellar Rays, New York, and *The Anthologist* at Dallas Contemporary in Dallas, Texas. His work *Portrait Landscape* (2015), which proposes a new reading of Michelangelo Antonioni's 1966 film *Blow-Up*, was exhibited in *Public, Private, Secret*.

Pauline Vermare: Your stunning piece *Portrait Landscape* is currently on view at the International Center of Photography. Would you describe it to us, and tell us more about its title?

John Houck: I wrote software that uses computer vision to find faces in Michelangelo Antonioni's movie *Blow-Up*. The software often misrecognizes faces and finds them in a field of grass or in the folds of someone's clothes, for example. The film is cut down to about ten minutes and only features scenes with the misrecognized faces. I also used editing software to pan and zoom into each face. It has a humorous and haunting effect. The title references two different names for the aspect ratio of pictures and it can also be read literally as a landscape of portraits. Whenever I think of the movie *Blow-Up*, the image of the lush, green parks around London comes to mind.

You traditionally work with painting and photography. What led you to create custom film-editing and facial-recognition software?

Prior to graduate school I worked as a software engineer for many years and I still program here and there for specific projects in my studio. This project started with an interest in the fact that images and film are now being scanned and "watched" by software agents. Images are now viewed and indexed more by machines than humans.

Portrait Landscape is composed of multiple scenes from *Blow-Up* and eerily resonates with what Antonioni said at the time: "I'm really questioning the nature of reality ... I always

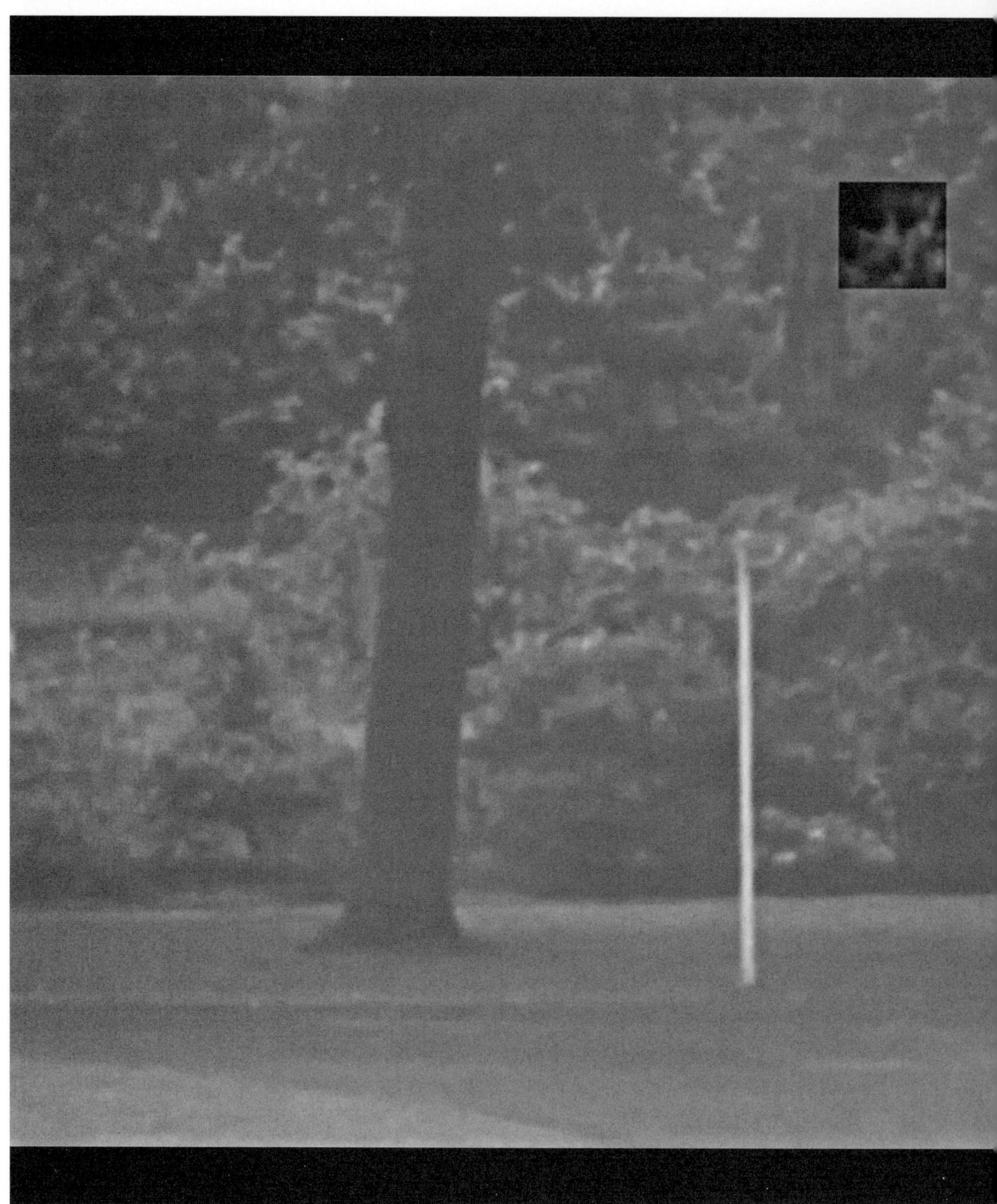

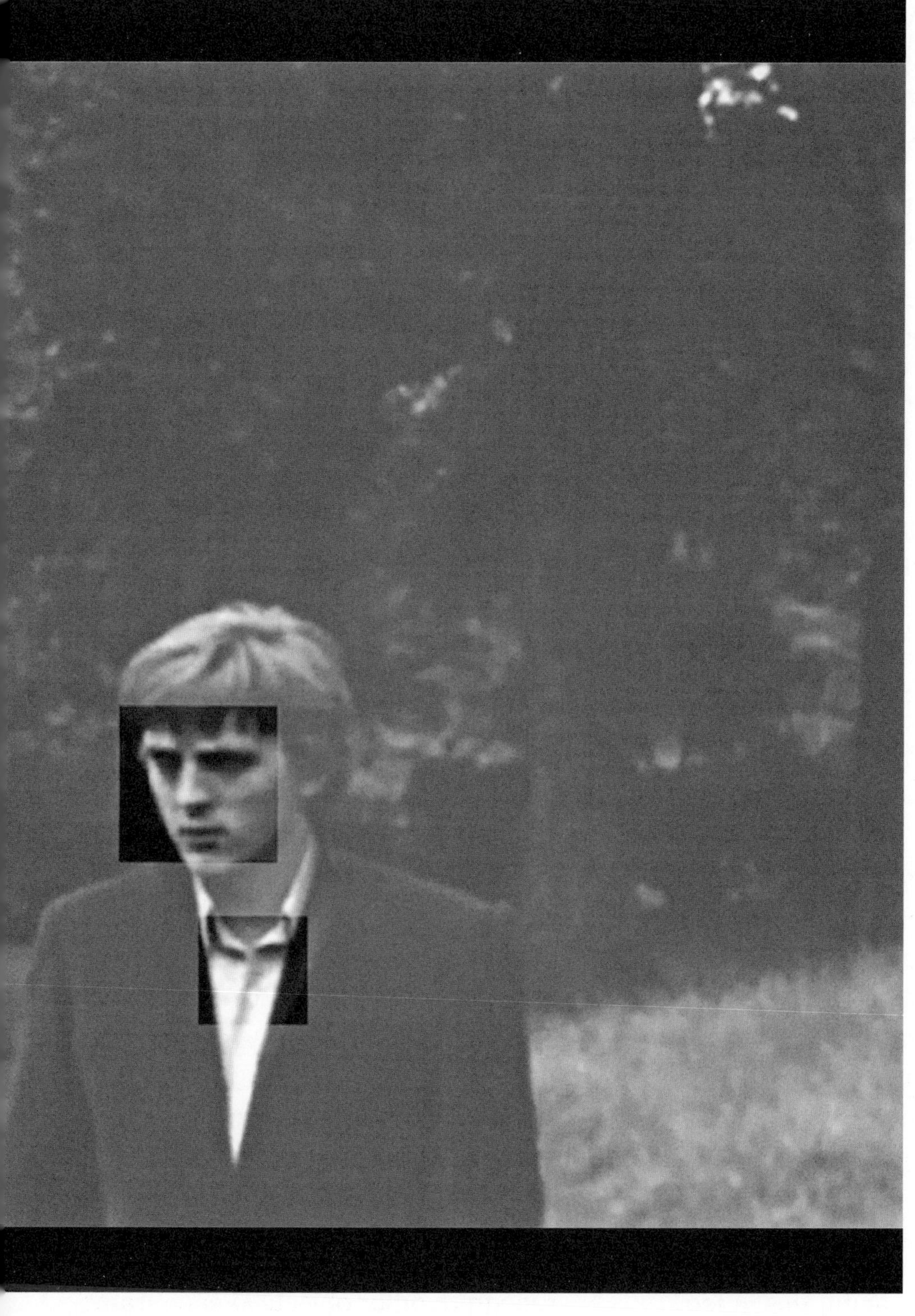

John Houck, *Portrait Landscape*, 2015

mistrust everything which I see, which an image shows me, because I imagine what is behind it. And what is beyond an image cannot be known." Why did you choose to work with this film in particular, and how did you select the scenes?

That is a great quote. Antonioni even painted the physical leaves and grass with green paint in the park scenes in *Blow-Up*, to make the film more vivid. This film came to mind because the main character is not that unlike the autonomous software agents that now scour the internet, indexing images. He is a kind of automaton, always on the move; he's constantly snapping photos, leaving abruptly, jumping up and running.

The scenes selected themselves, in a sense. I programmed my software to make a cut in the film anywhere a face was recognized in a scene. I then used editing software to go back in to pan and zoom in on the misrecognized faces. So there's this odd correspondence between my virtually edited camera moves and the ones from the original edit of the film.

In the film, the main character is trying to solve a murder he inadvertently photographed, but he keeps zooming into the pictures and is frustrated that it doesn't resolve anything. There's something in the futility of his search that is parallel to the futility of my search for faces in the film.

Your last show at On Stellar Rays, *Playing and Reality* [2016], dealt in part with the notion of the "analytic third," extending it to an interstitial third entity between painting and photography. With *Portrait Landscape*, the third entity resides between the film and the photographs—between one of the most iconic fictions of our times and an unsettling stream of surveillance-like images that look like human faces. The interstitial entity is the invisible, paranoid big brother that you created and who ends up guiding our gaze and subverting our psyche. Would you tell us about the psychological intentions of your work, and of this work in particular?

I wasn't thinking so much about psychoanalysis or the idea of the "third" when making this video, but the faces were interesting to me because of their emotive quality. They are also something that humans so readily recognize; the slightest suggestion of a face and we project all kinds of emotions on to it. I could have easily trained my software to recognize other objects in each frame, but we don't as readily project onto a misrecognized banana as onto a human face. I also didn't intend the film to be as funny as it is. The first time I showed it, people were laughing out loud as they watched it. It felt like finally my interest in comedy had come through in a work. Luckily I hadn't set out to make a funny piece! Had I intended to make it funny it probably would have felt too on the nose.

The end result is a striking, mesmerizing, and moving piece—and surprisingly melancholic. Did you expect this work to have such an emotional impact on the viewers?

You can never anticipate how something is going to be received, but I know that watching it over and over as I edited it, I certainly felt that haunting quality. It creates that same compulsive feeling we all have when life is lived through the lens of the camera. That obsessive feeling of walking around a city and snapping photos incessantly while knowing that we are continually being photographed, video-recorded, and digitally traced.

INTERVIEW: KATE COOPER WITH MARINA CHAO

Amsterdam-based artist Kate Cooper's recent series RIGGED explores the intersection of economy and psychology within an idealized, digital female body. Cooper is cofounder of Auto Italia South East, an artist-run organization based in London that works directly with emerging artists to commission and present new work, and was the recipient of the 2014 Schering Stiftung Art Award. Her video *RIGGED* (2014)—featuring an idealized CGI female figure whose inner monologue reveals acutely human feelings of anxiety, alienation, and fear—was on view in *Public, Private, Secret*.

Marina Chao: What were you working on and thinking about before you embarked on the RIGGED series, and how did the idea of working with computer-generated imagery and animation emerge?

Kate Cooper: *RIGGED* came out of a few projects. Through Auto Italia, I had been coproducing exhibitions, talks, and making films about ideas such as immaterial labor, creative work, and self-representation in our current, networked conditions. I was thinking about new forms of gendered positions, and considering what was at stake in these new economies and spaces of online distribution.

The works I produced just before *RIGGED* involved working with professional beauty models and online voice-over actresses. I was interested in the idea that the voice, like the image, contains one's capital. Through my work with the models, I was exploring the notion that their labor and source of capital is contained in their image, and that some measure of self-exploitation lay within that. I wanted to understand how we as creative workers might harness these new types of labor. A few years before embarking on *RIGGED*, I had been working with a women's film archive in London in collaboration with a group of female artists. In considering this historical archive in 2011–12, our question was how to negotiate the position of a female artist/filmmaker producing moving images today. It was this combination of projects and collaborations that really planted the seed for developing *RIGGED*. When I was commissioned by KW Institute of Contemporary Art in Berlin to produce a new exhibition, I knew it was a good opportunity to experiment and produce CG images, rather than referencing them or using found material. I wanted to get my hands dirty, so to speak, and work from within the material rather than at a distance.

When making *RIGGED*, I was questioning the ideas surrounding production, representation, and distribution of images. I wanted to understand these images and their position as material that is as much code as it is skin and pores. There is an explicit violence and desire within the images; I wanted to learn how to exploit and hack these images and understand the line in between—understand not only our relationship to them but also what they might be used for, and how they perform in themselves. I found it productive and freeing that the images didn't represent anyone in particular; they are fiction. This opened up wider possibilities.

Through the work I'm also examining ideas of class and gender, particularly related to beauty and representation, and how the body itself becomes an image-production machine. How do images accrue value and capital, and at what point do we withdraw or refuse our own labor—as workers and bodies, and within a certain collection of aesthetics?

There is a lot of moralizing surrounding women's relationship to social media and their own forms and language through representing themselves. I'm more interested in picking up on the complications in these positions, for instance how women through this self-awareness might be more in control of their own representation.

I'd like to ask you about the *RIGGED* publication [Sternberg Press, 2016], which was made in the style of a "lookbook." What interested you about this form of advertising specific to the fashion industry? I'm also curious about the enigmatic glyphs on the cover. They include a flag, an eye, a blended gender symbol, and a double-helix, among others. It's a word cloud but reduced to icons, similar to the way we communicate today.

Lookbook was a collaboration with photographer and filmmaker Theo Cook, designer Michael Oswell, and curators Catherine Wood and Ellen Blumenstein. The idea came from the desire to understand images within the format in which they are presented. I wanted it to be called "lookbook" to state what it is—an object you are viewing. I decided to keep the title descriptive because the format of a lookbook corresponds to a space in which bodies are "read." It was the first time I worked on a print publication and was excited that the book did something different with the material from the exhibition. For example, I was adamant to not include installation shots; instead, we produced new material. It was in many ways like making and editing a new film, and it was a new, complementary format to the exhibition.

The symbols came from a text by Catherine Wood—a response to the exhibition—and serve as a way to navigate and thread the publication. Michael Oswell and I liked the idea of the text becoming an image, as a framework to make the image perform a different set of prescribed rules. It was akin to a new type of code and language; in the same way, the bodies were functioning in the images. There was a desire for the publication to exist as a project that could be read on its own—separate from the exhibition—but that would also be complementary to the show.

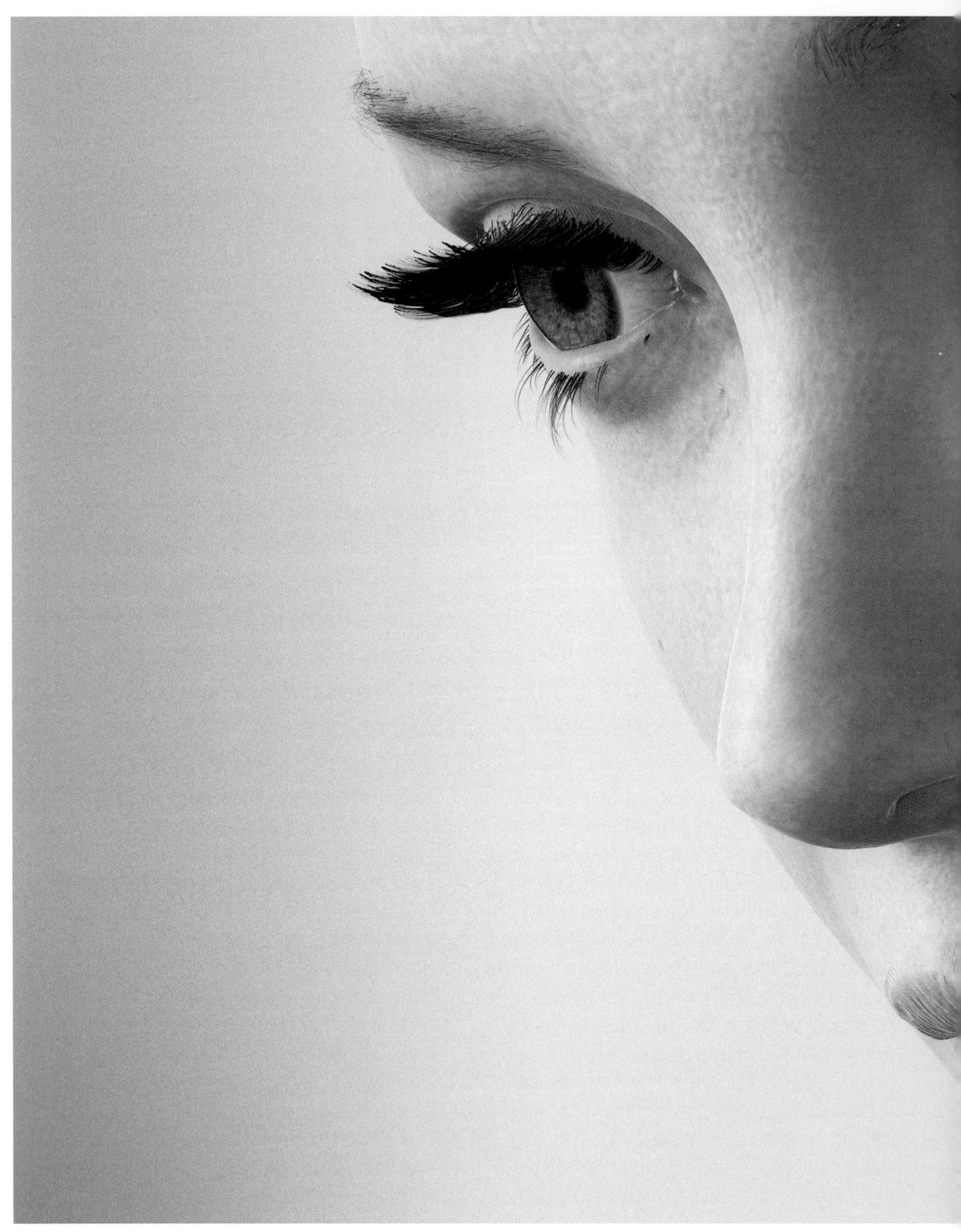

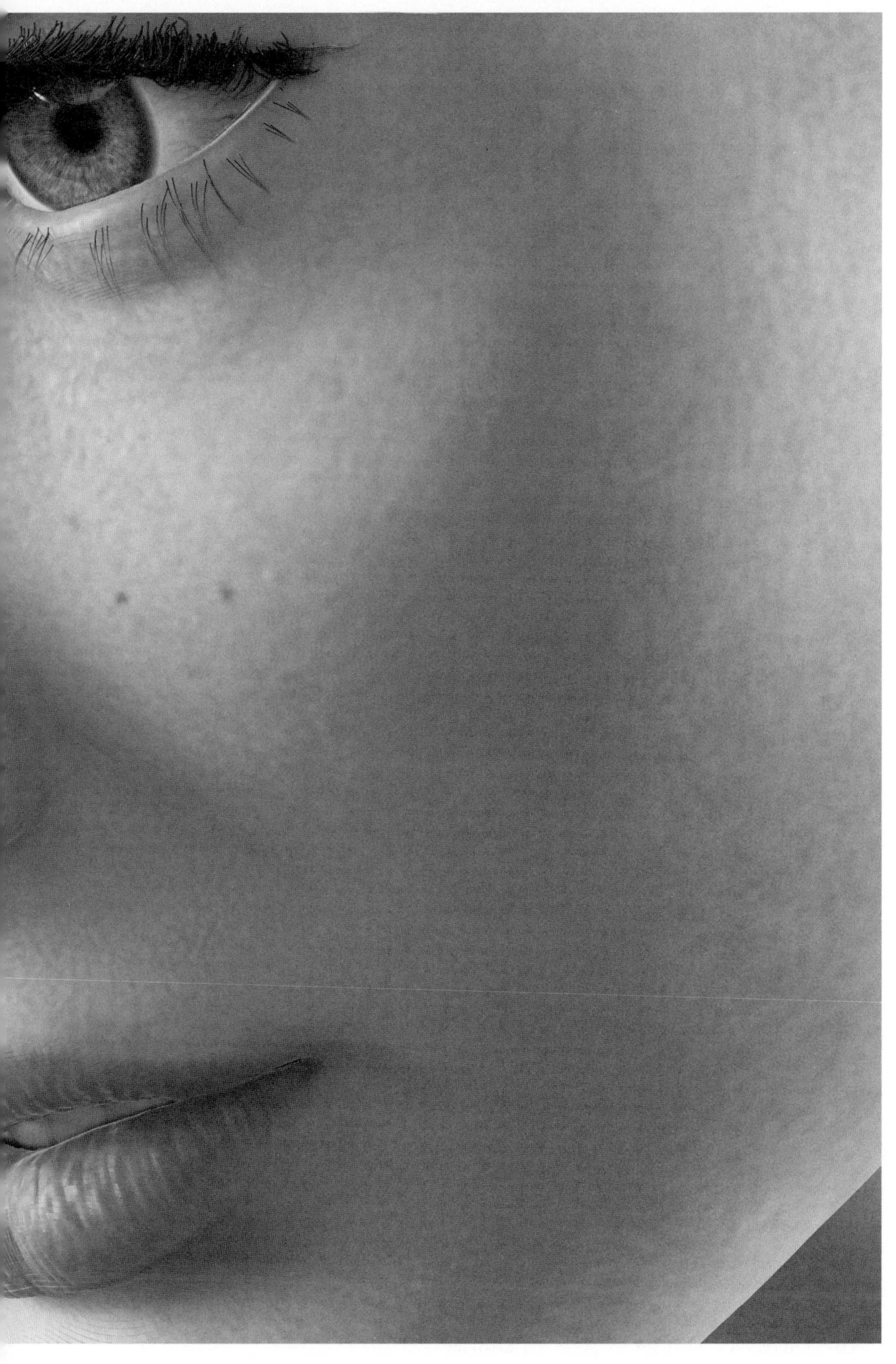

Kate Cooper, *RIGGED*, 2014

Lookbooks are more discreet than fashion magazines. They use bodies to communicate ideas through completely styled appearances. Maybe it's because I'm dyslexic, but I always loved lookbooks and still do; as a child, I was surrounded by them. I liked reading and misreading the visual language, which is sometimes very editorial. I'm always thinking of the impact the images have on us. I'm also interested in the mutability of this language as a space to present ideas and at the time I was thinking a lot of Paul B. Preciado's writing and the idea of "hacking the body."

The idea of images becoming language is also interesting, especially its allusion to the code or infrastructure of CG spaces. There is a collapse in making the images real, physical, and performing objects by rendering them in 3D. I liked inventing new languages through images. I guess most artists are trying to find a language. The book was a very playful way of doing this. It was an attempt to make the immaterial feel real, and for the infrastructure to become usable, physical. The politics of the body can be read through the lookbook.

In the context of *Public, Private, Secret*, we were especially engaged with how your work addresses visibility. We wanted to lay bare the power in being seen by others and how that power dynamic shifts when visibility is and isn't on one's own terms. In *RIGGED*, the voices in the woman's head repeat the phrase, "Disappear completely," simultaneously a menacing and mocking threat and a strangely appealing invitation. How does this relate to notions of camouflage?

Privacy is a position of privilege, but we also think of disappearance when we think of unrecognized people—undocumented people not recognized by the state—so I feel conflicted. There is also a different, long history related to a historical queer position of "passing," where someone in the LGBT community might present themselves as straight in order to self-protect and move freely within a wider society. And I think this work comes from a place of carving out a position of always being agile, of constantly pivoting and being in disguise. I feel it's essential to create strategies to withdraw as a way to refuse to perform certain modes of labor that are unrecognized by the state or the wider social framework in which we exist, from forms of childcare to creative labor. I'm thinking of the history of struggles such as Wages for Housework and interested in what the terms of negotiation might be today, how one might refuse, and what a withdrawal from representation might look like, or how such a strategy could be put in place.

1 Jeppe Ugelvig, "Kate Cooper: Hypercapitalism and the Digital Body," *Dis* magazine, n.d., http://dismagazine.com/dysmorphia/66668/kate-cooper-hypercapitalism-and-the-digital-body/.

You've said that for you "images are no longer representational in themselves," that they "perform another function,"[1] or have their own agency, which you wanted to explore in *RIGGED*. Could you expand more on this idea, break down for us what happens when the flat, silent, representational image gives way to (or is mapped onto) something else?

It becomes a combination of what things do versus what they are, a distinction at the center of this series. Thinking about this work now, several years later, I notice the political shift even in arenas like meme culture. I'm also thinking of writing by Hito Steyerl about the idea of the negative image. In her essay "The Spam of the Earth: Withdrawal from Representation," she proposes the idea that there is freedom in what images do or don't represent.[2]

When I was making this work in 2013–14, I was attracted to these politics and the rereading of our position toward images: Which politics are embedded in what space? What is our relationship to them? What fictions were being created and where did they land? There is a frustration in the essentialism that is presented to women, and that to me seems problematic, both in terms of my personal experience and that of working as part of a collective. What are we given permission to do, say, look like, and imagine? What are the terms of our representation?

Of course, there can be a problem and an inherent violence in these "hyper superhuman" presentations of female bodies, which was never the central focus of the work. It was more about exploring the possibilities of fiction when these images don't represent anyone. How can the images be hijacked and embedded with new meanings and politics that we give them? I was invested in the refusal of our images to do or perform a certain labor. In addition, I was trying to negotiate my own relationship to the images and what that might mean in terms of my own representation or ability to withdraw.

Finally, this relates to the idea of what it means to be authentic or inauthentic, or grateful or antagonistic within a capitalist system. Recently I was reading about how algorithms can fill in the missing pieces in images with slices of information; they can complete the picture with very little initial visual information. Where does this leave room to renegotiate these ideas, when we no longer fully create, let alone own, our images? Through their presentation I want to understand the particular aesthetics and representations attributed to images—their forms, logic, and autonomy—which are useful and productive for thinking through new politics and finding forms of shared empathy and affect.

2 Hito Steyerl, "The Spam of the Earth: Withdrawal from Representation," *e-flux journal* 32 (February 2012).

INTERVIEW: STEFAN RUIZ WITH PAULINE VERMARE

Stefan Ruiz's photographs have appeared in magazines worldwide, including the *New York Times Magazine*, *L'Uomo Vogue*, and *Rolling Stone*, and have been exhibited at the Photographers' Gallery, London; Photo España, Madrid; Les Rencontres d'Arles, France; New York Photo Festival; Havana Biennial; and the Contact Photography Festival, Toronto. *The Factory of Dreams*, his monograph on Mexican soap operas, was published by Aperture in 2012.

In addition to his decades-long global image-making practice, Ruiz has amassed a vast archive of vernacular photographs. A selection from his collection of mug shots was published by GOST Books in 2015. The prints—of which a selection was included in *Public, Private, Secret*—feature hand-written notes by police, yielding a fascinating taxonomy of criminals that includes bank robbers, murderers, robbers, pickpockets, swindlers, nannies-turned-thieves, etcetera. In addition to prints from his collection, the exhibition also featured some of Ruiz's own photographs.

Pauline Vermare: Your fascinating collection of Mexican mug shots, published last year by GOST Books, is exhibited for the first time at the International Center of Photography. Together, these beautiful photographs present us with a unique, thrilling, and moving social history of mid-twentieth-century Mexico. Can you tell us how you came across these prints, and how you ended up with such a unique collection?

Stefan Ruiz: I found the first few of these photographs at a stall in one of Mexico City's flea markets in the summer of 2010. The vendors were selling the photos for a friend, to whom I was introduced later that day. It turned out he had a lot more photos. We agreed to meet in one of the city's parks. He brought two plastic bags of photos. I looked through them, negotiated, and bought the lot. We met up two more times over the next year and each time he had more photos that I ended up buying.

Although I never found out the specific source, the pictures clearly came from Mexico City's police archives.

What led you to publish this collection?

As I was looking through the photos in the park, I thought that these could make a great book, but I wasn't sure it would ever happen. As the year went by and I collected more of them, I became surer of the project: there were plenty of strong photos and there was enough variety to make a good book. I showed the photos to my friend Stuart Smith, who was starting GOST Books, and he suggested that we do the book together.

I have worked on many projects in Mexico and Latin America. I have also taught art classes in prison. I am obsessed with portraiture. This project brought all of those elements together. Also, crime in Mexico at that time was at a historic high. The parallels between these old photos also have a modern relevance.

A beautiful surprise, working with you on this show, was also your incredible treasure trove of other mug shots—hundreds of them, from originals by Alphonse Bertillon to contemporary ones. When did you start collecting mug shots, and why? Are you more attracted by the aesthetics of the photographs, or by their social meaning and implications?

I started collecting mug shots around twenty years ago. I have always liked the fact that these are not voluntary portraits and that they are taken at what is probably quite a bad moment for the subject. The expressions feel very real. The portraiture is straightforward. It is a very private moment but they are a form of public record. Some of the subjects are murderers but some are only guilty of being on a street corner. Everyone is photographed the same.

Also included in the ICP show is a striking diptych of a "pregnant" drug mule—one color portrait and one X-ray photograph. Can you tell us about it, and how you ended up photographing suspected drug mules at the Bogotá airport in 2013?

I have been working with a writer on a project in Colombia for years now. The project is basically about crime and creativity—the extent to which creativity can often be used for a very negative end. This sometimes manifests itself in the drug trade, through such things as homemade weapons, guns, or landmines, or the objects themselves used to smuggle drugs—from sculptures to submarines.

On this day, we had access to photograph with the police at the Bogotá airport. Just as we were getting started we were called to the police headquarters. They had something to show us. We had no idea what it could be. When we got there they brought out a woman who was wearing a fake belly. And then they explained. She was a Canadian social worker who was trying to smuggle 2.25 kilos of cocaine stuffed into a false stomach.

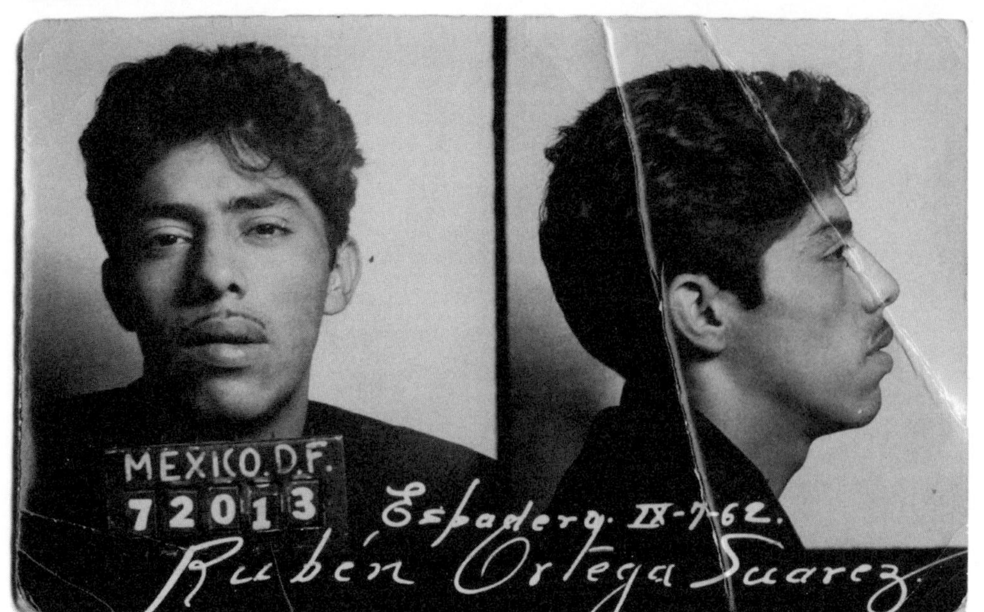

Stefan Ruiz, *Unidentified photographer mug shots, Mexico*, 1950s–70s

The X-ray portrait is particularly striking in the context of this show that deals with surveillance, privacy, and intimacy. What was your original intention when you started the project?

I have a whole series of drug-mule X-rays. I am interested in the fact that the body can be used as a creative vessel to transport drugs. Mules swallow around a kilo of cocaine pellets. If a pellet breaks open while inside, it will kill the mule. The subjects are selected based on suspicion or tip-offs. The X-rays are another type of forced portraiture.

What are you working on now?

I am currently finishing a book of portraits on a subculture in Monterrey, Mexico: a group of young people who listen to a slowed-down version of *cumbia*, and who dress and style themselves in a very unique way. They have become known as "cholombianos." The book should be published sometime next year.

INTERVIEW: MERRY ALPERN WITH PAULINE VERMARE

American photographer Merry Alpern is best known for her series *Dirty Windows* (1993–94), a controversial set of photographs of an illegal sex club that she took through a bathroom window near Wall Street, New York. In 1994, on account of this series, Alpern was rejected by the National Endowment for the Arts in a controversial vote that also refused applications by artists Barbara DeGenevieve and Andres Serrano. Over the course of her career, Alpern's work has been exhibited at museums around the country, including the Whitney Museum of American Art and Museum of Modern Art in New York; the National Museum of Women in the Arts, in Washington, DC; the Museum of Fine Arts, Houston; and the San Francisco Museum of Modern Art.

Pauline Vermare: *Your Dirty Windows* series is currently on view at the ICP Museum. Would you tell us more about the story behind the photographs?

Merry Alpern: The project began one night, in 1993, when a friend led me to a back room in his loft in New York City's Wall Street district. From his window, one flight down, maybe fifteen feet away, I saw a bathroom window and felt the vibrations of a pulsing bass track. Suddenly, a body in a sparkling harness appeared, then disappeared. It turned out that a private lap-dance club had newly opened and been secreted away in the building.

I was transfixed and spent the next six months sitting in the dark, dressed in black, camera on tripod, watching the goings-on of perfect strangers. I had to use fast black-and-white film in the dim light, which gave the photos a grainy quality reminiscent of low-grade peep show reels. What began as the desire to get a single, great picture became an obsession, and even found its way into my dreams. As the project continued, a sense of paranoia set in—was anyone watching me?

During that time I had little connection to the art world, but I submitted some of the photos to the National Endowment for the Arts. Months later, I received a baffling phone call notifying me that my work had been approved for a grant but that it had been overturned. The caller added that I'd be reading about it in the paper the next day. Overnight, fueled by news of the NEA's rejection, the pictures gained notoriety and took on a life of their own.

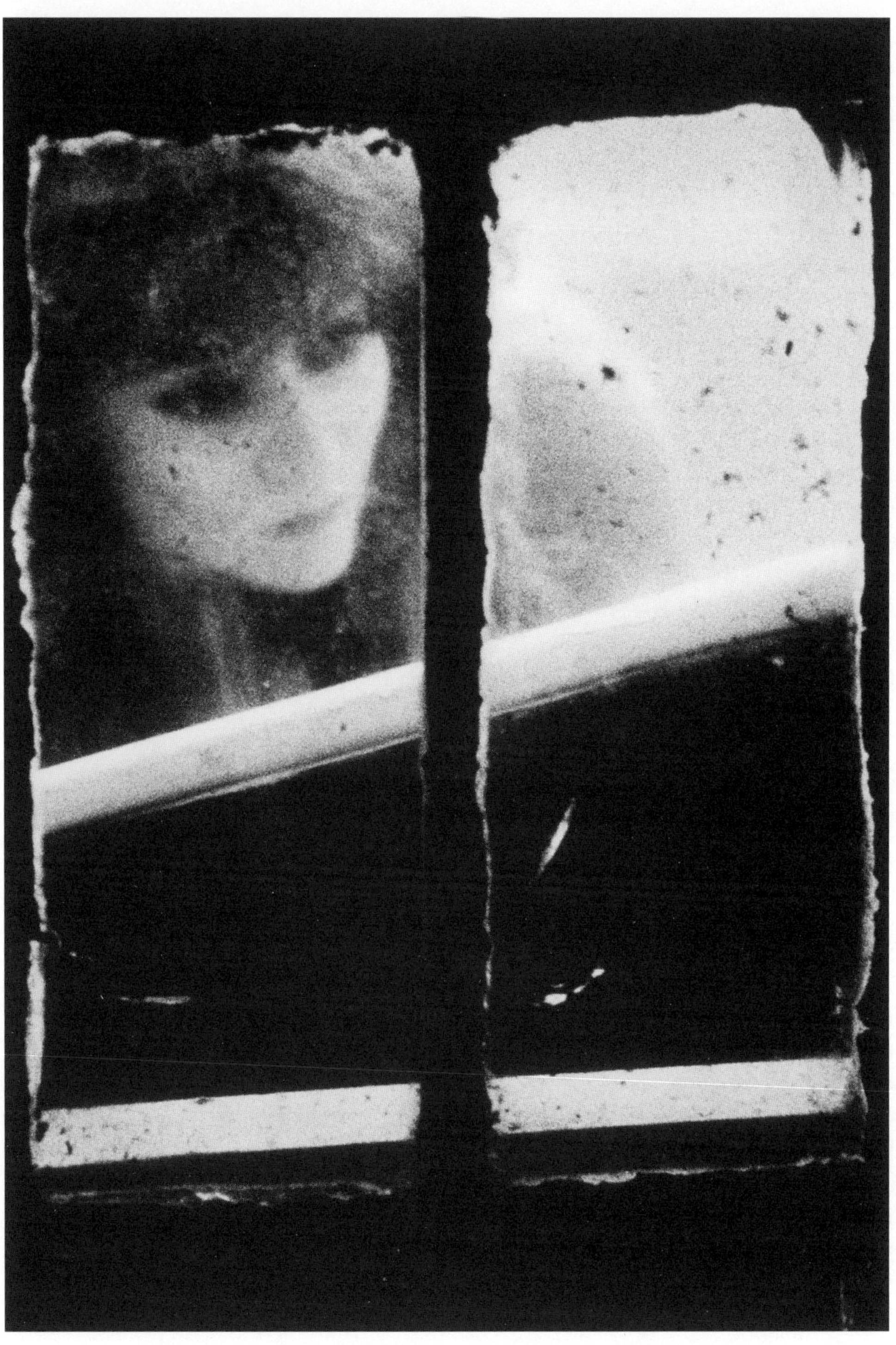

Merry Alpern, *Dirty Windows Series #19*, 1994

Your photographs are taken from a distance, in complete secret. Did you at any point meet with members of the club, or go into the space that you photographed?

One evening, a workman in the building escorted me into the club (without a camera), when I expressed curiosity about the place. In the middle of a huge empty room, folding chairs surrounded a low, makeshift platform. A handful of young men in suits were in attendance and the dancers were friendly and conversational. I was surprised by the intimacy and informality of the situation. The women drifted over and teasingly invited me to join them "onstage." I was hoping at that time to view the bathroom, but it would have required a very conspicuous walk across the space. And as the only female patron there, I felt I'd drawn enough attention to myself already.

It wasn't until the club had disappeared—busted one night—that I was able to investigate the bathroom, my access granted by a real-estate agent. It was a minuscule powder room, hardly the Hollywood set I'd imagined all those months. I realized that the tiny proportions had aided my photos, forcing subjects to squeeze in close to the glass pane. Most surprisingly, I could see that my former perch, above and across the airshaft, was practically invisible.

In your brilliant essay, "Dirty Windows" [1995], you wrote at the time: "Finally, there's nothing left to do but examine my motivations: Why am I sitting alone again in a darkened room, waiting to watch strangers fuck?" Did you ever find an answer to that question?

Perhaps it had something to do with wanting to understand how people connected, no matter the circumstance. I was single, so within that framework the smallest details of the couples' interactions became obsessively interesting. How and when did the money change hands? Who made the first move? Was it reciprocated? Was there a condom? A kiss? Would they meet again? There was a soap-opera quality to it all, with recurring characters and a good measure of entertainment. After long stretches of staring at empty windows, it was an adrenaline rush when a body suddenly appeared. I felt like a trophy hunter waiting in the blind. Shooting on film, there was no sure way of knowing what I'd captured until the film was processed. It was very exciting!

Some of the photographs in the series are surprisingly romantic (I am thinking of *Dirty Windows* #2 [1994]). Some of the portraits are very melancholic. You visibly had a lot of respect for the women you photographed. How did you feel, as a woman photographer, witnessing some of these scenes?

Although the notion of the “female gaze” has never really interested me, as a woman I could project some of my own experiences onto the pantomime in the window. I recognized the ruse when a dancer reached in her purse and brandished a tampon in the face of an overeager, undesirable patron. On the flip side was the anthropological experience of viewing scenes that are quite ordinary in a man’s world. It was a revelation to watch the bathroom habits of the opposite sex....

You were very sensitive to not include any markers when you published your portraits, so that none of your subjects could be identified. Would you tell us about this?

Faces and identifying marks such as tattoos were not included, or were digitally altered in the book *Dirty Windows* [1995]. The publisher was worried about a lawsuit. I was hoping nobody would come looking for me. Nor did I want to compromise the identity of any of the subjects. For the safety of all concerned, it was probably a good idea!

When did you become a photographer and what were your first stories?

In 1977, I left college, where I was a sociology major, and headed to New York with the idea of becoming a photographer. I began working in a commercial lab as a black-and-white printer, which led to a job as a rock-and-roll photo assistant and then a position at *Rolling Stone* magazine. In the 1980s, I ventured out on my own as an editorial/corporate freelancer, but my personal projects on the side always provided the greatest satisfaction. The camera was my proverbial ticket to explore whatever interested me, and my early subjects often focused on the city’s fringe cultures.

A.J. and Jim Bob [1988] was a documentary-style series that sprang from my fascination with an Upper West Side prostitute and her companion. For two years I photographed the couple, who lived in the streets during the emergence of New York City’s crack epidemic. Pressed by a photographer friend to “do something” with the photos, I showed them to magazines and museums, applied for grants, and was surprised by the positive reception. MoMA purchased a group of the pictures and in 1989 I had my first solo show at the Camera Club of New York.

What are you working on now?

One project is a photo series of abandoned spaces. There is a line fragment in a poem by Amiri Baraka: “traces of dead used up.” It sticks in my head.

INTERVIEW: TREVOR PAGLEN WITH PAULA KUPFER

Trevor Paglen's research-based practice spans image making, sculpture, investigative journalism, writing, and engineering, among numerous other disciplines. His work is structured around learning how to see the present historical moment and using art and images as a way of understanding the complex and invisible forces that surround us. In 2014, he received the Electronic Frontier Foundation's Pioneer Award for his work as a "groundbreaking investigative artist." Paglen's work has been showcased in solo exhibitions at the Vienna Secession; Eli and Edythe Broad Art Museum, Los Angeles; Van Abbe Museum, Eindhoven, the Netherlands; Frankfurter Kunstverein; and Protocinema Istanbul. A retrospective of his work will take place at the Smithsonian American Art Museum in Washington, DC, in 2018. At the time of this conversation, Paglen was inaugurating new work in the exhibition *A Study of Invisible Images* at Metro Pictures, New York.

Paula Kupfer: To start, I want to ask you about the work, *Blue #3 (Chelsea)* [2016], included in *Public, Private, Secret*, in which you photographed a detail of the courtroom drawings of the trial of Chelsea Manning. The work underscores physicality, materiality, and even human touch. What were you hoping to extract from such a close viewing?

Trevor Paglen: That work was almost gestural for me; it was trying to look at this event that obviously had an idea of political context around it, but of which there was no sort of direct representations. There was no actual media produced around that trial, no photos or recordings, only the courtroom artist's. So the gesture is looking as closely at those representations as you can. And of course there's a kind of opacity that emerges from that.

You're about to open a new show, *A Study of Invisible Images*. Two ideas embedded in this work have become central to your recent research: that computers are being taught to see and that "images" are produced daily, intended to be legible by computers only, without human intervention. Do you think this shift calls for a renaming of technology? Is the word *photograph* anachronistic at this point?

I guess it's a metaphysical question. I don't really know. I think about *images* at this point and I don't make a distinction between a photograph or a painting or a metadata signature. To a machine, a sound is the same as a digitized image of a painting. The traditional discourses that we have to think about photographs seem useless today. I don't know whether we should have a different word, but we definitely need new analytical tools.

You worked with "training sets" of images to teach AI how to recognize different shapes or objects. Did the process of teaching a machine to see uncover any notions of the ways humans learn to see? Did teaching a machine activate a cognizance of how humans learn—in a similar or a completely different manner?

This is a big question. When you start looking at computerization, with the kind of background I have, you start to understand that human vision is basically two things: It's the basic ability to navigate through space, be able to reach your arm out and kind of accurately judge the distance to an object. There's a very physiological thing that every animal that has vision has, right? It's a mechanistic form of vision.

But vision is also the meanings—or readings—that one makes of that world. In other words, two coffee cups can be identical in terms of the physiological relationship you have to them. But they can mean entirely different things, like if one says, "World's Greatest Dad," and another has a skull on it.

This second layer—that construction of meanings—is tangible in the ways that humans see; in other words, meanings can continually change. Art is an obvious example of where this kind of thing happens all the time: you take an image that's familiar and you make it strange. And that is precisely something that computers or AI systems cannot do. When they're taught to see, the kinds of meanings that tend to be fluid for us become fixed in automated systems.

Say you want to train AI to see an image of a CEO. The training images that you have of a CEO are going to be stock photography of white people because that is historically how that image has been created. And so if you use that training set, you are going to reproduce that stereotype and that AI system is going to enforce that stereotype. And it will literally not even recognize a woman CEO. That's what I mean: it creates a situation where it creates meaning and those meanings are derived from the past, and those meanings are kind of enforced and it's not possible to challenge or reshape them. That is something that I've thought a lot about. And so in a way—when you're training AI systems—you're training them on a racist and patriarchal past, and you're going to reproduce that racist and patriarchal past.

Can that sort of teaching not be challenged?

It could be challenged in a number of ways. But first of all there's the person who's deciding what these things mean, and that is usually going to be some young man in Silicon Valley who has a particular sets of interests, etcetera, etcetera. The thing is, once a network has been created, it subscribes to a certain set of meanings and it doesn't evolve. It can't make its own rules. It can only operate according to pre-programmed rules.

That's a pretty fundamental difference between how humans and machines learn, but it suggests something further about the way stereotypes develop.

Yeah, humans can say, "I am a man or I'm a woman or I'm queer or I'm not a man and I'm also not a woman." And that kind of ability of thinking fluidly about definitions is precisely what automated vision systems cannot do.

If the way machines are taught seems predetermined and to some degree unalterable, what recourses are we left with? Where do we go from there? Do you feel any responsibility as an artist, from an activist point of view?

It's not my job to tell other people what to do. People can do whatever they want with this technology. I, for myself, am trying to understand how these systems work and work alongside people working in ethics and AI and policy. There are many people collectively trying to understand how to think about formulating policies or regulations, or legal and ethical norms around the deployment of artificial intelligence and learning systems.

It's a really hard problem: there are no obvious answers at the moment. Nobody knows. But I think there are many different kinds of people trying to think through what some of this might mean. And I definitely think that artists have a lot to contribute to that, precisely because we understand images and we understand how meanings are generated and how pernicious interpretation itself can be.

If we consider the history of art as the history of seeing, then this re-education—learning how to see—seems quite urgent.

I think a good first step is to start trying to understand how some of these systems work—what is this paradigm of vision that's being constructed?—and try to understand the nuts and bolts of it, which is a necessary first step to starting to think about the wider-scale implications.

Will you continue your research on AI?

Yes, it's a big body of work, and for me one project always leads to the next. I see a smooth continuum from one project to another. When I was working on the project about NSA infrastructure and undersea cables, it's almost as if this body of work is going into those cables to see what other infrastructures are in place, like the digital infrastructures and the software infrastructures within these physical infrastructures. So it feels to me like a very logical kind of progression.

Are there any writers or theoreticians focused on this subject that you find particularly elucidating or clarifying at this moment?

Kate Crawford is a good friend and really smart in terms of how she's thinking about this kind of thing. Mostly it's conversations that I'm having with people. There's not a whole lot of writing yet.

Hopefully that will also ensue from the show, in the sense that the artwork will open up different lines of inquiry.

You know, I hope so. That's a very high bar to set for an exhibition. It's stuff that I am looking at and that I think is important to look at. And if other people agree with me, then maybe it's a way to start a conversation.

INTERVIEW: DOUG RICKARD WITH PAULA KUPFER

Doug Rickard was born in San Jose, California, and studied US history and sociology before beginning to work with photography and video. In his *A New American Picture*, Rickard used Google Street View to look on the parts of America left behind in a contemporary economic and social divide; it was published in a limited edition by White Press in 2010 and by Aperture in 2012. His project *N.A.* (2015), shown in *Public, Private, Secret*, expands this practice toward video, using appropriated YouTube clips to virtually access forgotten and economically devastated locales in America. Rickard's work is part of important museum collections, including the Harry Ransom Center at the University of Texas at Austin; Los Angeles County Museum of Art; Museum of Contemporary Photography, Chicago; the Museum of Fine Arts, Houston; the Museum of Modern Art, New York; the San Francisco Museum of Modern Art; and Yale University Art Gallery, New Haven, Connecticut.

Paula Kupfer: In describing *N.A.*, you've said that it "painted a picture of American violence, anger, frustration and rage, targeted at economic isolation that is pervasive." You portray a very dark vision of America. What underlies the desire to show such an image?

Doug Rickard: The work channels a subconscious compulsion that I can't help. I've been an artist for all of my life; my mom's father was a painter, and so was her brother. I grew up making art almost obsessively, and I found a camera in my early thirties. My intellectual provocation and questioning were fueled by two things: growing up with a father who was a devoutly conservative, patriotic mega-church creature, and having a world view of America amplified in my household that was in conflict with what I studied. I was looking at the history of segregation, the Civil War, etcetera, and felt anger about these juxtaposing, conflicted views of America. All those things were percolating in my mind as well as my love for photography; I had the artistic desire as well as the anger, amid an intellectual compulsion.

How are these contradictory emotions channeled in *N.A.*?

The video channels the zeitgeist, our toolsets, and how people are using the media. We're seeing radical shifts in people's habits, how people consume media, even how they communicate. Everyone's a voyeur, everyone's obsessing over their phones—our phones are voracious, ravenous beasts for our time. I can't put mine down. I also love technology. I have one leg in the generation of my fifteen-year-old son and another in the generation of William Eggleston. I'm immersed at the edge of what youth are doing with technology. I'm forty-nine; I can see both worlds.

In terms of *N.A.*, I feel there has been a mountain of adversity dealt to a large part of our population and I wanted to show that in a way that is jolting. I didn't want to hold any punches. I do feel that a large part of society has avoided it as well as minimized it, taken an out-of-sight out-of-mind approach. I have wanted to say: This is America. This is America. This is America. I'm also attracted to dark subject matter as a mode of expression.

That's a feeling that's carried over from *A New American Picture* to *N.A.* How did you transition from still imagery to video?

Even when I was toying with *A New American Picture*, I was seeing if still images from YouTube could be used. I wasn't doing video editing but I was working with video. So the video work evolved out of that experimentation. There's a difference in that the Street View project [*A New American Picture*] feels more isolated, alienated, ostracized from much of American society, while the video work jumps right into the hands of the people living in the environment.

How do you describe your method? What reaction do you seek from your audience?

The actual material I select can lend itself to both directions. In *A New American Picture*, because everything is in daylight and the aesthetic is softer, even with dark subject matter there's space for people to breathe, there's a way for people to be pulled into the beauty of the imagery and come to some conclusion themselves. With my intentional use of darkness, night, and more intimate camera angles in *N.A.*, I knew this other material was going to bring into it a different feeling and vibe. I don't think I can give any answers to people who are viewing it. I can't tell them, This is what I want you to feel. I think darkness is a running component because I have a lot of empathy for people faced with adversity—such as racial hate—but in the video work I wanted to slightly toy with the archetypal things that white Americans fear—or that they maybe size up as wanting to avoid—and almost push those buttons.

Can you speak to the intent behind the editing in *N.A.*? I was struck by the moody sounds and the repeating motifs, such as swerving cars and dollar bills.

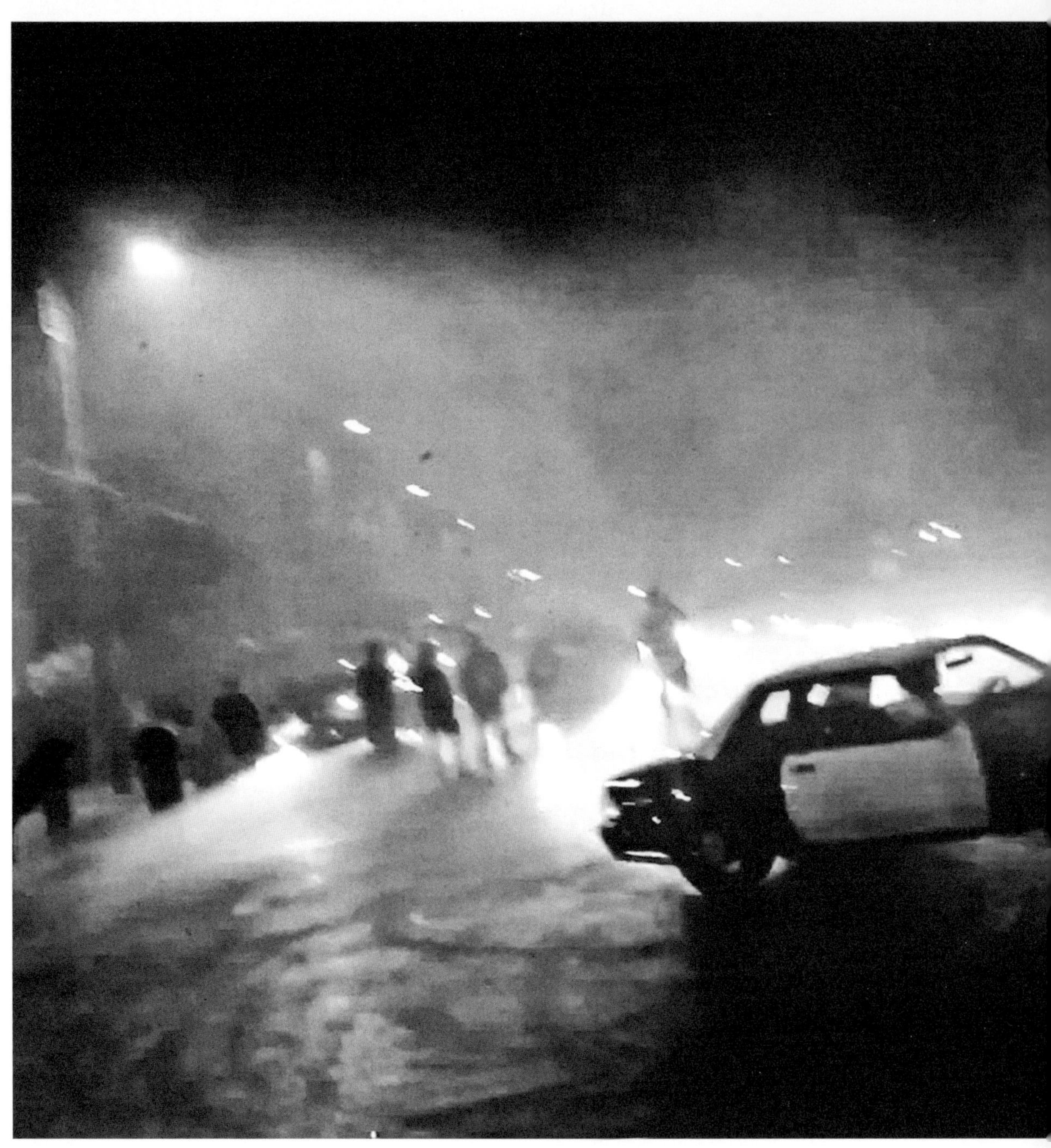

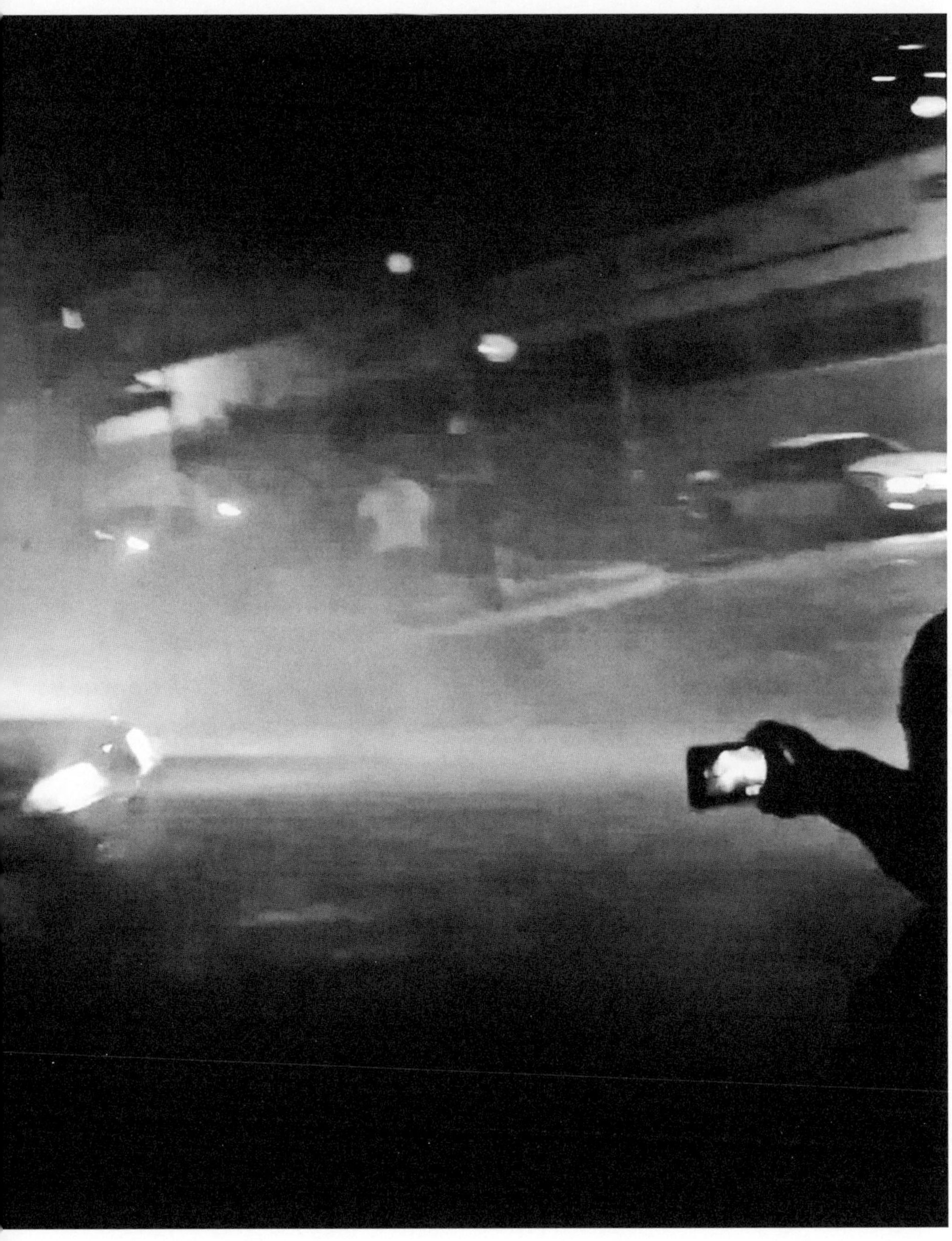

Doug Rickard, *N.A. 3*, 2012

The sound is the national anthem, slowed down to the level of noise. It is a generic recording; the singing is a US military version. In the editing I tried to emphasize authorship and maintain an aesthetic connection. I wanted to edit the videos as photographers work with books. The notion is almost that of a pattern, where color threads together visually. Other videos are also starkly arranged by color. Color is an important component.

In other interviews relating to this work, you've described yourself as a "hijacker." Do you see yourself as a participant in the violent discourse by choosing such a label for yourself?

Part of me goes back to being the son of a pastor—there's a part of me that has a rebellious streak and is antiauthoritarian. But here, in a sense, I'm hijacking the phone and the device of someone who held it in their hands. I didn't use the word in the way of hijacking an airplane but I did select this word because it is provocative; that comes with my personality and my mental framework.

The hijacking is an interesting thing for me, more than viewers would ever ponder. I find it really interesting—the fact that I could be a fly on the wall and "take" other people's phones and use them for my own devices, and the power that comes with that. Even if someone else says that I'm curating, I'm synthing, I'm extracting—it's fascinating to have access to the material.

I also use "hijacking" because I'm getting at situations that may be in between of the intent of showing. I'm going for still images and extracts of some of the videos that seem to put me in situations where I was not supposed to be. It is about how I treat the section that I select, pulling in those points of view—out the window, inside the car. By choosing how I grab it—what I show—I have the ability of telling my own tale. It's a form of authorship.

Since we're talking about words, I want to talk a bit more about the keywords you used to find YouTube clips for *N.A.* You've described using terms such as "hood fight," "crackheads gone wild," "passed out white girl," "gangstalking," "sideshow," "racial profiling," "illegal search," or "police brutality."

I was able to unearth more material that way than other avenues. Now, to be fair, I didn't search, say, "Detroit job hire." There's not a lot of amateur footage on that. I had a certain intention in terms of finding what I found. I was also committed to finding video only by people who posted it for some reason that had nothing to do with production. I didn't want edited video content. Part of that was the aesthetic was dark, grainy, visceral, potentially real and raw. I was trying to unearth a certain darkness. There's a whole underlayer of that in amateur video.

What are some of the critiques you've received? Don't you feel that you are reinforcing stereotypes?

Based on my point of view—of what has resonated with me about the lives of people in communities such as Detroit; North Philly; Gary, Indiana—there are certain themes that they all are facing that people outside of these communities don't face. That's the point of view that drives me.

I've not done many in-depth interviews to get more information of what it's like on the ground. My project is not about engagement or intimacy, but rather a way of painting an architectural picture. I feel that people shouldn't confuse my projects with what is possible with both photojournalism and journalism. You can possibly confuse it with street photography and connect the dots. But the reality is that if you can go there physically with your camera, you incorporate people's personal stories.

My work isn't about that and people shouldn't hold it up to that lens. It's intentionally, and because of the technology, at an extreme distance. With *A New American Picture*, I'd rather have the people blurred—as archetypes, constructs—and I've tried to do that with *N.A.* The blurring is intentional. I don't need to show them as recognizable; it's not the point of this work. How could I possibly give context without talking to them?

Did anyone in the videos contact you? Have you ever shown the work to an audience closer to the subjects?

No. This is because of the limited audience in which the work is shown. The audience is not the same as the subject matter. There's definitely a disconnect between my subject matter and the art world that sees the work.

Once I showed this work in North Philly, but it was still pulling a distinct audience: art students drove over, but it didn't draw in the community. I'd love to show it in other settings, like Detroit, and offer Ubers or Lyfts and solicit an audience and response to get a greater mixture of points of view.

Have you visited any of these places in person, or only virtually?

Some I've been to: Compton, Watts, Camden. But even in person, my impression is generally from the outside. As I mentioned, a journalist or photojournalist might see the inside, how people are trying to live normal lives. I'm only seeing the exterior of a car. I can only make that judgment from the outside.

I've talked to some young men living in the projects in Atlantic City. They gave me a view that was really interesting, that their feeling is they live in a "trap." They say it's a trap, because it has walls like a prison but they are invisible. I talked to them at length and asked candid questions; they said everyone in their community feels they're placed into areas cordoned-off from where whites live. The predominant feeling was that this was orchestrated and sanctioned by the government. These conversations reinforced some of my own feelings.

INTERVIEW: JON RAFMAN WITH MARINA CHAO

Jon Rafman is a Montreal-based artist whose work explores the psychological, philosophical, and moral dimensions of technology. Since 2009 he has been archiving Google Street Views on his widely followed Tumblr project *Nine Eyes* (2008–). Through deep dives into online subcultures and avatar-led travels across virtual landscapes, he examines the fantasy worlds that technology fosters and what our behavior within these virtual spaces reveals about us. Rafman's video *Mainsqueeze* (2014), composed entirely of appropriated online content offering a haunting glimpse into the technology-addled human psyche, was on view in *Public, Private, Secret*.

Marina Chao: The video *Mainsqueeze* was included in *Public, Private, Secret*, but your project *Nine Eyes* is ostensibly the natural point of entry into your work for a photography-based institution. The title references the nine cameras that Google used on their Street View cars when the program first started in 2007. What drew you to working with the Street Views?

Jon Rafman: Google Street View reveals a world in which you are watched by everyone and by no one, a world in which everything is being recorded, but the meaning of everything is equivalent.

Like any old photograph, Street View images will gain power and ambiguity over time. The photos simultaneously demonstrate a concrete reality that cannot be denied and highlight that knowledge of the past can never be complete.

I'm interested in the moral aspect of the disembodied, impartial camera, which you've spoken about before. You've noted the objectivity of the Street View cameras as they record potentially violent and unlawful activity without a moral agenda and without judgment. Could you speak more about that? Do you think it's liberating to consider these images as untethered to human intent, or is it alienating?

I'm interested in using the technology that alienates us to make art that gives us insight into the nature of this alienation. Google's mode of recording the world reveals how we already order our perception: our own mode of interaction parallels this detached, indifferent mode of capturing the world, leading us to question our own significance. This contradiction—the tension between the roving Street View camera robotically gathering data, connected only by contiguity, and the empathic human observer who seeks human connection and meaning in the image—is what gives the project its force. The idea of Google as a "neutral" corporation is deceptive; Silicon Valley controls how data is gathered, organized, and consumed online. Google, like the internet as a whole, is both revolutionary and totalitarian.

A final point on the *Nine Eyes* project: photography's relationship to memory. You've described these images as lacking a connection to the memories of picture-taker and subject, a defining aspect of photography. These are nobody's memories. Can you expand on this relationship between consciousness, memory, and meaning?

Like other media before it, photography changes how we experience reality. When you photograph something, you alter your vision of it. Despite the impersonal nature of Google photography and the fact that the subjects of the *Nine Eyes* photos are being captured in the absence of a human photographer, they resist becoming objects of the automated camera's gaze. Through my screenshots, I stress the importance of the human individual and the fight against the loss of autonomy and meaning.

By your own account, *Mainsqueeze* was a shift away from the romanticism of *Nine Eyes* and the Kool-Aid Man in Second Life series (2008–11), in which your Kool-Aid Man avatar travels through *Second Life* environments. There's the tradition in the earlier works of the street photographer and the flâneur, the wanderer-spectator who luxuriates in looking and passing through. Do you still identify with that kind of figure in your most recent work?

Yes, very much so. However, the World Wide Web of my childhood is completely different from the internet today. The web browser still remains my portal. But the chance of random encounters and discoveries occurs less and less. Everything is filtered through the same few companies. This loss recalls Walter Benjamin's bemoaning the end of the Paris arcades as they transformed into department stores.

Public, Private, Secret was interested in the internet and its—and photography's—desire-machine nature. It produces desire from our own, sometimes scary and therefore repressed, urges.

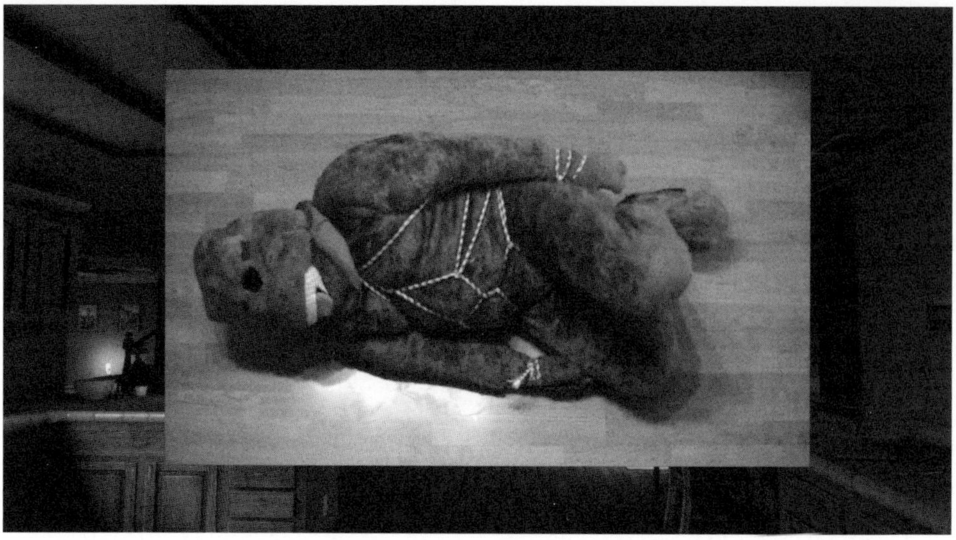

Jon Rafman, *Mainsqueeze*, 2014

After having gone through so much online material, what have you learned about what people want from these alternative spaces and bodies we've created?

On one level, the explosion of fetishes, subcultures, and political identities means that increasingly more obscure or marginal desires and interests can find an audience, a community. What is surprising, however, is that rather than unifying us, the internet has actually had a polarizing effect. Yes, you can find like-minded people on the internet but at the same time you can avoid meaningful interaction with people outside of your belief system. Nihilism and the desire for destruction is emerging out of the contemporary social climate at the same time as waves of cyber-utopian sentimentalism. My more recent films, such as *Poor Magic* [2017] and *Open Heart Warrior* [2016], highlight the particular alienation associated with technology and the virtual world.

Our relationship to technology, as expressed in literature and in the visual arts, is overwhelmingly dystopian. You've described aspects of digital space as a kind of waking nightmare. For you, is there anything optimistic to be found in the growing reach or sophistication of technology—or is that some Silicon Valley Kool-Aid?

That new technology necessarily leads to human progress is dubious. Rather, we may be sliding more and more toward ignorance and darkness. The legal and political history and structure of the internet allows individuals to express extremely divisive, hateful views and desires that hitherto were socially constrained. The widely acknowledged increase in information is ironically paralleled by a decrease in meaning. It is increasingly difficult to grasp the real, to make sense of everything, and to distinguish between truth and falsity. We sense that everything we are experiencing is predigested. All activity is pseudo-activity. Subjectivity is compromised.

The animation *Poor Magic* looks at artificial intelligence and the idea of technological singularity represented by phalanxes of anonymous figures running headlong into walls and marching off ledges. You described it as the most distressing, worst-possible singularity scenario. Can you speak more about the advance toward technological singularity and what you think is at stake? And what are other, less terrifying possibilities?

Each era's vision of the future reveals something about its present. I'm less focused on singularity as a possible future and more on what this posthumanist dream of the future says about contemporary society's desires and fears.

In *Poor Magic*, I imagined a future in which an AI tortures what is left of humanity for all eternity, and doesn't allow us to die. Humanity will have finally achieved immortality, but as endlessly suffering, voiceless avatars. This postmodern, dystopian vision of the future is an exaggerated reflection of what has already occurred. After all, do we not spend much of our life online, tortured in front of screens, that is, in a flattened, virtual world? The idea of having your consciousness uploaded and being abused for all of time by an evil AI is not so far off to me.

What are you working on now? Are you continuing to look at AI and virtual-reality spaces, or are you tackling something else? Will you return to making physical sculpture?

I'm currently working on several immersive video installations. I just made an essay film about Leonard Cohen using virtual landscapes from videogames. It continues the meditation on memory and history that I began with films like *Remember Carthage* [2013] and *A Man Digging* [2013]. I have become increasingly interested in creating sculptural seating systems that are in dialogue with the imagery of the videos.

INTERVIEW: NATALIE BOOKCHIN WITH PAULA KUPFER

American artist Natalie Bookchin has long cast a critical eye at media, investigating ways in which new forms of broadcasting and self-expression on the internet serve as barometers to measure political attitudes, economic tendencies, and the evolution of the concept of self. In her video work *Testament* (2009–17), included in *Public, Private, Secret*, Bookchin searched for common themes in online video diaries, while her recent documentary *Long Story Short* (2016) recorded over a hundred people discussing their experience of poverty. Her work has been exhibited widely, including at MoMA, LACMA, PS1, the Walker Art Center, the Centre Pompidou, and the Tate. Bookchin has been the recipient of many grants and awards, including from the Guggenheim Foundation, the Rockefeller Foundation, and the MacArthur Foundation. She is a professor of media and associate chair in the Visual Arts Department at Mason Gross School of the Arts at Rutgers University, New Jersey, and lives in Brooklyn.

Paula Kupfer: What connections do you see between traditional photography and your video work?

Natalie Bookchin: I think my video work makes lots of sense in a photo show. For my entire twenty-five-year teaching career, until I moved to Rutgers two years ago, I have been situated within photography departments. Although I don't make photographs anymore, the photographic is an essential element as I work with lens-based recordings of actuality that I find on social-media sites. I search in the video documents for poses, stances, and gestures.

Just as a street photographer might go to the street to document people in public, I go to the internet. The videos I collect are documents that reveal how people perform to the camera and present themselves in public—a few steps removed from the candid shot of the street photographer.

Audio recordings are equally important. I listen for tone, language, and word selections. I collect documents in which people perform for the camera, in both rehearsed and seemingly spontaneous ways. I look to these documents for what they might reveal about who we, as a culture, think we are, and how we present ourselves to the world as we perform in front of real and imagined viewers.

Different forms of performance are embedded into your work, particularly in *Mass Ornament* [2009] and *Testament*. How did you arrive at discovering the common, perhaps limited, lexicon of words and movements that people use to express themselves and perform?

My videos try to make visible repeated and shared tropes and scripts that people perform and reenact as they present versions of themselves and their lives to the world through networked cameras. The videos can feel raw and spontaneous, but each one is also a performance. People frame themselves against unmade beds, in bathrooms, or in a car as they drive. People often don't even bother to make the bed first. There is an urgency to the filming, a rushed quality, even a kind of desperateness. It seems to suggest such longing, for some kind of connection, and to be seen and heard.

The strangeness of the activity is also in how common and repetitive each one is. People say similar things in similar ways. By placing many videos side by side, the cultural scripts—of language, of narrative, of gesture, and, ultimately, of identity—that people rehearse in spontaneous ways, start to emerge. The collection starts to reveal the reciting of shared scripts as both personal and habitual.

The contrast and contradictions between the scripted, the staged, the intimate, and the vulnerable, together with the witnessing of raw desire, is what makes the video document so strange and compelling to me. The imperfections in performances and in the forms themselves can allow for a texture of humanity, vulnerability—maybe something similar to Roland Barthes's punctum.

Can you tell me about the title *Testament*? Why did you choose it for this work? Were you thinking about religion at all, or invoking spirituality?

No, it's the camera! Vlogs can function as a kind of testimonial or confessionary, of the self to the world. People confess to a networked camera. As they look out to an imagined audience, they also look at themselves on the screen. It's a kind of confession to the self, and at the same time, to the world of potentially millions of future viewers. It's such a strange thing that it's all of those things at once. It's both confessing to the mirror, or dancing to the mirror, and dancing to the self, and also dancing to the potential, limitless audience.

When I started making work with found online videos, YouTube hadn't been around that long. DIY videos from those days were often raw. Not just poor quality and low resolution, but the production was much less polished. Today, people can make money off their YouTube channels. As a result, many vlogs have higher production values, and individual channels often have commercial sponsorship. In the early days, it wasn't entirely clear how the platform was going to be monetized, either for Google (who bought YouTube in 2006, a year after it was launched) or for its participants, who freely provided its content.

Was there one instance or confessional video that compelled you to use this as source material? Or was it a natural transition from people dancing in *Mass Ornament*?

I wanted to move from the contagious physical gestures of *Mass Ornament* to language, to look at how ideas, words, and phrases circulate and become viral. I was interested in choreographing language in the way that I had choreographed movement.

I began to notice how people were performing not just language and phrases but identity itself, including racial and gendered identity. In *Now He's Out in Public and Everyone Can See* [2012–16], I focus particularly on conflicted performances of racial identity.

You say people *perform* gender or race—how can we understand this?

In *Now He's Out in Public and Everyone Can See*, vloggers narrate a series of media scandals involving unnamed African American celebrities. They repeat familiar racist and racialized tropes associated with blackness—specifically black, male identity. They describe and evaluate the men in question—their masculinity, their racial authenticity, their private lives, and their moral codes. The montage depicts race and gender as continually reconstructed through expressions of collective spoken language. There is heated emotion and rage in the vloggers' performances, suggesting just how much is at stake in these words and their public articulation.

It also uses the theatrical device of the chorus, which can hover in the background, or come to the foreground—

It's a particular kind of chorus. Looking back now at works like *Mass Ornament* and *Testament*, I was thinking about the way it both reiterates this kind of self-branding and self-performance where there's never an erasure of the individual: In *Testament*, there can be something hopeful and unifying about seeing and hearing a chorus of speakers sharing similar sentiments and revealing commonalities. Yet, at the same time, people are alone—isolated—in their rooms, in their video frames, and in front of their individual screens, talking to themselves.

In *Now He's Out in Public and Everyone Can See*, when vloggers appear to speak together in concert, it can feel more like a mob than a collective, each charging or judging an unseen and composite black, male celebrity who apparently has (as one vlogger says) "stepped out of line."

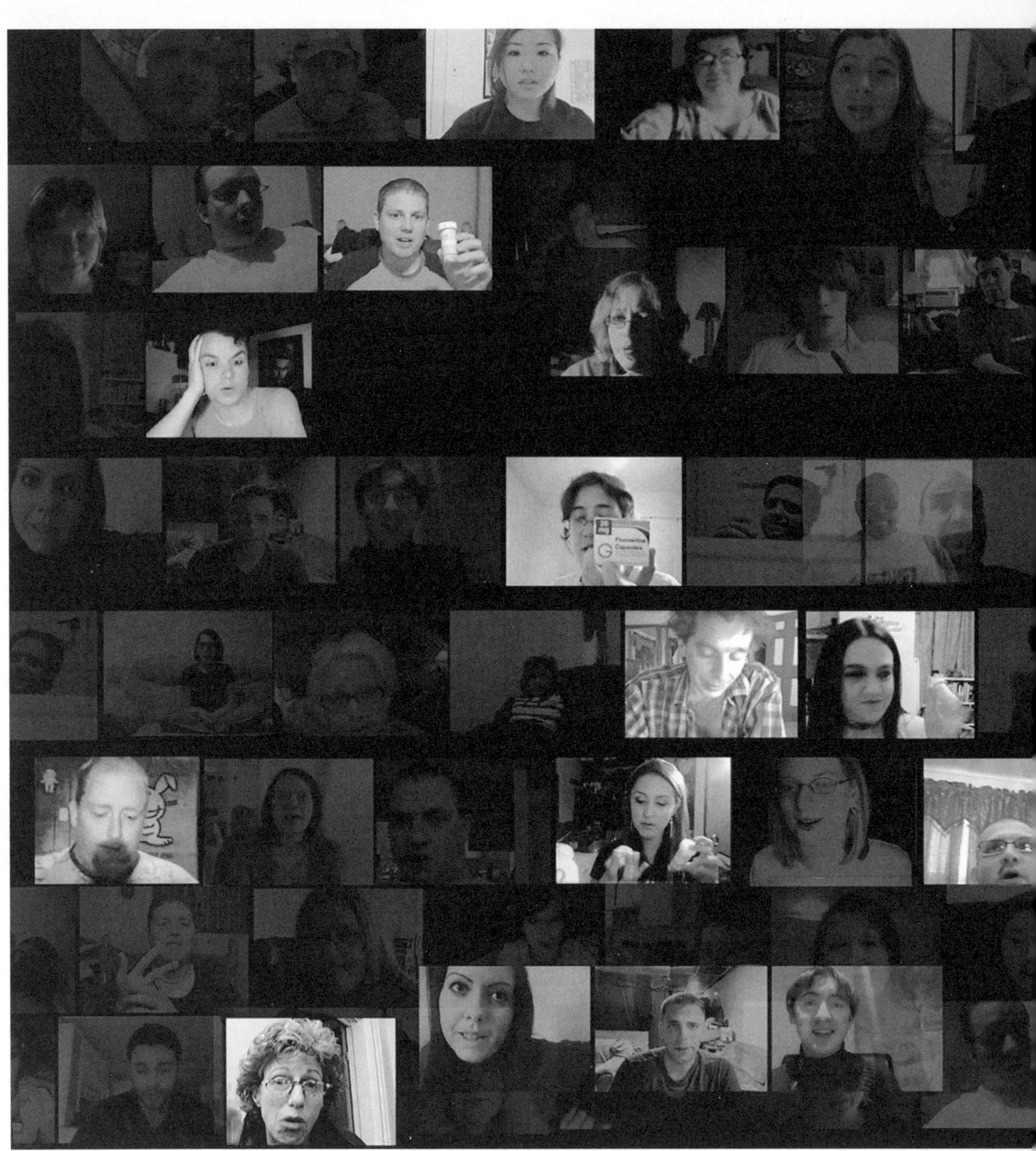

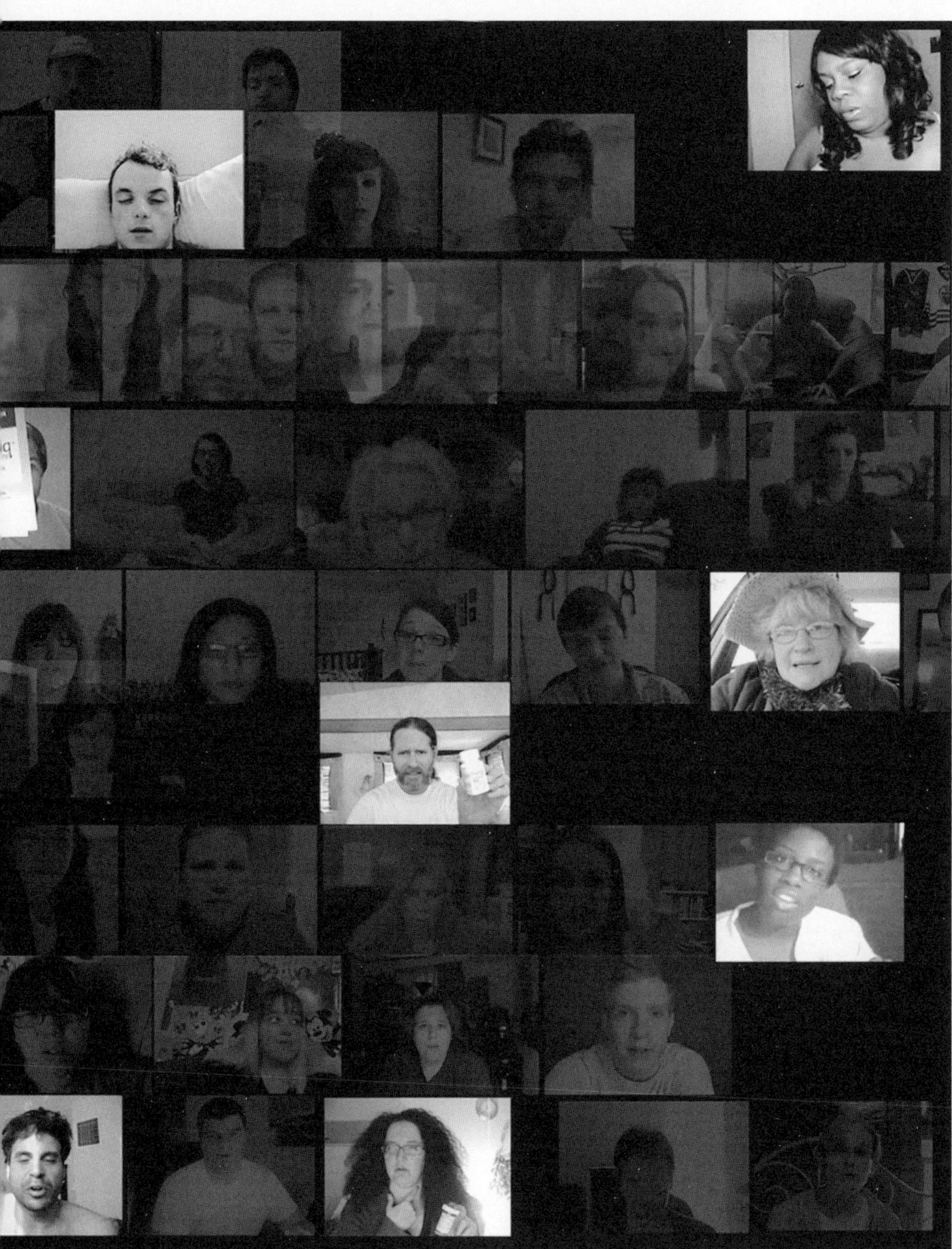

Natalie Bookchin, *My Meds*, from the Testament series, 2009–17

Mass Ornament is often discussed in the context of the 1920s and '30s when the idea of the common was at the forefront. How do ideas about the economy figure into your work? Where does the artist's labor fit into the economy of the entrepreneur today?

I made the piece during the 2008 financial crisis and wanted to contrast the depression of the 1930s to the recession of 2008. In 2008, more people worked from home, in temporary and freelance jobs. I was reflecting on post-Fordist labor, a mode of work different from factory work, where people gathered en masse; now it's freelance, temporary, and private labor, as well as free labor done in the name of individuality and self-expression online. It is a different understanding of labor, but it's work all the same, even though those getting paid are the platforms (Google and Facebook, etcetera) not the individuals.

My work focuses on the shared self—its combination of private and public, scripted and authentic, empathetic and opportunistic. I explore elements and contractions of the pact between the self, the social, and the so-called sharing economy, and examine its forms and constraints. Putting the word *sharing* next to *economy* would have once been considered oxymoronic, but today sharing has been monetized. On Airbnb, we rent our homes; with TaskRabbit, we rent our labor; with Uber, we rent our cars; and on Facebook and YouTube, we rent our selves—our identities, our images, and our opinions.

A number of political theorists following Foucault, including Wendy Brown and Michel Feher, define neoliberalism as not only a set of economic tendencies that include a shriveled welfare state, free markets, privatization, and job insecurity, but also as a condition that presupposes a particular form of subjectivity. According to the neoliberal condition, as they term it, human beings are redefined as human capital, and all aspects of existence are seen and understood in economic terms. Under this regime, the market has come to infiltrate all aspects of daily life and humans are seen as market actors who must invest in themselves as they participate in the marketplace of life. In the past, the market player aimed to fit in and conform, but today it is the artist/entrepreneur who is poised to succeed and who has the potential to compete by standing out from others, thinking differently, and being disruptive. Under this logic, artistic labor is the quintessential form of entrepreneurial labor.

This is quite a grim view of society, and in my work, I search for cracks and fissures, gaps in this oppressive logic, instances of sharing that conflict with, interrupt, or make visible an otherwise seamless flow of the so-called market share.

Speaking of visibility, did anyone whose videos you used ever contact you? In general, are you concerned with privacy issues when working with found video material from the internet?

After I made *Testament* and *Laid Off*, I posted the video as a "video response" to some of the original videos. Only a few people responded, although those who did were pleased to be included. With *Now He's Out in Public*, a screengrab of one of the narrators was published in the *LA Times* before the show opened. The person depicted enthusiastically posted the clipping on his blog.

In terms of the question of privacy, I think about the internet as a space similar to the street, in the sense that you can photograph people in the street because they're in public. I try not to use anything that people wouldn't want to see of themselves but I also think there's free rein because it's become a kind of a public space.

In *Long Story Short*, a forty-five-minute film, you addressed a different public space, one that is invisible to many people. How did the concept and work process differ from earlier pieces like *Mass Ornament* or *Testament*?

Instead of looking online for what's commonly shared, I produced a missing archive, one that didn't appear to exist on social media. I went to food banks, adult literacy programs, and job training centers in Los Angeles and the Bay Area in Northern California and asked people to discuss and reflect on their experiences of poverty—how it feels, how they cope, and what they think should be done. I used the same forms—the webcam, the vlog, the amateur video—where people present themselves and their expertise to the world. My aim was to contrast this material and put it in conversation with contemporary social media, to reflect on the images and voices we usually see and those that are starkly absent.

Are you concerned about the longevity of your video works? People always seem to be asking, Is photography dead? How do you see the dynamic playing out with video?

I am creating an archive of a particular moment in time. I find beauty in their materiality, in their pixilation, in the "bad" lighting, and in how it locates them in a particular historical moment and technological regime. My work preserves something that would otherwise be lost or buried. You can't find those videos online anymore because what rises to the top are the Drake videos, or whatever is most popular at any time. Google's algorithms favor the popular. The rest sink to the bottom of the database. I rescue the unloved, unseen, and unwanted videos from the dustbin of history.

INTERVIEW: LYLE ASHTON HARRIS (AS TOLD BY PARISSAH LIN) WITH MARINA CHAO

Lyle Ashton Harris's artistic practice spans photography, collage, assemblage, video, and performance. He mines an extensive personal archive to explore the intersections of individual and political histories. Harris's large-scale mixed-media collages bring together hundreds of elements—including photographs, textbook illustrations, magazine and newspaper clippings, letters, and other personal ephemera—to explore the complex and recursive connections between identity, collective memory, and political and cultural ideology. He debuted the collage *Appunti per l'Afro Barocco* (2015) in *Public, Private, Secret*.

Marina Chao: Can you tell me about *Appunti per l'Afro Barocco* and how you began working on it? It came out of an invitation from the American Academy in Rome in 2015, where you were a fellow in 2001, right? You and Robert Storr organized the exhibition *Nero su Bianco* [Black on white] there that summer.

Lyle Ashton Harris: I was indeed a fellow and am now on the board of trustees of the American Academy in Rome. *Appunti per l'Afro Barocco* is a multilayered, multimedia collage originally produced as a visual essay for the catalogue *Nero su Bianco* [2015]. The original collage was constructed early in 2015 so that photomontages could be extracted for the catalogue. Though it began as an organic and meditative project with the intention of being the foundation for a photomontage series, as it grew and took shape in my studio it became apparent that the work had weight and presence on its own. As an exploration of the relationship between Africa and Europe, the work is highly specific and situated, although it references my earlier body of work—the Blow Up series [2004–6]—and positions itself in relation to *The Watering Hole* [1996].

Could you describe the *Nero su Bianco* project and what you and Robert Storr wanted to accomplish with that show?

Nero su Bianco—cocurated by fellow trustee Rob Storr, Peter Benson Miller, and myself—was an international survey of artists' perspectives on the shifts in perceptions of identity within the African American, Afro-European, and African spheres. The show featured the work of international artists—including Terry Adkins, Carrie Mae Weems, Nari Ward, Fred Wilson, Stanley Whitney, Senam Okudzeto, Meleko Mokgosi, and Theo Eshetu—and spanned across multiple decades to demand a reconsideration of the historical canon. The show coincided with *Black Portraiture{s} II: Imaging the Black Body and Re-Staging Histories,* a conference hosted by New York University in Florence. With both this and the crucial placement of the Academy in mind, the exhibition and accompanying catalogue sought to raise questions and present multiple perspectives on perceptions of identity, subjectivity, and agency within both the African and African diasporic cultural spheres. It was a space for the academy to reexamine its position as an institution with regard to cultural hybridity and autonomy.

I'd like to know more about some of the individual elements in the *Appunti* collage and how they relate to each other, however unfixed those links might be. Just to pick a few, can you speak to some of the connections that bring these images into the same constellation: the photograph of you in bed with a *Caravaggio* poster behind your head; the Dolce & Gabbana men's underwear ad; the photograph of the Malcolm X T-shirt; the pictures of a nude man on a kitchen counter pulling something out of his foot (in a reference to the classical *Spinario*, or *Boy with Thorn*, sculpture); and the small clipping of the infamous Abu Ghraib prisoner-abuse photograph, with the hooded figure balancing atop a small box?

As my forthcoming book with Aperture Foundation, *Today I Shall Judge Nothing That Occurs* [2017], shows, I have throughout my practice and since childhood been an avid and almost obsessive archivist and collector. *Malcolm X T-shirt, Rome* [1992] is a photograph from *The Ektachrome Archive*. The image is from the first European road trip with my then-partner and close friend Tommy Gear. This T-shirt was from a street vendor in New York or LA, post–Rodney King riots of '92—to quote my studio manager Parissah: "These institutions still exist." The sign painters, street artists, etcetera did a lot of the work of advertising and disseminating information prior to the digital medium. The *Caravaggi*o image is also from *The Ektachrome Archive* and is a photograph in the guest room of Isaac Julien's apartment with a film poster of legendary Derek Jarman. The Dolce & Gabbana advertisement relates to the readymade piece at the center of *Blow Up IV (Seville)* [2006]: an Adidas advertisement depicting a black man, who bore a similarity to me, putting a shoe onto a white soccer player. The homosociality in this Dolce & Gabbana advertisement was deeply related to the racialized, ambiguous desire of the Adidas advertisement. Finally, the Abu Ghraib image is obviously from the 2003 story of the violence against prisoners in Iraq. The images of this violence were to me almost pornographic. The story was broken to major news sources through social media and through the sharing and trafficking of these images. What does it mean for us as Americans to experience our fellow citizens acting out violence on the bodies of others?

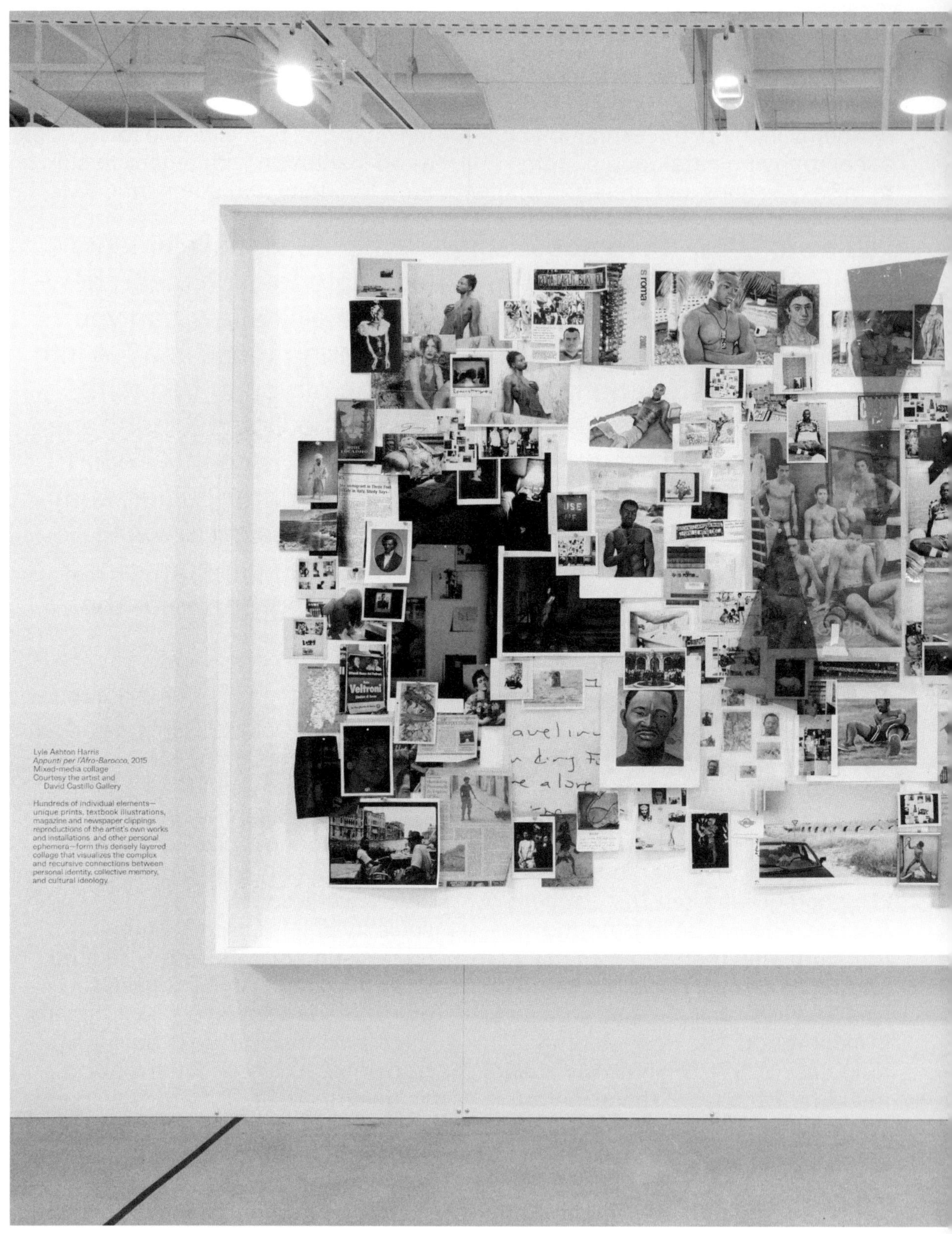
Lyle Ashton Harris
Appunti per l'Afro-Barocco, 2015
Mixed-media collage
Courtesy the artist and
David Castillo Gallery
Hundreds of individual elements—
unique prints, textbook illustrations,
magazine and newspaper clippings,
reproductions of the artist's own works
and installations, and other personal
ephemera—form this densely layered
collage that visualizes the complex
and recursive connections between
personal identity, collective memory,
and cultural ideology.
roma
Veltroni

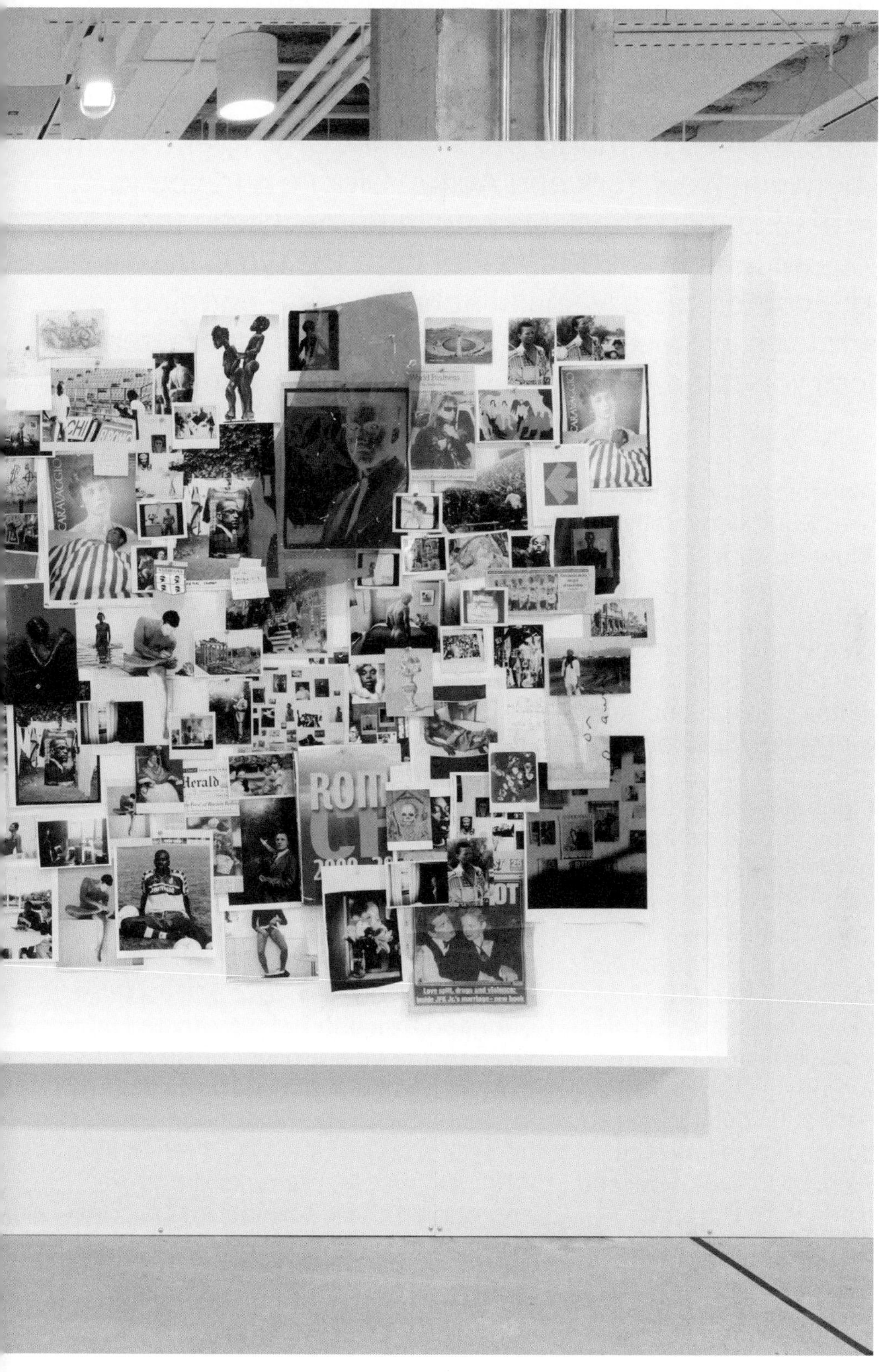

Lyle Ashton Harris, *Appunti per l'Afro Barocco*, 2015. Photo © John Berens

And what is the relationship between this image and the contemporary saturation of similar images in the media of state violence against people here at home?

You've lived and worked primarily in New York City; spent seven years living between New York and Accra, Ghana; and you've had a couple of extended stays working in Rome. Given the way you work, you must have thought a lot about the ways in which you fit into the contemporary social networks and ongoing historical narratives in those places. How would you characterize the differences you felt most acutely, from New York to Accra to Rome?

Specificity of place has always been an element of my work, especially present in the Blow Up series. Through these connections of news clippings, organic remnants of my own life, journal entries, etcetera, I am able to start to draw connections across national boundaries, generations, and public and private space. Each place has a specific texture, a way that time passes, and languages. Each has its own version of cosmopolitanism. New York, of course, has undergone so many changes in the last thirty years, with neighborhood upheavals and the elimination of much of the semi-public space that used to be home to LGBTQ people and artists in the '90s. Accra, in many ways, is at the seam and junction of many histories and worlds. There are still vestiges of the neocolonial imprint, as well as legacies of colonialism, the slave trade, and autonomous trade with Europe. Accra is a blooming metropolis with a multitude of languages, textures, and religions—all resting on the edge of the ocean. Rome is shrouded in vestiges of antiquities. While in Rome, I frequented churches and museums and collections to see Caravaggios and antiquities.

After returning from Los Angeles to New York in the mid-to-late 1990s, I helped my grandfather make his transition. I had been residing in New York for a couple of years when I won the Prix de Rome. Originally, I was to do portraits for this project; however, a *New York Times* cover story on racism against African soccer players in international soccer changed my direction; I became fascinated with the dynamics of masculinity, crowds, power, and violence. Upon my return to New York on the eve of 9/11—a tense but good transition—I was invited in 2005 by the vice provost of New York University and Nancy Barton to go to Ghana for the semester and develop an arts program for NYU. I fell in love with the people, place, and culture and stayed there for half a year every year until December 2012. I had an in to the city and communities—such as gyms, churches, and funerary culture—through my former Ghanaian partner.

Something I love about your practice is the reappearance of images across works, in different forms, and in achronological ways. Can you describe what that gesture means to you? Are there particular images that you find yourself drawn to again and again?

I would say it's more about the process for me, about the image slippages than the images themselves. What does it mean to have them recontextualized over time? What does it mean for them to be rejuxtaposed at different scales? How does it change from an image to an object? They offer different ways of teasing the multiple readings.

It's also significant that identical images at different scales repeat across and within the same collage, as is the case in the *Appunti* work. That's the aspect of your work that led me to think about the idea of recursion, an essential characteristic of the logic of language: we can embed ideas indefinitely, not only retaining but building meaning as we go. Is that a fair reading of the echoing of images within a single work? Or is it less about language and more about repetition and highlighting certain visual tropes?

Yes, that is a good reading; it is definitely about language. It's about both those things. How can we recontextualize and repeat within a final frame? How can it change the narrative of the work?

I was at a group studio visit in your space recently and somebody asked whether homoerotic imagery featured in most of your work. Your response was to ask what he thought from what he had seen. Then you spoke about the notion of the homosocial. Can you articulate the difference between those two related but separate ideas—the homosocial and the homoerotic? Do you identify much with the use of the latter term? Is it at all useful to you?

They have parallel tracks that may intersect and intertwine. Obviously there are technical differences between "homosociality" and "homosexuality." There is an impulse with contemporary photography—especially when the artist's sexuality is known—to label many images as "homoerotic" when in reality they are often about more subtle and present interactions: gestures of masculinity, public and private performance, intimacy. They may have parallel tracks and sometimes they may intersect but they are still distinct.

Your work is rooted in the performative. How would you say you engage with performativity differently in your iconic self-portraits from the 1990s as compared to later pieces, in which the physical body is less central?

I think it was necessary to somehow remove and deconstruct the figure, exemplified in my deployment of montages in *The Watering Hole* [1996], as a way to decentralize the subject and incorporate the viewer in the conception of—let's say—the Jeffrey Dhamer-esque and the consumption of images. It is about implicating the viewer.

Public, Private, Secret was very much about performativity and considered the performance of identity through circulating images—from the nineteenth-century practice of distributing cartes de visite to today's ubiquitous sharing within social-media culture. What do you think about juxtaposing artistic practice and popular acts of performance? You've incorporated web content into your work before, such as in *Deceivers and Money Boys* [2013]. Do you think about social media in a serious way?

It's important to take a break from social media, first of all. But, secondly, I do see social media as part of the legacy of personal archives: it offers a multiplicity of narratives and histories to supplement the dominant one. It is important to have both.

GALLERY 02

Public, Private, Secret, ICP Museum, 250 Bowery, NY, June 2016–January 2017

Gallery 02 constellated a diverse range of historical and contemporary works with streams of real-time images from social-media sources. The aim was to heighten our attention toward the social implications of the contemporary image-centric world—staged against the backdrop of the factors that define our media environment—which we internalize and naturalize through our own image usage and behaviors. *Public, Private, Secret* takes into account the extent to which the virtual game of being seen and seeing others creates slippages between our physical bodies and behaviors. But these ostensible freedoms are overshadowed by the ways in which automated imagery—captured and interpreted for surveillance purposes—is now used as the standard of identification, enabling us to be digitally measured and objectified. These automated renditions of identity are inevitably restricted; the exhibited works embody the disruptions, resistances, and subversions that artists propose to these limited versions of race, gender, sexuality, and autonomy populating popular culture. Whether historical or contemporary, these creative practices and their authors counter the restraints on identities established by society. In so doing, and by invoking photography, they anticipate a future for our image-world rich with diversity and alterity, one that can be shaped and influenced by the agency of self-representation.

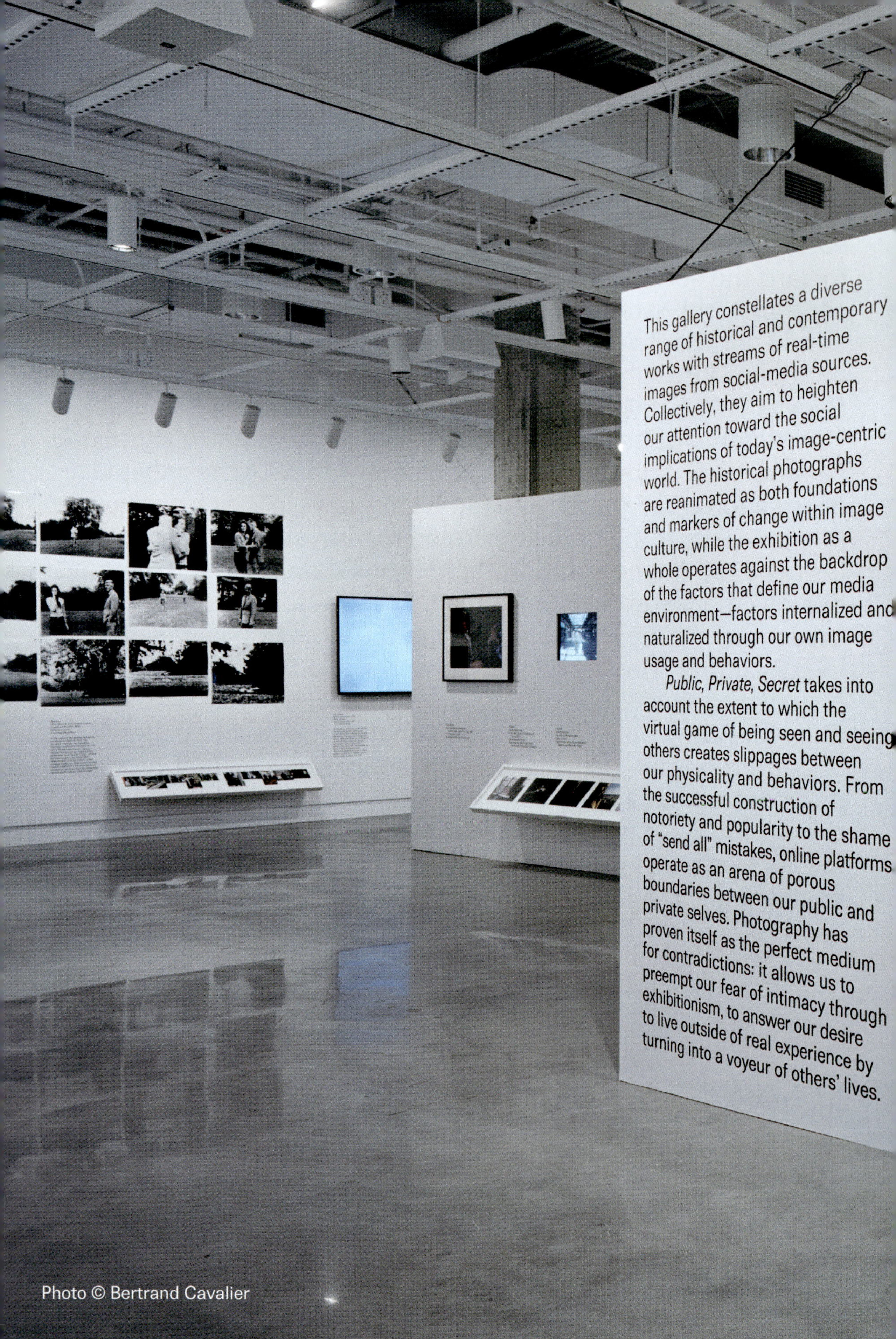

Photo © Bertrand Cavalier

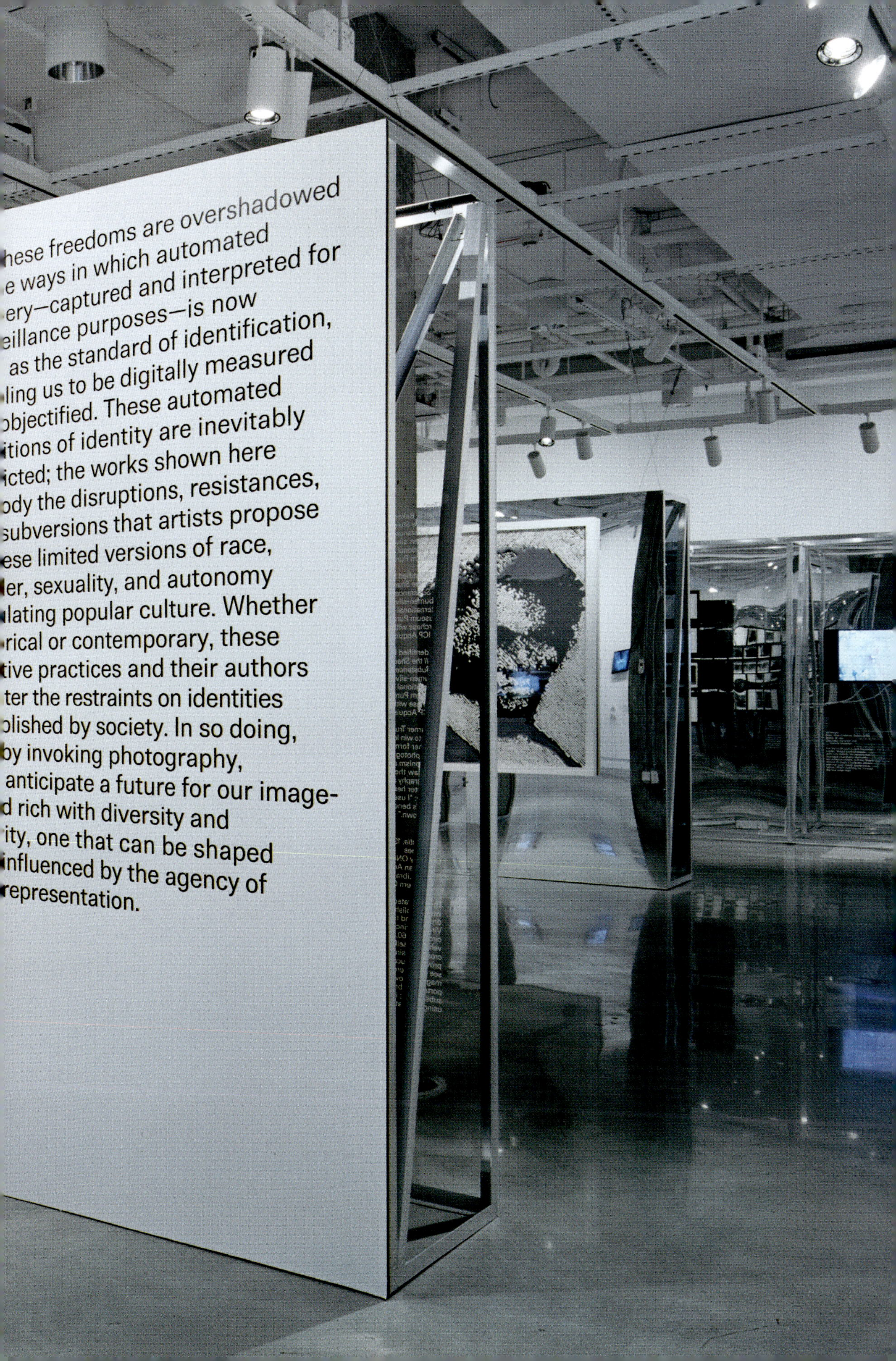
hese freedoms are overshadowed
e ways in which automated
ery—captured and interpreted for
eillance purposes—is now
as the standard of identification,
ling us to be digitally measured
objectified. These automated
itions of identity are inevitably
icted; the works shown here
ody the disruptions, resistances,
subversions that artists propose
ese limited versions of race,
er, sexuality, and autonomy
lating popular culture. Whether
rical or contemporary, these
tive practices and their authors
ter the restraints on identities
blished by society. In so doing,
by invoking photography,
anticipate a future for our image-
d rich with diversity and
ity, one that can be shaped
influenced by the agency of
representation.

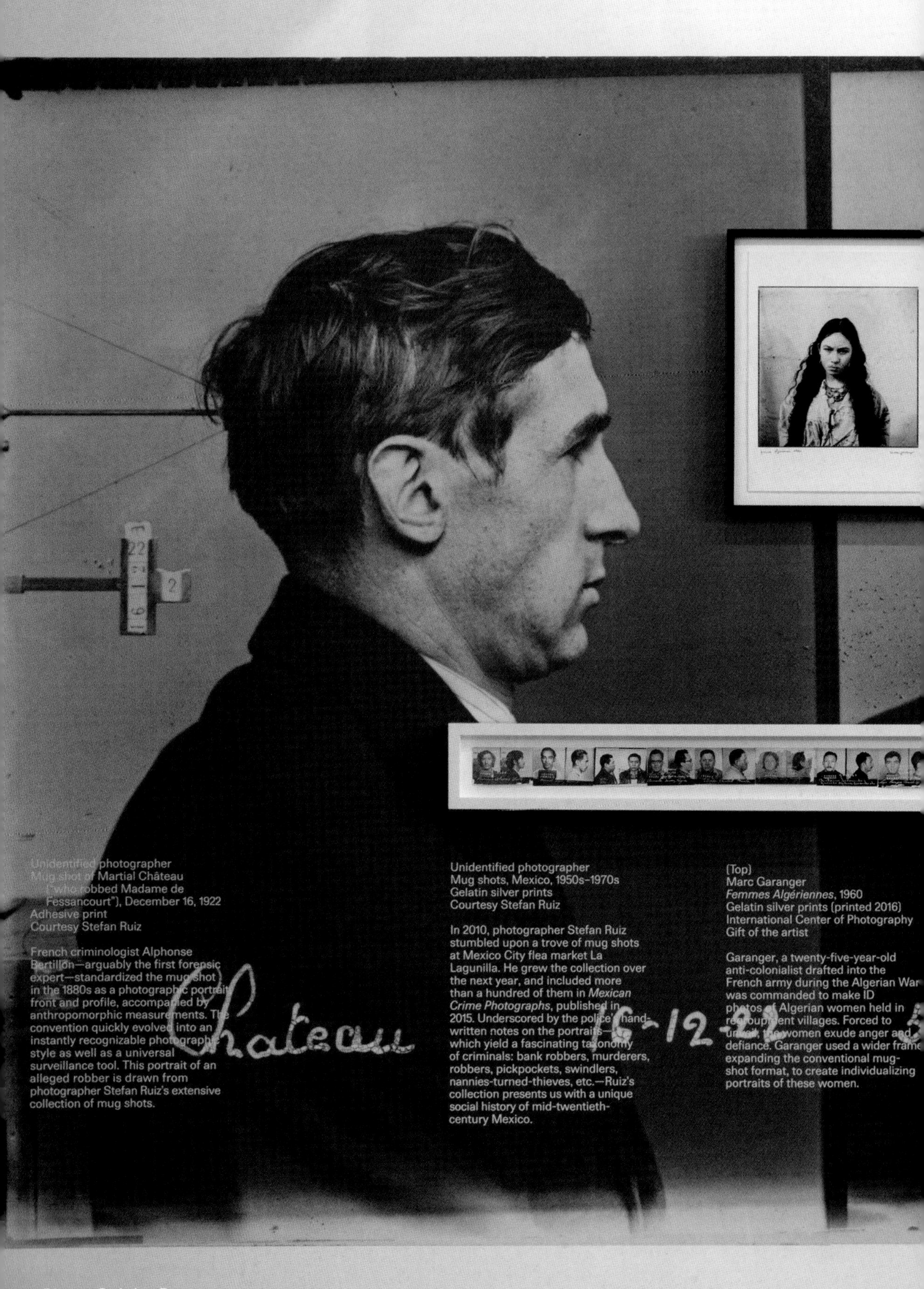

Photo © John Berens

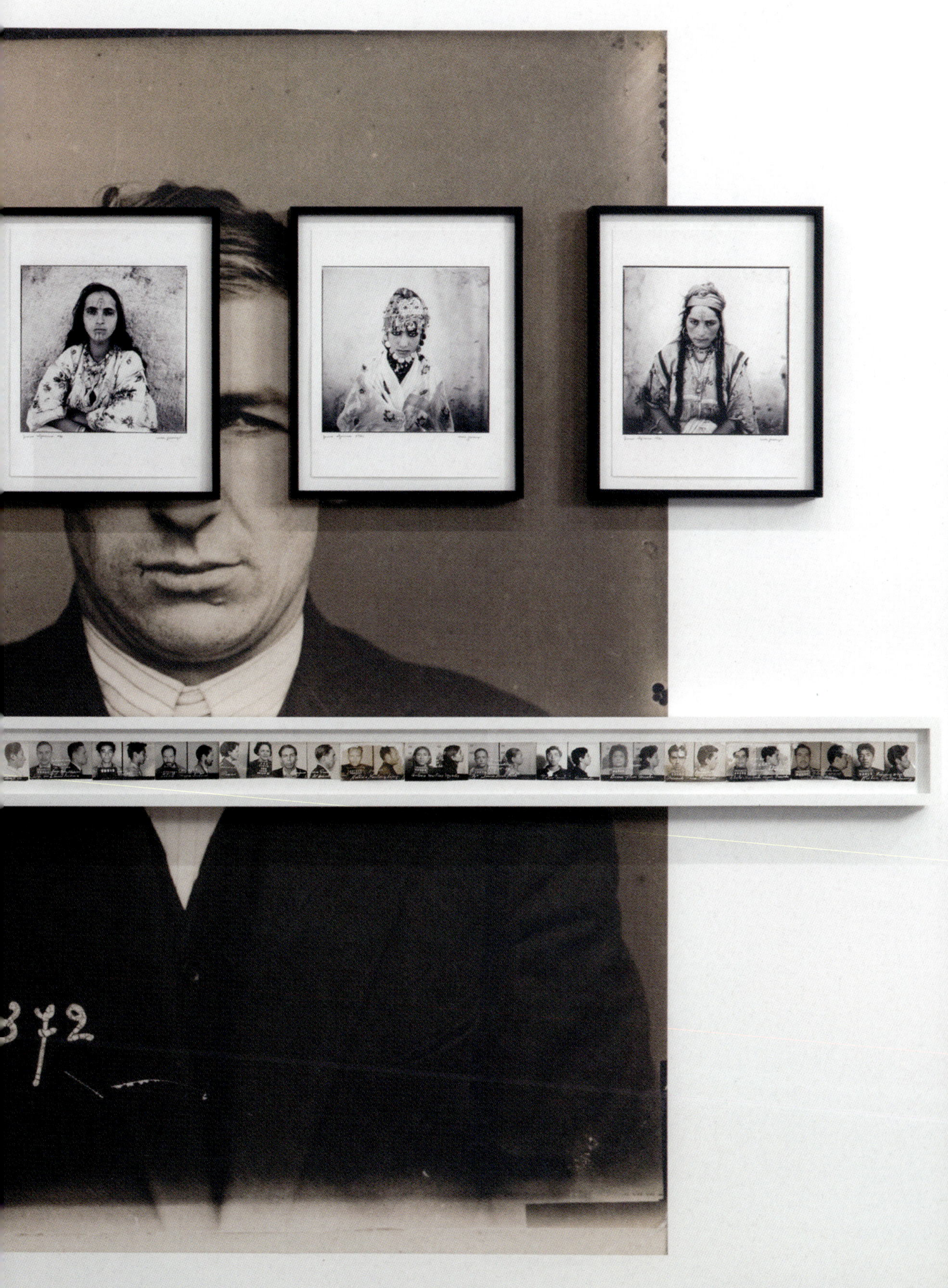

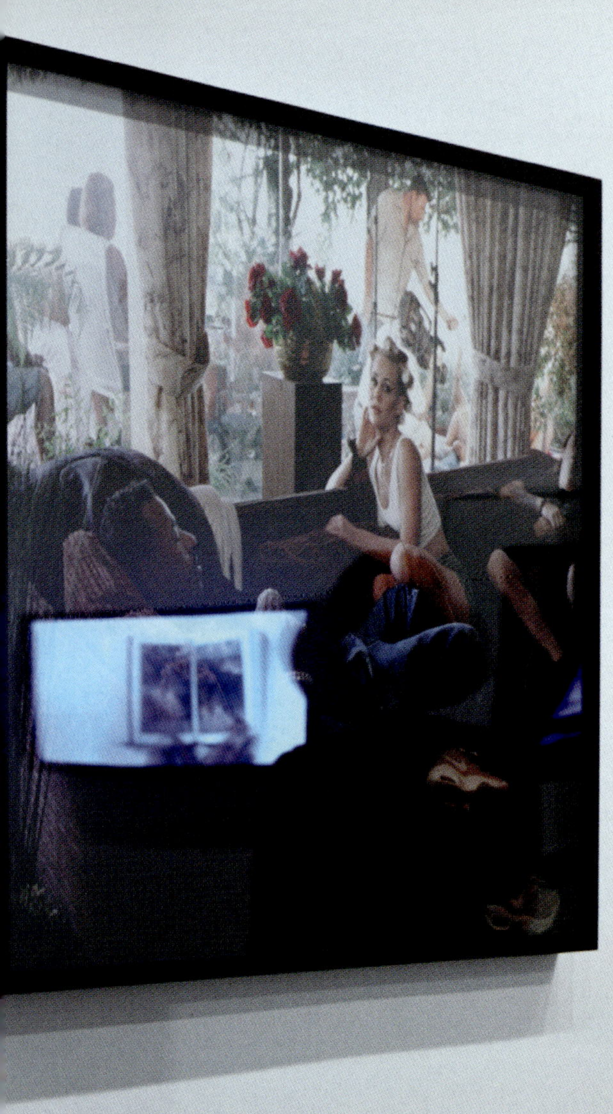

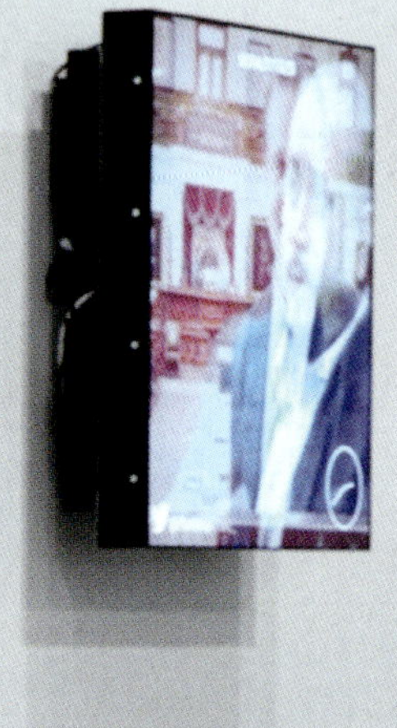

Photo © Bertrand Cavalier

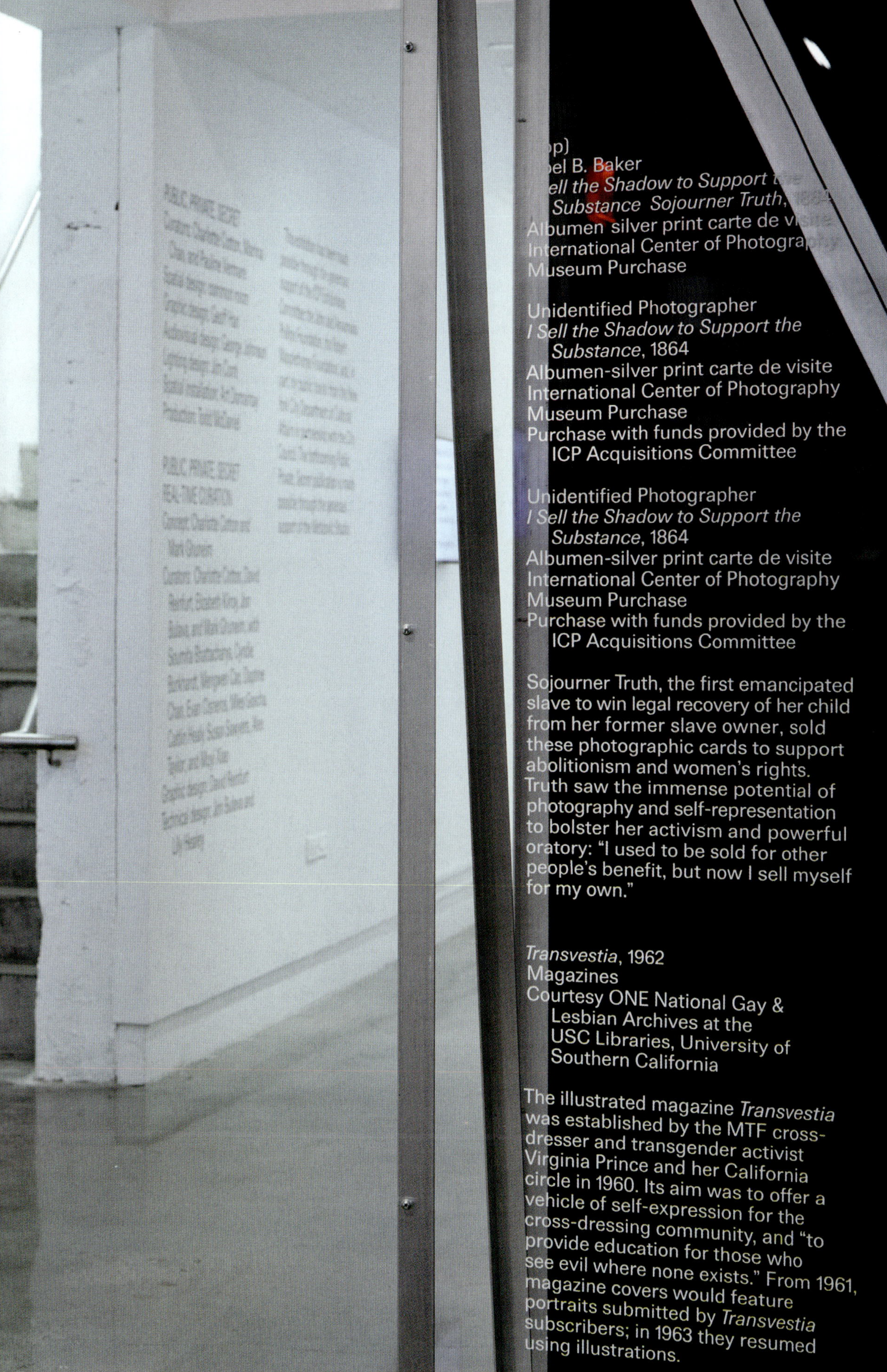
Albumen silver print carte de vi
International Center of Photogra
Museum Purchase
Unidentified Photographer
I Sell the Shadow to Support the
Substance, 1864
Albumen-silver print carte de visite
International Center of Photography
Museum Purchase
Purchase with funds provided by the
ICP Acquisitions Committee
Unidentified Photographer
I Sell the Shadow to Support the
Substance, 1864
Albumen-silver print carte de visite
International Center of Photography
Museum Purchase
Purchase with funds provided by the
ICP Acquisitions Committee
Sojourner Truth, the first emancipated slave to win legal recovery of her child from her former slave owner, sold these photographic cards to support abolitionism and women's rights. Truth saw the immense potential of photography and self-representation to bolster her activism and powerful oratory: "I used to be sold for other people's benefit, but now I sell myself for my own."
Transvestia, 1962
Magazines
Courtesy ONE National Gay & Lesbian Archives at the USC Libraries, University of Southern California
The illustrated magazine Transvestia was established by the MTF cross-dresser and transgender activist Virginia Prince and her California circle in 1960. Its aim was to offer a vehicle of self-expression for the cross-dressing community, and "to provide education for those who see evil where none exists." From 1961, magazine covers would feature portraits submitted by Transvestia subscribers; in 1963 they resumed using illustrations.

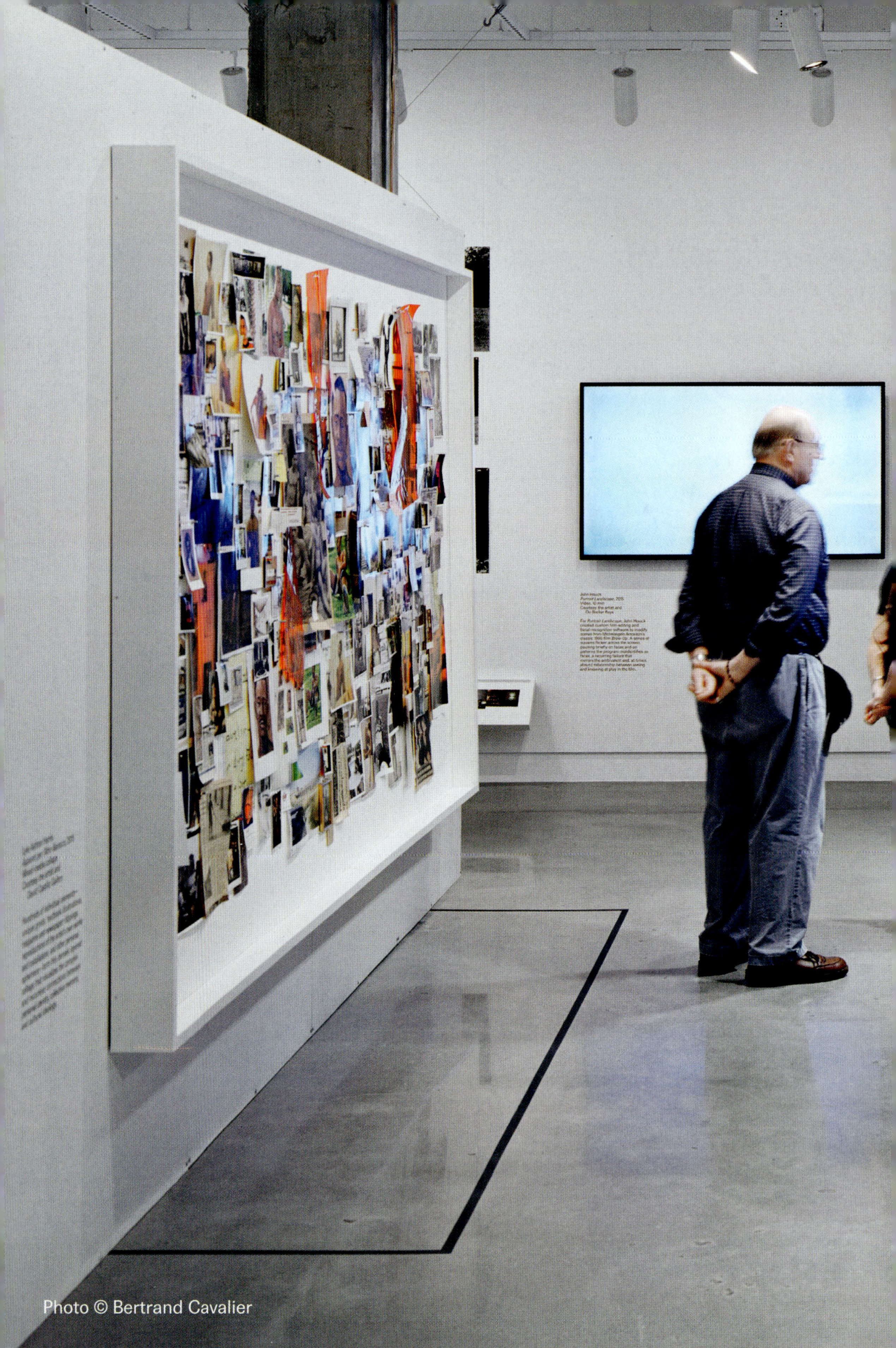

Photo © Bertrand Cavalier

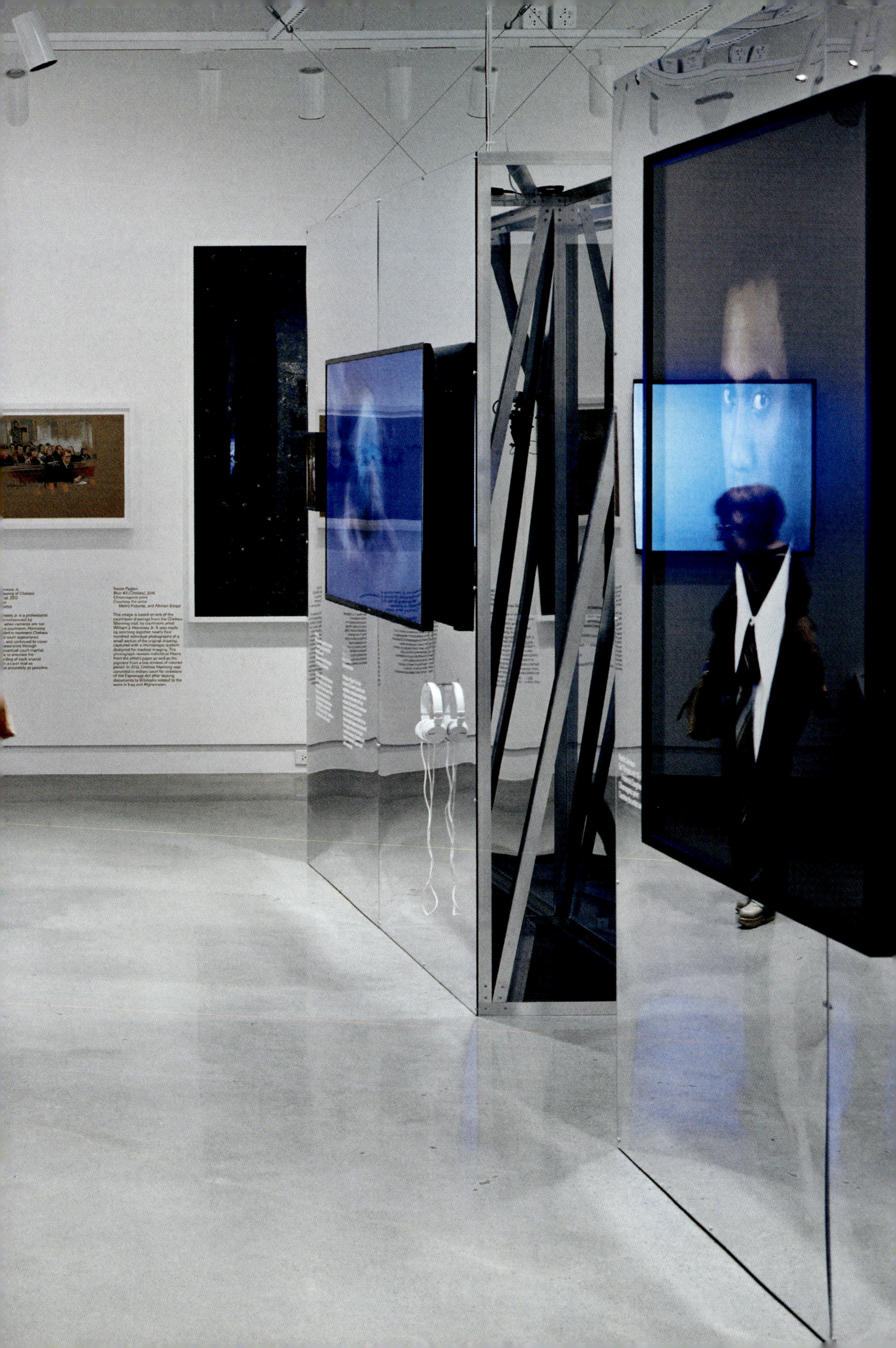

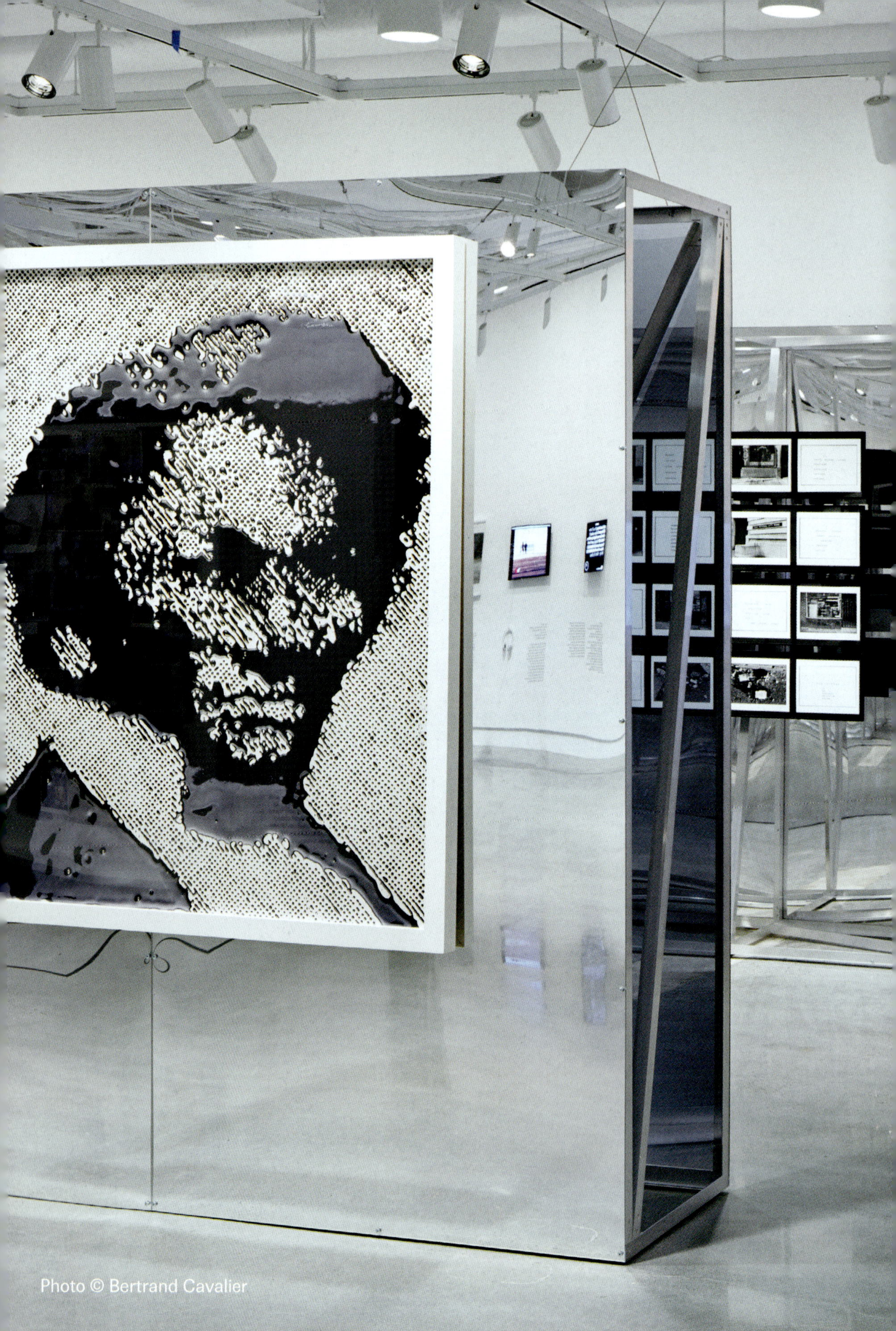

Photo © Bertrand Cavalier

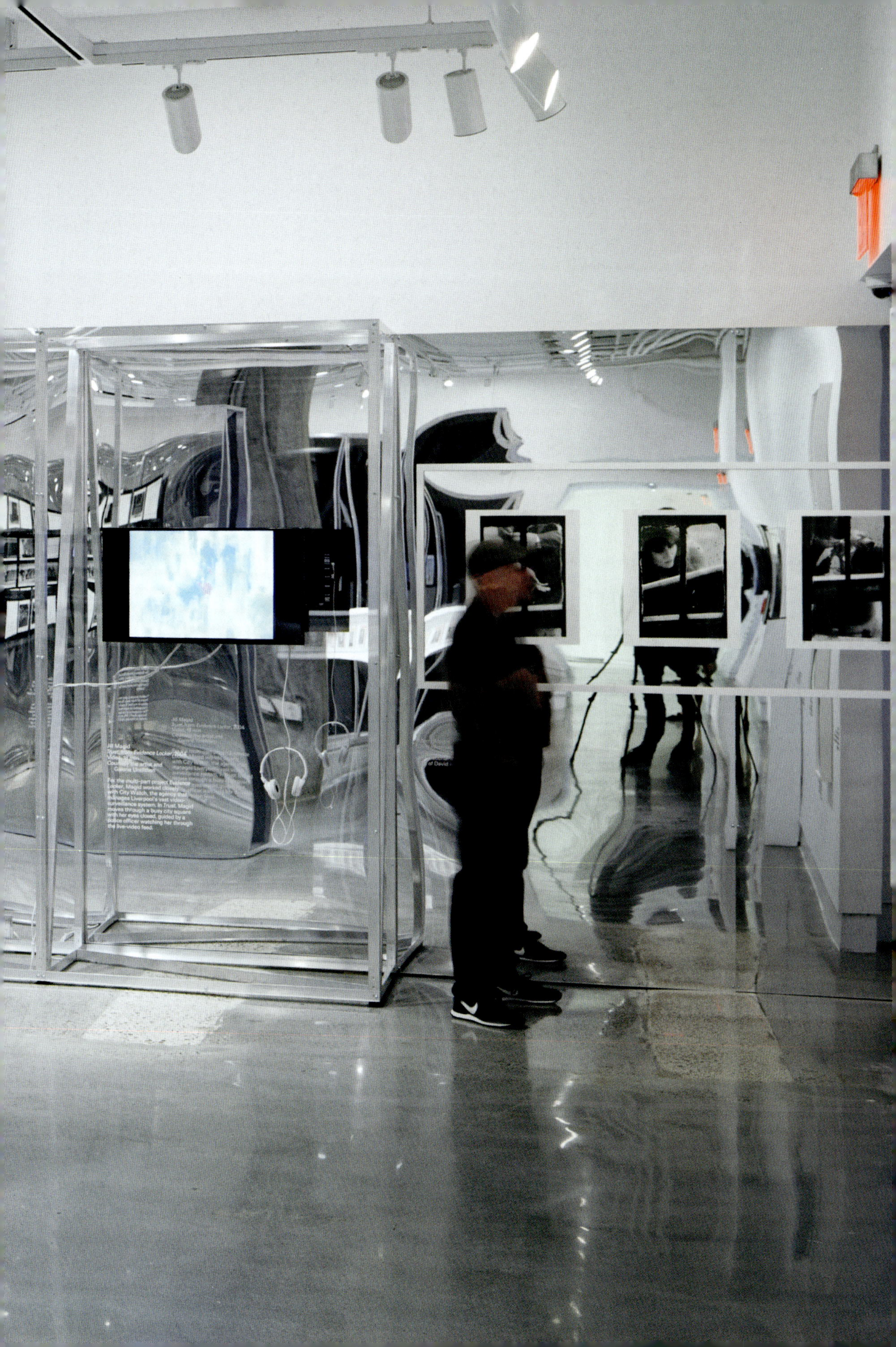

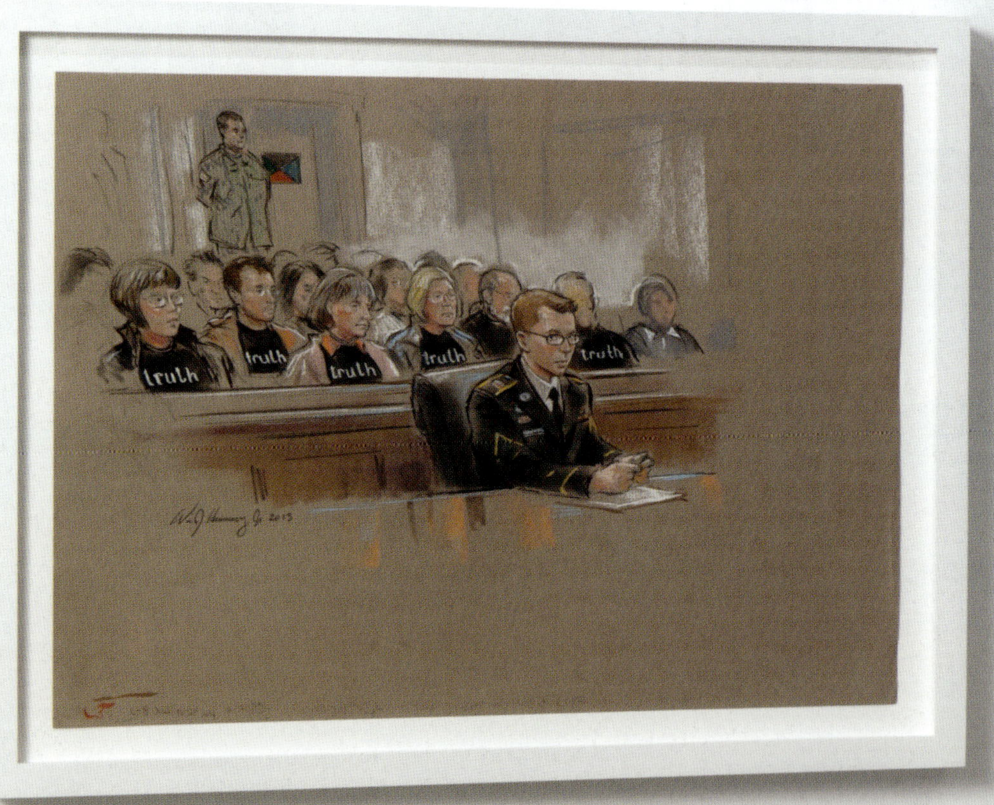

Artwork depicted: Trevor Paglen, *Blue #3 (Chelsea)*, 2016 (shown with an official courtroom drawing of the Manning trial by William J. Hennessy Jr.). Photo © John Berens

Trevor Paglen
Blue #3 (Chelsea), 2016

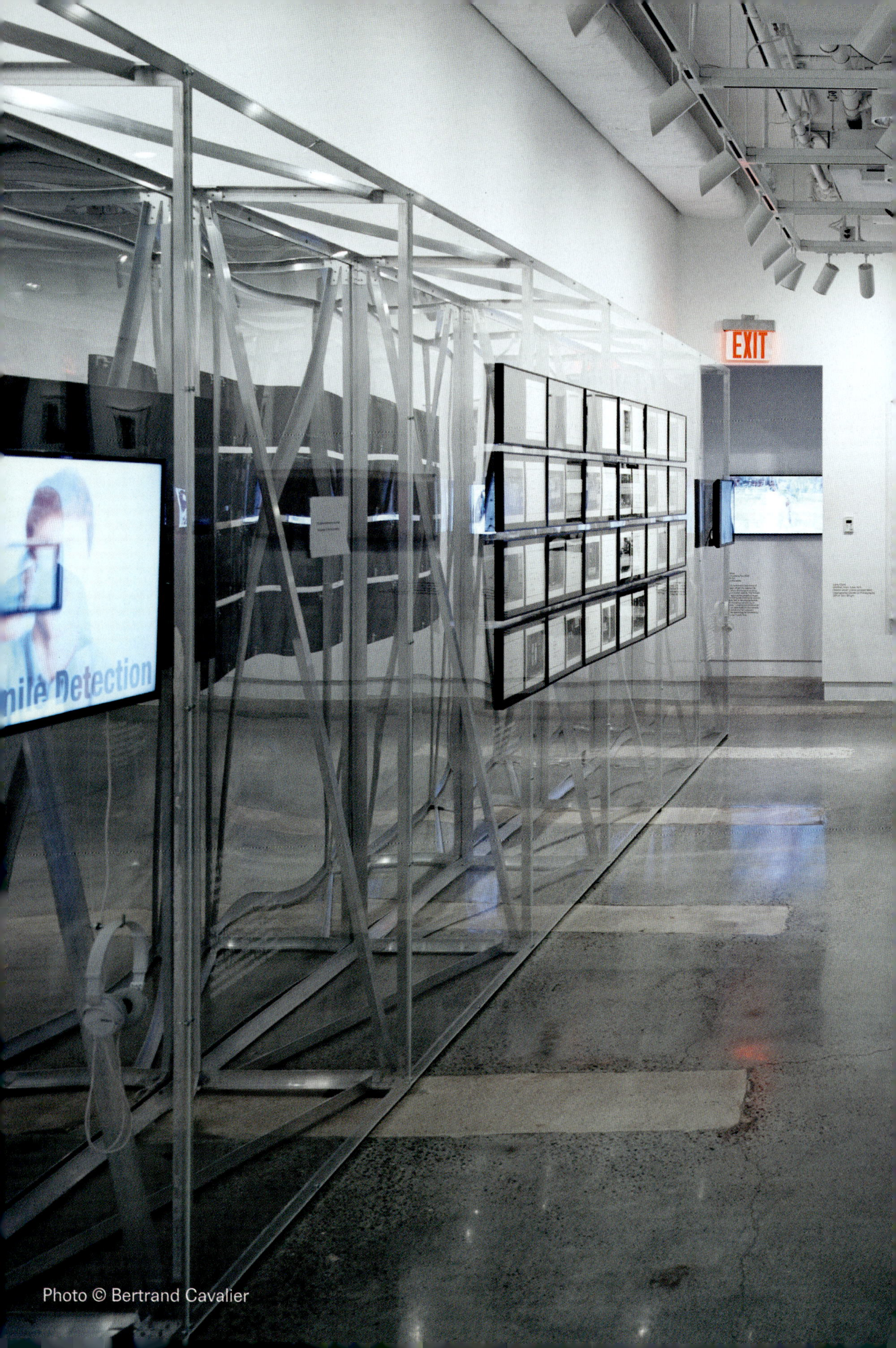

Photo © Bertrand Cavalier

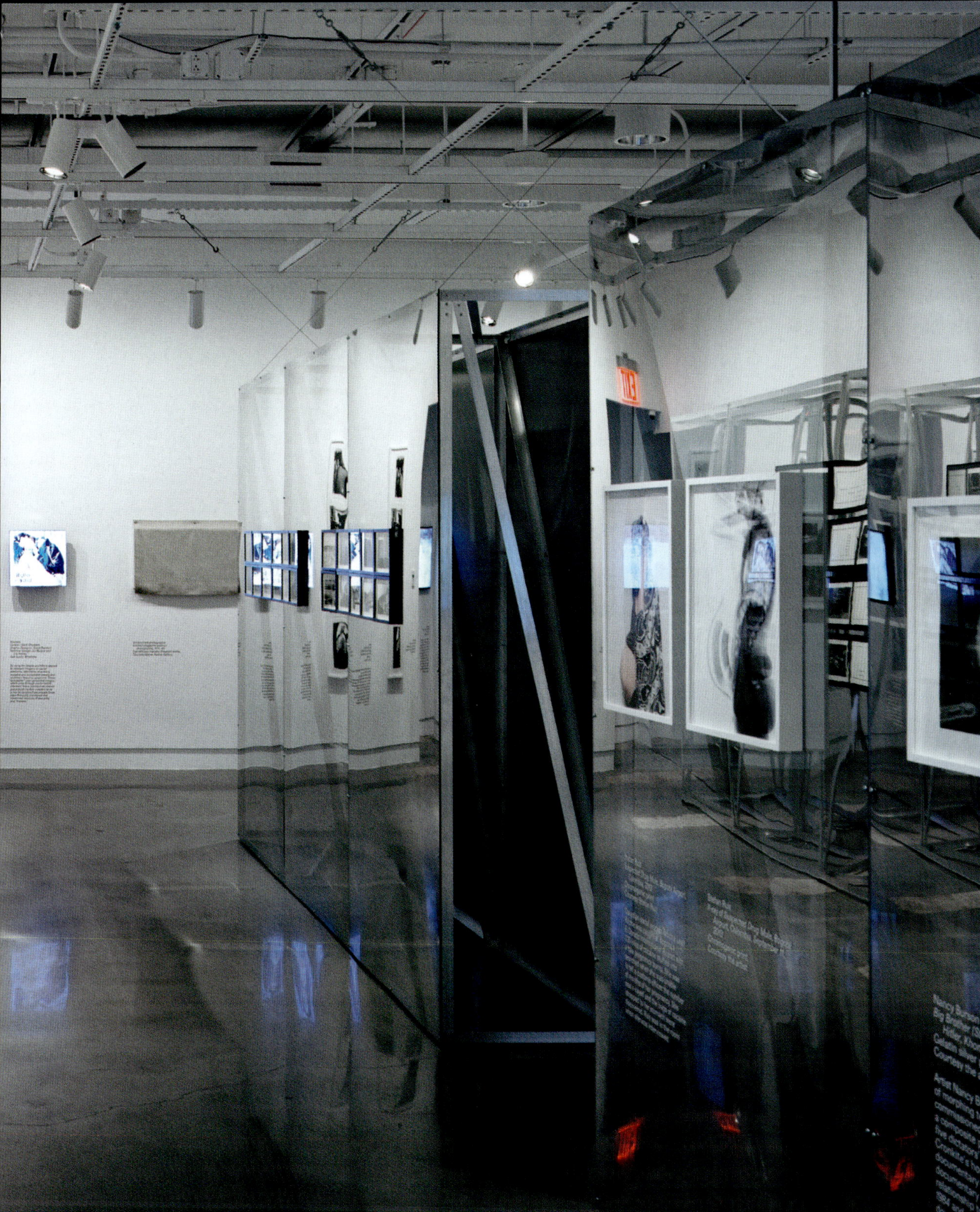

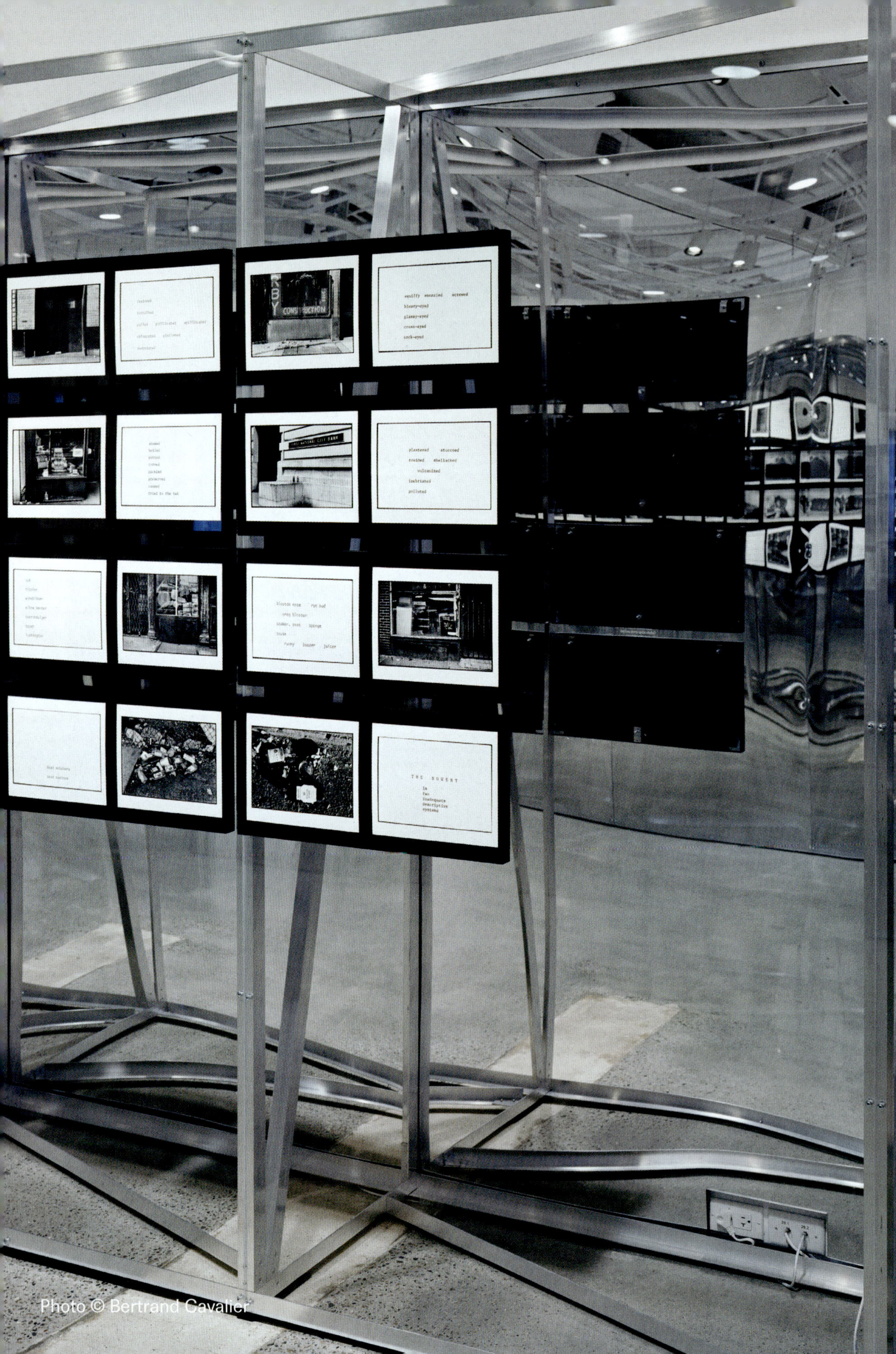

Photo © Bertrand Cavalier

Reflections

Transparent and Opaque, common room

Correspondence, David Reinfurt

Every Image Found, Mark Ghuneim

Students in the New Media Narratives Program Curate Real-Time Social-Media Collections for *Public, Private, Secret*, Elizabeth Kilroy

Making *Public/Private/Portrait*, Romke Hoogwaerts

Urgent Archives, Paul Soulellis

Belonging in the Mess, Johanna Hedva

Spooky Action from a Distance, Lucas Wrench

Pictures without Words, Joseph Maida

Redefining What and Who We See and Don’t See, Lacy Austin

REFLECTION: TRANSPARENT AND OPAQUE, COMMON ROOM

Common room is an architectural practice with a publishing imprint and an exhibition space. It is a collaborative platform based in New York City and Brussels, and is comprised of architects Lars Fischer, Maria Ibañez de Sendadiano, and Todd Rouhe; Rachel Himmelfarb; and graphic designer Geoff Han. Common room created the spatial design of the first iteration of the ICP Museum at 250 Bowery, including the *Public, Private, Secret* exhibition design, with visual identity by Geoff Han.

> *Architecture has always represented the prototype of a work of art, the reception of which is consumed by a collectivity in a state of distraction.—Walter Benjamin*[1]

As architects, the significant provocation of *Public, Private, Secret* was the recognition that there is a new way of differentiating the public from the private, a distinction that is not as powerful as it once was. As we were introduced to the exhibition's vision and content by its lead curator Charlotte Cotton, we had to accept that a clear difference between public and private space has probably collapsed. To use Mies Van der Rohe's glass and steel ("skin and bones") Farnsworth House as an example, the voyeur—real or imagined—is no longer outside peering in through the glass walls. You don't need to be outside of the house or even near it. Through new forms of media you are able to see inside; the architectural charge has been dispersed.

Still, our practice is invested in the material conditions of the event. The concrete conditions of the built environment still shape experiences and social interaction even as users find new ways to represent themselves through social media and its virtual forums for public engagement. The exhibition design for *Public, Private, Secret* approached this in two ways: through self-consciousness and simultaneity. The spatial organization of the exhibition was simple. Modular metal frameworks were used to create freestanding walls with different surface materials: painted plywood, clear acrylic, and single-sided and two-way mirrors. The materiality of the support surfaces explored the different ways that the public—the viewer—could interact with the work, regardless of whether it was intimate, public, or private. We simply set up the conditions for the work to be viewed.

Upon entering the exhibition, the viewer faced a wall of mirrors, immediately seeing both their own reflection (a confrontation between the viewer and the physical environment) and a virtual image of themselves (an

1 Walter Benjamin, "The Work of Art in the Age of Mechanical Reproduction," in *Illuminations: Essays and Reflections*, ed. Hannah Arendt (New York: Shocken Books, 1968).

absorption of the viewer and physical environment into something new and dubious). Gallery 01 was nearly empty, displaying only the introductory text panels and looping projected works in two locations. The digital nature of the projected works in this space confronted the material qualities of the installation but reinforced a condition of self-awareness and presence. As viewers continued to move through the gallery, the single mirrored wall with which they were initially confronted multiplied and took on the effect of a hall of mirrors that distorted the video works, the textual graphics, and their own presence.

As they moved downstairs to Gallery 02, there were several conditions to navigate. A series of parallel walls defined the space and created a system for display. The artworks were mounted directly onto the various panels. The transparency and reflectivity of the surfaces meant that as viewers moved through the exhibition they were literally reflected in the work, never able to adopt an entirely detached vantage point. The participation of the viewer was thus mediated through reflections and glimpses beyond, separated from but visually connected to the rest of the gallery. The works the curators selected, combined with the spatial design and our chosen materials, created for viewers both an increased sense of agency and of surrender to the spatial conditions of a mediated society. They could not see the work without seeing themselves and other visitors. One could not view the work without subjecting oneself to being on display.

The wall surfaces varied in transparency and reflectivity but revealed their supporting structure. At the far wall of Gallery 02, for instance, a mirror was mounted behind the work mounted on a transparent frame. It reflected the backside of the artwork and the monitors hung in front of it. This almost irrational configuration revealed more than the visitors expected to see, while continuing the spectacle of the exhibition into the depth of the wall, reflecting the gallery back onto itself and exposing the underlying infrastructure. This sense of exposure emphasized the presence of the individuals while underscoring their increased dependence on the surroundings to define themselves.

The sequence of opaque, translucent, and transparent surfaces and their varying degrees of reflectivity created an environment where layers of visual information were superimposed. The eyes would see through one surface and the spaces between partitions only to be reflected in another parallel surface. The partitions served both as obstructions and mediators, subjecting the viewer to multiple simultaneous visual and spatial understandings. Although the material layers were set in a fixed sequence within the gallery, their relationships to one another changed as the viewer moved through the space. While the curators organized the work according to their themes and modes of agency, the simultaneity of the visual experiences discouraged a linear reading of the exhibition. Visitors were encouraged to wander and create their own narrative.

In contrast to the exhibition, which proposed a personal experience, the common area in the front of the house emphasized collectivity and a shared or common identity. Much of the content in *Public, Private, Secret* was related to media-technical conditions that have allowed for new forms of subjective representation of individuals or virtual communities. Charlotte Cotton envisioned an actual place—a lived commons—where face-to-face interaction would take place and a new, or relocated, group of users would gather. We put an interior infrastructure in place to facilitate and locate these interactions and to suggest ways that the public space might be programmed or appropriated. The infrastructure—a rail system made from aluminum tubes—frames the large space of the common area while also defining more specific zones of program and activity. Between and around the infrastructure, an assortment of furniture created from the same

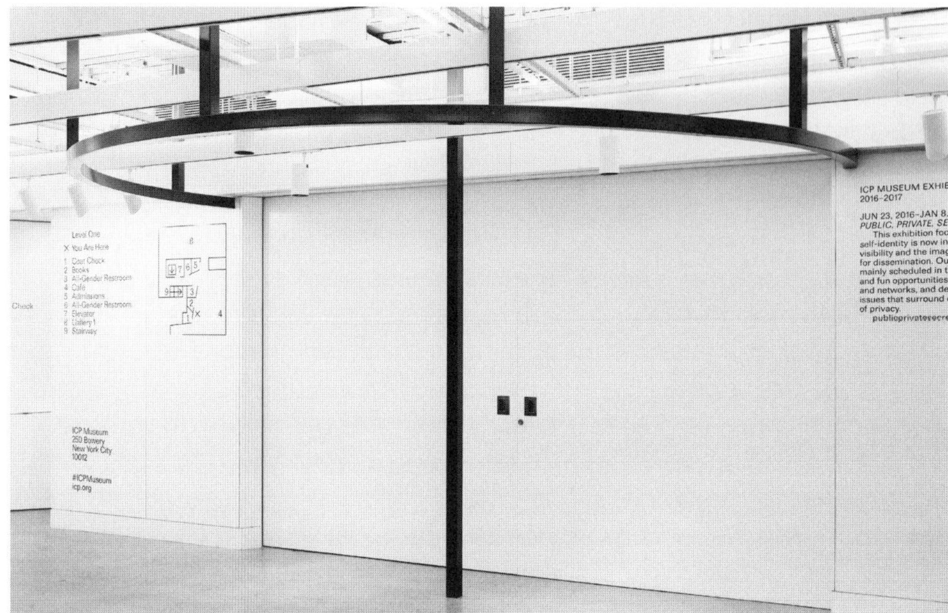

Photos (pages 180–81) © Bertrand Cavalier

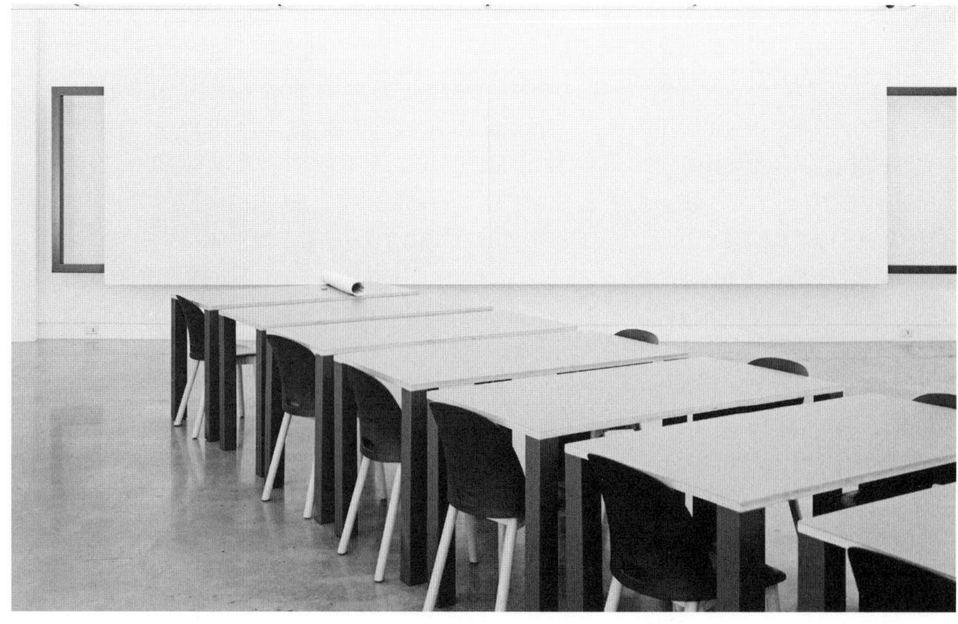

aluminum-tube material allowed for an inhabiting of the common museum area.

There is a more conventional separation between public and private represented by the plate-glass facade of the ICP museum building. The facade extends directly from the pavement and allows passersby to visually occupy the museum's interior. Conversely, sitting at a café table on the interior is almost like sitting outside on the sidewalk. This final observation is a note to ourselves that the distinct conditions of public, private, and secret space don't disappear as life moves on; they just become layered and interwoven.

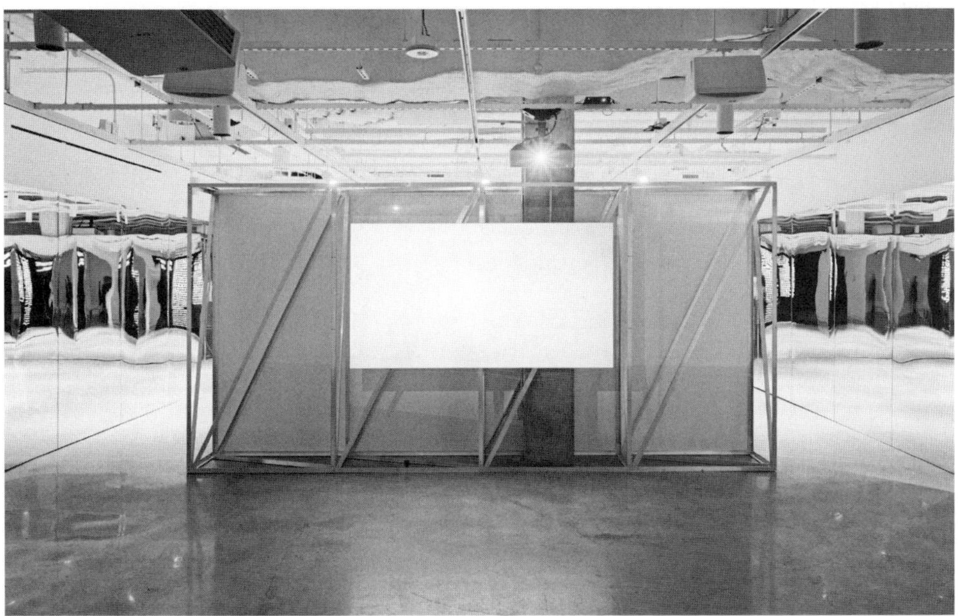

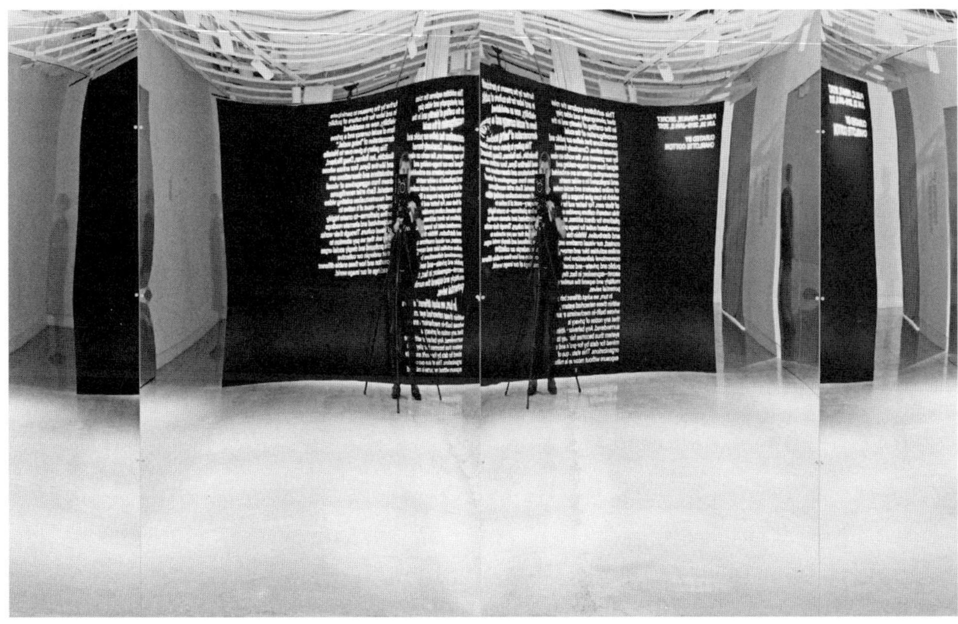

REFLECTION: CORRESPONDENCE, DAVID REINFURT

David Reinfurt's *"Clock"* was commissioned for *Public, Private, Secret*, and consisted of two parts: a digital monitor at the front of the building, facing the street, and a pair of projections in the rear of the space. The wall-mounted projections streamed live-video data drawn from six cameras in the front and in exhibition spaces, positioned by artist Sean Donovan. Custom software stripped the position information—the x and y coordinates of visual data—and organized the remaining data into an abstracted grid of reorganized pixels. By altering the original pixel positions, any immediate reading of the space was frustrated. Instead, these new images registered as dynamic data, more legible by a machine than a person. Custom software created a digital rendering of an analog clockface as a marker of the consistent back-and-forth play between the continuous and discrete—analog and digital—that describes the way we live with images today. David Reinfurt compiles his correspondence with curator Charlotte Cotton during the *"Clock"*'s creation and reflects upon the project in retrospect.

On Apr 28, 2016, at 6:42 PM,
David Reinfurt
<reinfurt@o-r-g.com> wrote:

charlotte,
it is, predictably, a productive exercise to think through the design of the clock in another medium—words instead of pixels. i've written more than you need here and i'm quite happy for you to redescribe what i've written, or to work with you on revising what i've started. here is a fairly concise description followed by a lengthier aside, which you can read at your leisure. i can imagine this long trawl is not what you want to go through at the end of a long day, so feel free to skim, collect the "Clock" description, and save the rest of this for the future. it should still be as true as it is now, then.

ok, here's the description:

David Reinfurt, O-R-G
"Clock" (2016)
"Clock" is commissioned for Public Private Secret as a piece of social furniture at 250 Bowery. It consists of two parts: a pair of projections in the rear of the main public space and a digital monitor at the front, facing the street. The wall-mounted projections stream live video data drawn from cameras in the lobby and in the exhibition spaces. Custom software strips the position information (x and y coordinates) from this image stream and reorganizes the remaining lo-resolution data in an abstracted grid of sorted pixels. By dropping the ordered pixel positions, any immediate reading of the space

is frustrated and, instead, these new images register more forcefully what has changed—the resulting, scrambled images are pictures of that changing data, more readable by a machine than a person. Instead of pictures of the space, these are images of what has changed in it.

The abstract screens are accompanied by a concrete clock face, a flag-mounted digital monitor installed on a pole directly in the street. Here, custom software creates a digital rendering of an analog clock face as a marker of the consistent back-and-forth play between continuous and discrete, between analog and digital, that describes many of the images we live with now.

ok, that may all be a bit of a stretch, and could likely be more simply said, but it is a useful start. i'd like the chance to make it clearer and more concise.

i'm also including two page scans and two images which are meant for you, not for a broader audience. i realized, while working on this from the comfort of my computer's command-line—which i stare at while programming the various bits—that the genesis of all this was right in front of me. if you look below at this obscure image of my command-line prompt, you see that the name i gave to my computer is "David Hume." anyway, that Scottish Enlightenment ur-empiricist philosopher is a big one for me.

David Hume's philosophy is completely concerned with perception as the basis of reality. to very crudely capsule some of what he wrote: he was convinced that the world only arrives to us through our perceptions of it, and these are the primary—in fact the only reliable—sets of data for understanding reality. he goes at least one, maybe two, steps further to assert that "reality" is one of these collections of perceptions. there is no further truth beyond what the individual subject can and does perceive, and this perception has its limits. he suggests that there is some point past which we are unable to perceive something as existent. and this threshold that marks the smallest possible perceptual atom is, in fact, concrete reality. furthermore, these perceptions are not continuous; they are perceptual steps—in a gradient of colors, for example—and these steps *are* the reality of a transition from one color to another. he was truly discrete and truly digital in his arguments.

he was also the most hardline of empiricists, insisting on the absolute priority of perceptions above any other kind of truth claim. some years ago, i came across this book cover for a book that visually summarizes what Hume was arguing:

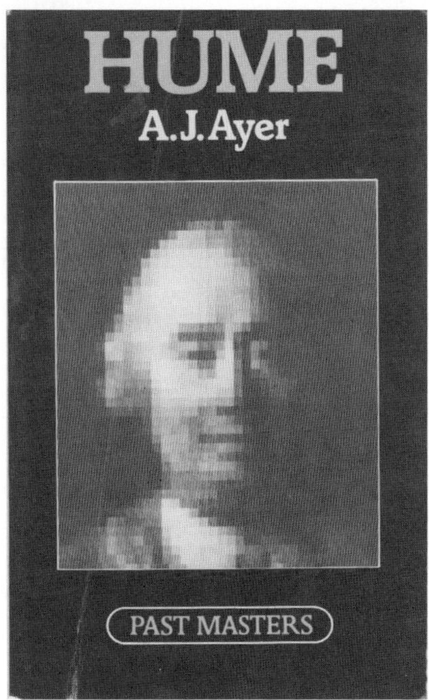

the 18th century in pixels! i love it.

Hume's discrete, digital, perceptual orientation led to some pretty radical ideas about how time works. he reasoned something like if the world only exists through its perceptions by a subject (i.e., objects as such don't properly exist) then it follows, via many twists and turns, that cause and effect are not as tightly linked as we have been brought along to think. and further, if the world is only built from discrete perceptions ("sense reports") and objects don't as such exist, then time, like things, can only exist as it is perceived. time is then, according to Hume, actually *produced* by changes in our perceptions. it is manufactured by our perceptions of how things change! here is the money page from Hume's major work on the matter, where i've marked the relevant passage:

80 *Treatise of Human Nature Book I*

our perceptions of every kind, ideas as well as impressions, and impressions of reflection as well as of sensation, will afford us an instance of an abstract idea, which comprehends a still greater variety than that of space, and yet is represented in the fancy by some particular individual idea of a determined quantity and quality.

As it is from the disposition of visible and tangible objects we receive the idea of space, so from the succession of ideas and impressions we form the idea of time; nor is it possible for time alone ever to make its appearance, or be taken notice of by the mind. A man in a sound sleep, or strongly occupied with one thought, is insensible of time; and according as his perceptions succeed each other with greater or less rapidity, the same duration appears longer or shorter to his imagination. It has been remarked by a great philosopher,[8] that our perceptions have certain bounds in this particular, which are fixed by the original nature and constitution of the mind, and beyond which no influence of external objects on the senses is ever able to hasten or retard our thought. If you wheel about a burning coal with rapidity, it will present to the senses an image of a circle of fire; nor will there seem to be any interval of time betwixt its revolutions; merely because it is impossible for our perceptions to succeed each other, with the same rapidity that motion may be communicated to external objects. Wherever we have no successive perceptions, we have no notion of time, even though there be a real succession in the objects. From these phenomena, as well as from many others, we may conclude, that time cannot make its appearance to the mind, either alone or attended with a steady unchangeable object, but is always discovered by some *perceivable* succession of changeable objects.

To confirm this we may add the following argument, which to me seems perfectly decisive and convincing. It is evident, that time or duration consists of different parts: for otherwise, we could not conceive a longer or shorter

[8] Mr. Locke.

see you tomorrow at 10.

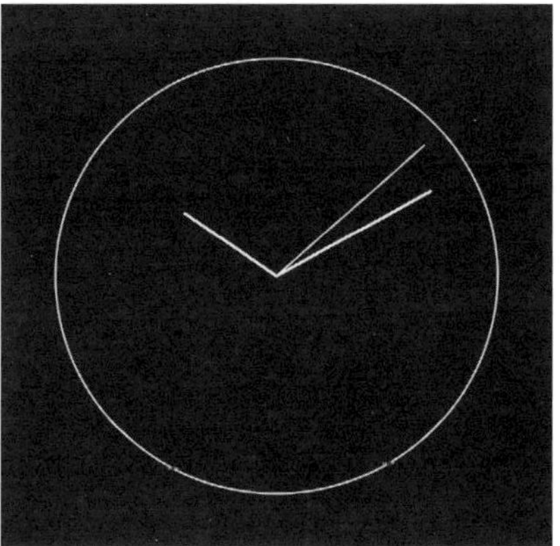

d

On Aug 7, 2017, at 2:55 PM, David Reinfurt <reinfurt@o-r-g.com> wrote:

charlotte,

picking up this thread after more than fifteen months, i thought it might be useful to write a bit more about "Clock" from the temporal distance afforded here. you'd asked me to write a reflection on this project, so that gives me an excuse.

three days after *Public Private Secret* closed at the ICP on January 8, 2017, i left New York for Rome to live and work for six months. it was two weeks before the presidential inauguration and it was (perhaps) a good moment to leave. i've just moved back now to the U.S. two weeks ago and i am having the distinctly uncanny temporal sensation that i both never left and also that i was away for a lifetime. this is, i'm sure, a common reaction to being away for a chunk of time and then returning. still, i find this jump cut in my life both jarring and worth thinking about some more.

while i was away in Rome, i also turned off all my social media. i muted Twitter, stopped checking my Instagram, and i have never been on Facebook, so that was not an issue. it wasn't meant as a statement to abandon these for that time, but rather more of a practical necessity to open up some room for my thoughts. however, i am certain i was also motivated to do so by what i had just witnessed (and been complicit with) for the previous six months of the presidential political campaigns. for me, it seemed a good idea to tune out of these noisy channels and spend some quiet time in my own head. as you can imagine, Rome is not a bad place for such a temporal recalibration, as cut-through with time as the city is. no other place i've experienced is quite as persistently stubborn about both retaining what has come before and also adapting these physical facts into contemporary, daily life. here's a favorite example of mine below—it's a small electrical shop (*ferramenta elettricita*) whose sign happens to be set in Chicago, a distinctly digital font designed for the original Macintosh operating system. this butts up to a much older sign, set in a serif typeface carved in stone, a marker of the city limits from nearly two thousand years before, as declared by the emperor Claudius and inscribed on this stone, which remains roughly in place now next to the electricity shop:

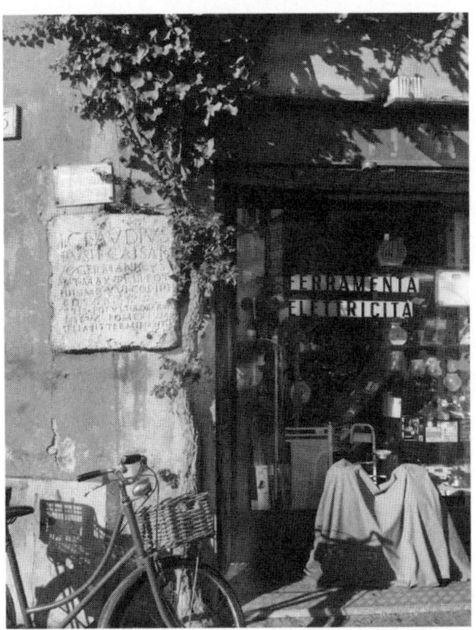

amazing, no? two times, two thousand years apart, sitting side by side and registered by the physical facts of their signage.

well ... i'm back in the basement today and i've just turned my Twitter feed back on for the first time since January 8, with the express purpose of collecting some images from "Clock" to include with the reflection text for you. as you recall, during the six months of the exhibition, "Clock" fed a stream of pixel-sorted camera images from the ICP Museum to an automated Twitter bot which would release one image per hour through the @pblcprvtscrt handle. although this bot didn't have a huge following, these abstract images, released as incremental tweets, are still kicking around the back alleys of the internet where they will remain on redundant servers, cloud backups, and in the tangled and distributed databases of likes, retweets, repostings, and so on. it is no wonder that social media is so often compared to an echo chamber given the promiscuity of digital media which reproduce their data each time they touch a computer (electronic files physically duplicate themselves as identical digital copies every time they are transferred through or viewed on a particular device).

over roughly the same period, when the presidential candidates were waging image wars through the media (and, most consequentially, over digital social media), @pblcprvtscrt simply plodded along, quietly populating its feed with a ceaseless string of abstract, pixilated images. here's a sequence of five hours on the last day of the exhibition:

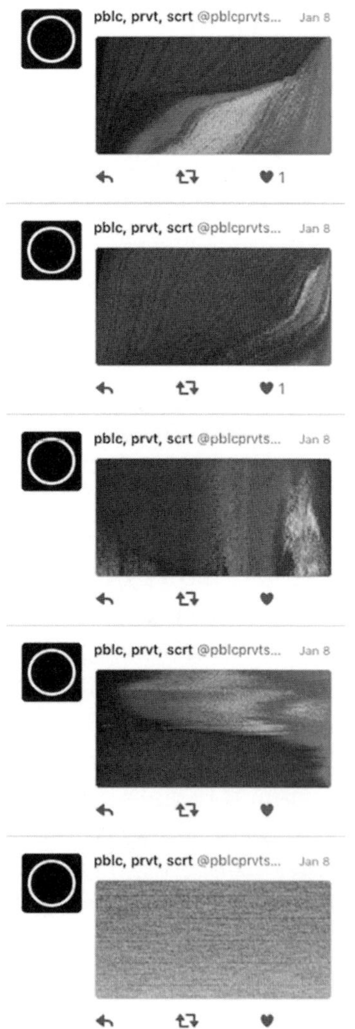

we can then return to David Hume, who i mentioned to you more than a year ago now, and ask what he would make of any of this. i'm pasting a bit of his argument about the relation between the perception of images and the perceived passage of time here:

> *If you wheel about a burning coal with rapidity, it will present to the senses an image of a circle of fire; nor will there seem to be any interval of time betwixt its revolutions; merely because it is impossible for our perceptions to succeed each other with the same rapidity that motion may be communicated to external objects. Wherever we have no successive perceptions, we have no notion of time, even though there be a real succession in the objects. From these phenomena, as well as from many others, we may conclude, that time cannot make its appearance to the mind, either alone or attended with a steady unchangeable object, but is always discovered by some perceivable succession of changeable objects.*

that seems to me to offer an easy enough explanation for how it is possible for me to feel simultaneously like i have been away forever and also that no time has passed at all.
i didn't *see* anything change in New York for six months, and so practically, or in Hume's account anyway, for me, nothing did. lacking a daily stream of sensible differences, i was simply unable to feel the passage of time in New York.

for now, "Clock" has stopped. when it was live, its steady progression of software abstractions marked out the passing of time as a series of discrete moments. Hume would argue that in some sense they *produced* the time that passed! i realize that is a large mind pill to swallow, but i suppose i am happy to believe it. the time in between then and now, between the first email and this one, also gives me a chance to reflect on these images. i think their relative muteness, their coded visual language, their de-facto digital default-ness, are their strength. one isn't tempted to read too much into or from any one image. instead, it is their persistent progression that is their strongest quality. these images are necessarily a sequence. and i suppose these kinds of images are precisely what i would call for, now, in a moment when so many of the images that pass in front of our eyeballs have been weaponized to transmit a particular political ideology. quiet, discrete, persistent images are in too short supply.

thx for the chance to think out loud.

for now,
david

REFLECTION: EVERY IMAGE FOUND, MARK GHUNEIM

Mark Ghuneim was the instigator and lead creator of the real-time social-media streams that punctuated the *Public, Private, Secret* exhibition. From the vantage point of a longtime creative responder to online and surveillance culture, Ghuneim here contextualizes ICP's incorporation of "no net" media streaming in the exhibition and comments on the narratives that developed throughout the six-month duration of the exhibition.

This image is no longer available

My history of working with information as it is created was applied in *Public, Private, Secret* to the challenge of bringing real-time media streams into a cultural space. My apprenticeship in the early-1980s video-jockey craft—at a time when the great visual menagerie of sound and real-time images could turn any situation from a riot to a party—has a presence in the harnessing of media streams for *Public, Private, Secret*. The growing omnipresence of cameras and screens became clear to me in the early 1990s as I observed the beginnings of CCTV systems becoming a presence on the streets of New York. I started to ask questions: Who owned these cameras? What are they there for? A wall had symbolically been taken down and I wasn't comfortable with it. I documented every camera pointed down onto people in public areas of Manhattan—cameras owned by the city or private individuals—and published a map of the camera positions with the New York Civil Liberties Union. When I set up my first company in 2005, I employed people to pull images from live-media streams, and started to see and assess what we were collectively doing with images.

What excites me about what we created for *Public, Private, Secret* is that this is the first time that any cultural institution has hosted this kind of real-time exploration of our image world at scale. The precise ways in which we used real-time curation in this exhibition—to siphon off social observations and commentaries to literally see them as they unfolded—was a radical act. We attempted to create the right constructs of language and computer code to offer a subjective and objective reading of the visual information that circulates in our social media. We actively anticipated that no two people would have the same experience of this exhibition because everyone would bring their own truths to bear on these highly subjectivizing *and* objectifying media streams. There was real beauty in the meeting of the ephemeral and the empirical in the concept for this exhibition. Each real-time image had the same importance for the moment it appeared on screen. It all happened in the moment—real time only matters in the moment; it's inherently ephemeral—and every viewer's experience was unique. It brought to the viewer a mirror that reflected contemporary and historical expressions of privacy within visual culture in real time.

The defining moment in our process was the decision to run curated real-time media streams without a net of saved "safe" content, and with full transparency of how we were algorithmically searching media. We attempted to fully face this inflection point in culture, which coincided with the rebirth of the ICP Museum. There were many levels of collaboration, and a shared responsibility in being the (albeit noninstitutionalized) arbiters and creators of the curatorial structures. We became the first viewers of what we were discovering. We understood when we needed to come together as a team to discuss—with Lily Healey and Jon Bulava on technical design, and David Reinfurt on visual representation and design of this real-time information and the clock overlay. We also learned when we needed to go into our separate corners and reflect, before coming back in and making a measure of it.

It was incredibly personal and intense: I was hung in the suspense of the relevancy of each image. It was a quest for perfection at scale for a system that would be live for over half a year. As a perfectionist, this demanded of me a continuous sense of zen, both programmatically and personally. Finally, our collaboration with the first graduating class of the International Center of Photography's New Media Narratives students was immensely helpful to research and craft ideas, and shape the project.

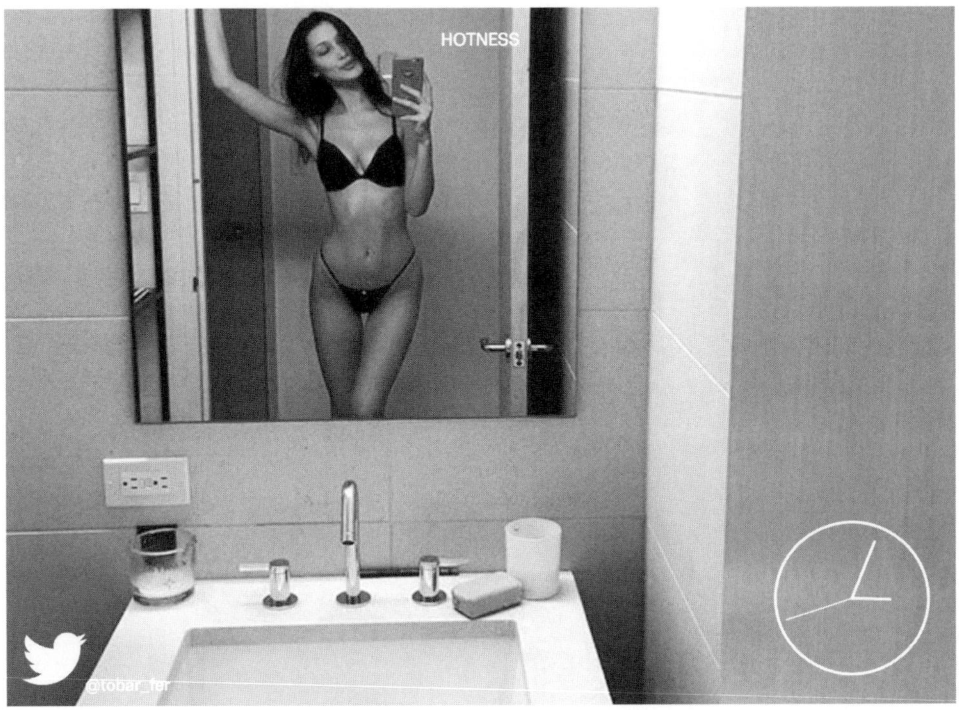

Hotness, Sole query: #Hotness. Source: Instagram 2016

Privacy
Who's your daddy

Underneath Tiane Doan na Champassak's Looters series (2014) and close to Trevor Paglen's project reflecting on Chelsea Manning's 2013 trial, and Zach Blas's searing perspective on the biases of biometric recognition, *Privacy*'s uninterrupted base feed of unmanned surveillance-camera footage depicted computerized vision and machine readership. This unfolding cache of images could only be viewed when actively sought, or when the AI—the logic of the programs we ran to identify, sort, negate, and display the most relevant pictures—picked up the information as an anomaly. This feed perhaps conveyed the greatest distance from a camera to a human viewer, intended to illustrate a small but potent group of live camera feeds that are hidden from public view yet are always capturing the public.

These orphaned surveillance images were interspersed with key privacy Twitter accounts that were actively debating the implementation and impact of our new surveillance statehood. These accounts included lawyers from the American Civil Liberties Union (ACLU), hackers, the National Security Agency (NSA), and the Electronic Frontier Foundation (EFF), through to a bot that monitors multiple sites for password dumps and other sensitive information, and of new accounts that had been breached and whose information was shared online. During the six-month "life" of this stream, we saw many of the current issues that dominate our discussions about privacy rendered live, and left to play out.

"Hotness"
Hold a mirror up for all to see

This stream aimed to visualize the shift in a segment of society that moved from, "Don't look at me" to "Look at all of me all of the time." I think we all unknowingly fell down the rabbit hole of social media and started sharing what we used to protect. Concurrently, we took the reflection that we most liked of ourselves and shared it for all to see.

This level of "look at me"—at scale—had not been seen before. This feed found a delicate line that exists within social-network platforms where our bodies—and some specific bodies—become heavily prescribed

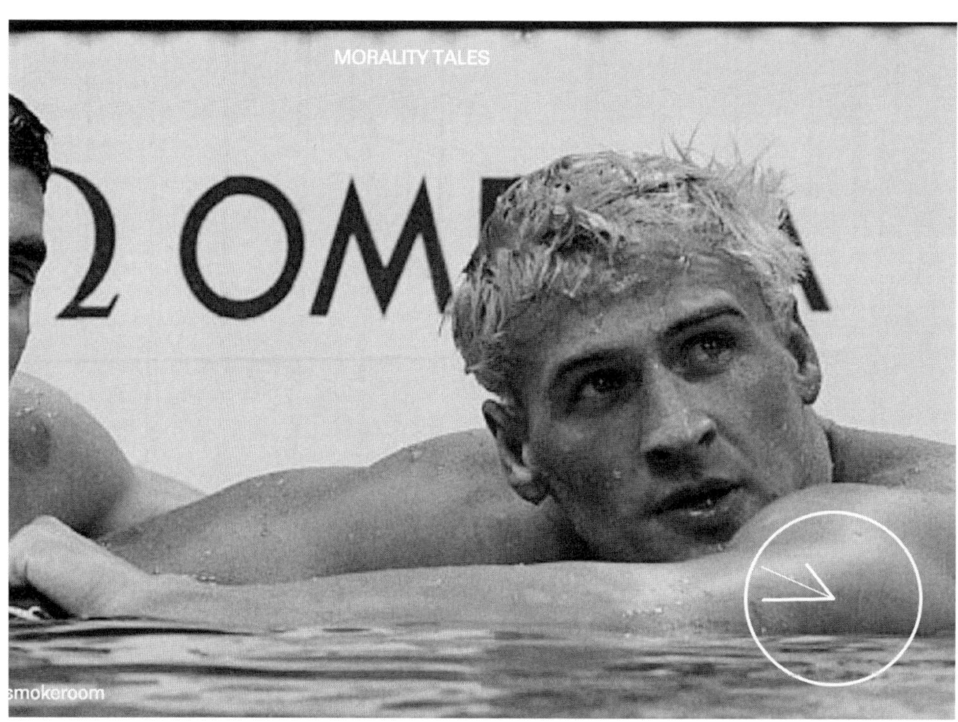

Morality Tales, Starter Queries: Victim of social media; internet justice; morality tale; Martin Shkreli; Laremy Tunsil; Belle Gibson; Sam Rader; Josh Duggar; Julia Cordray; Kim Davis; Rachel Dolezal; Walter Palmer; Anthony Weiner; Lance Armstrong; Sinéad O'Connor; @dumpmon. Source: Twitter, 2016

fantasies. The curatorial process began with a single word, *hotness*. It returned a bounty of NSFW images that were tooled and recursively trained to filter into the tropes of contemporary "hotness."

color images and footage from governmental sources.

These motley descriptions were shared with the public who then set its unified gaze within the surveillant act of identifying, locating, and apprehending our perceived "Other." The idea of crowdsourcing from the public at large—a nineteenth- and twentieth-century phenomenon—got reworked in our social-media era to a startling effect, a relentless reminder of the way in which our bureaucratic structures obfuscate and control identity, and expect us to participate in the act of othering.

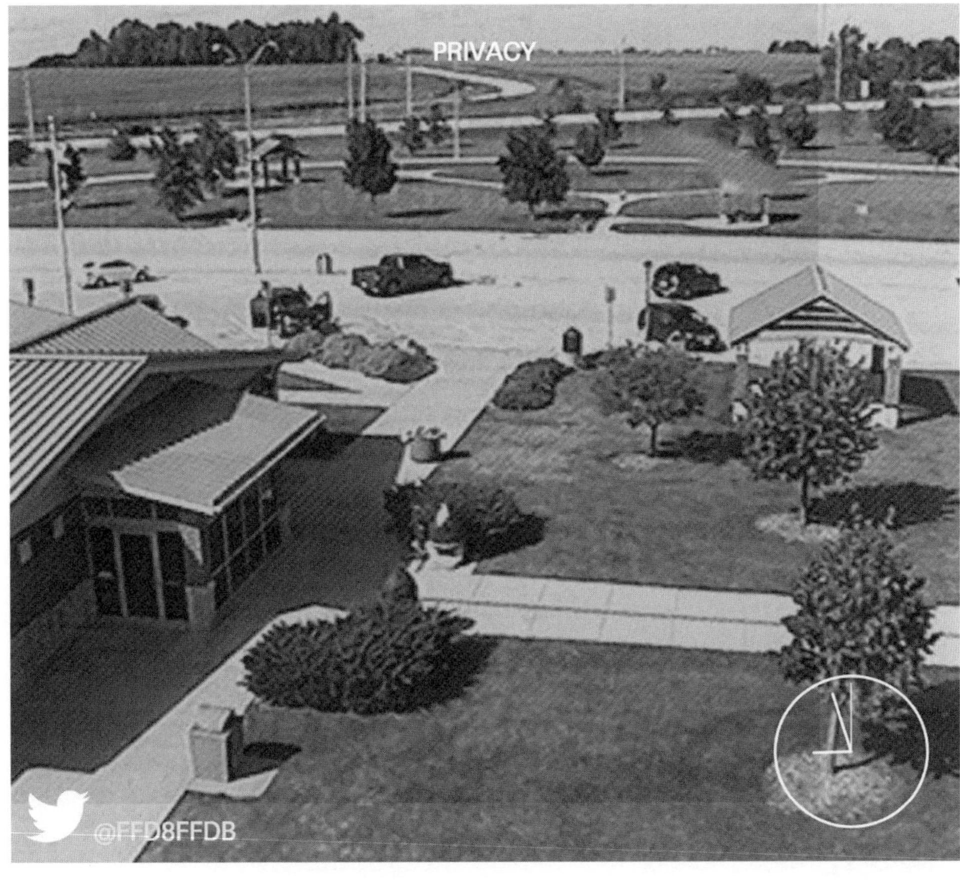

Privacy, Starter Queries: surveillance; encryption; mass surveillance; privacy. Source: Twitter, 2016

The "Other"
Seeking to capture an unknown actor

The "Other" rendered, more than any other feed, the capacity to capture what does not want to be captured. It created a textured mosaic of resolutions and picture qualities that mirrored the last several decades of technology and surveillance infrastructure. These reproductions ranged from early 1980s SLP VHS, glitchy, grainy, and black-and-white footage—often a byproduct of its intended environment—to high-res

Transformation
The capacity for change

The goal here was to identify an important subset of transformational images at a transformative time in our social realm. What we hoped to capture was how we see ourselves at a time when gender fluidity has known no greater acceptance, public awareness, and practical manifestation. This was the most empowering livestream when it hit on the arrival of the unabashed, historic "We're here, we're queer, we're proud" as a rallying anthem of legions and now part of a mainstream lexicon.

Morality Tales
Shame, shame, shame, shame

Alongside *The "Other,"* this feed performed with deadly accuracy, producing a steady stream of individualized portrayals of societal shame and revilement. Digital culture adds amplification and resonance to each epic drama and to personal embodiments of the struggle between good and evil. More than this, *Morality Tales* silently observed the narrative arc, typically over the course of just a few days, as individuals or corporations became public prey on social media—our real-time cast of politicians, media-tech titans, and celebrities acting out failure and shame. The AI created for *Morality Tales* did not just focus on individuals, it also sought out and found the corporations, organizations, and unseen conglomerations that engaged social-media participants in the chorus of outrage and defamation.

Celebrity Leaderboard
"You love me, you really love me"

This ranked leaderboard of the most popular people on social media was situated in the exhibition just before a collage of Patrick McMullan's analog *Face Book*, used to identify subjects at New York Fashion Week events in the pre–social media era. Together, they marked a line in time—the pre- and post-selfie versions of celebrity dissemination. The *Celebrity Leaderboard* listed the celebrities at the top of the tight popularity contest that permeates social media. Movement was constant, and we could see the rankings shuffle many times per hour, interrupted at times by the immediate swell of someone catching the collective gaze. For instance, Congressman John Lewis joined the ranking of Rihanna, Taylor Swift, and Justin Bieber when he took the House floor and cameras were cut during a gun control sit-in. This type of attention occurring in real time would pierce the popularity carousel with relevant, current meaning.

REFLECTION: STUDENTS IN THE NEW MEDIA NARRATIVES PROGRAM CURATE REAL-TIME SOCIAL-MEDIA COLLECTIONS FOR *PUBLIC, PRIVATE, SECRET*, ELIZABETH KILROY

Elizabeth Kilroy, chair of the New Media Narratives program at the ICP School, and her first graduating year of students, collaborated with Mark Ghuneim and Charlotte Cotton in the realization of the real-time media streams in the *Public, Private, Secret* exhibition. Her reflections center on the working process of the New Media Narratives team as well as the issues within the field of new-media storytelling that this collaborative project raised.

> *This media experience has become the norm for all aesthetic experience. Hence in art there is no longer anything beyond the media. No one can escape from the media. There is no longer any painting outside and beyond the media experience. There is no longer any sculpture outside and beyond the media experience. There is no longer any photography outside and beyond the media experience.*
> *—Peter Weibel*[1]

In January 2016, the New Media Narratives (NMN) program at the International Center of Photography was six months old. NMN is a one-year certificate program that offers a strong foundation in photography and visual storytelling with digital and interactive media. Students expand the role of photography as a collaborative process, creating art and telling stories using a variety of new tools, platforms, and opportunities for engagement.

At the start of the second term, I received an email titled "Real Time Curation" from Charlotte Cotton, curator in residence, who was deep into planning the first exhibition at the new ICP Museum. The message extended an invitation to myself and our pioneering class to join Charlotte and Mark Ghuneim in the research and development phase of devising real-time curation elements for *Public, Private, Secret*. Charlotte's vision was to create an exhibition that made the curation of the present moment in image culture an integral part of the visitor experience.

At the time, students were beginning to investigate integrative modes of interaction with audiences, challenging notions of social presence and exploring interactions in virtual spaces. One student was experimenting with using a life-logging, narrative clip camera to consider whether continuously recording and uploading photographs had the potential to enhance memory for Alzheimer's patients. Another noted that as we struggle to define ourselves online,

1 Peter Weibel, "The Post-media Condition," in *AAVV, Postmedia Condition* (Madrid: Centro Cultural Conde Duque, 2006).

a personality is automatically created for us based on collected data. His work focused on exploring how to step away from being the consumer version of the "self" generated by technology, and into the shoes of the creator. Students were excited to be involved in a project for the new museum that explored how people communicate and present themselves online, in real time.

New-media art, photography, and storytelling are deeply interwoven into our networked, wired information society. Network structures and collaborative models create new forms of cultural production and profoundly shape today's cultural climate. Media tools facilitated by rapid advances in technology allow us to create, view, and interact with photography and the moving image in ways that change how ideas are formed; how work is created, viewed, and understood; and how research is developed. When artists and creators make work in virtual spaces or upload work to the cloud, they invite collaboration with audiences who interact, comment, share, and imitate, emulating real-life conversations. People find each other online based on shared interests—transcending geographic proximity—and curators in turn can explore these shared interests as clusters.

Mark joined our seminar class on February 8, 2016, to present the tools needed to access selected application programming interfaces (APIs) for social-media platforms, and to discuss search terms and organizing principles for creating live-media streams. Soumita Bhattacharya, a dedicated teaching assistant and ICP graduate, acted as the project coordinator for the students. The group communicated through a Slack channel. With suggestions from Charlotte, students chose their research areas based on themes also explored in the exhibition at large. Susan Sawyers, Caitlin Healy, and Evan Cisneros focused on "Makers"; Soumita Bhattacharya considered "Hotness and Beauty"; Muyi Xiao and Miles Goscha tackled "Celebrity"; Cyndie Burkhardt and Alex Taylor researched "Morality"; Mengwen Cao and Daphne Chan looked at "Transformation"; and Mark Ghuneim and myself explored the idea of "the Other."

The students' process consisted of searching Twitter and Instagram using queries that would reveal recent or popular posts and tweets. Each query could have operators that modified its behavior. For example, searching for two words strung together would return different results than searching for the same two words enclosed in quotation marks. To search images and video, other parameters were put in place. Queries could also include hashtags, @ symbols and the word *or*, and various other options to filter out retweets and reposts. Opposite are some examples of the searches for each area.[2]

The students then compiled these search results into collections, which are defined by Twitter's Developer Site as "editable group of Tweets hand-selected by a Twitter user or program-

2 For a full list of possible search parameters, see dev.twitter.com/rest/public/search.

matically managed via collection APIs." Each collection—curated data, created by users—had a name and a description with new entries constantly rising to the top. Students compiled their collections from exploring multiple lists, search parameters and queries, and from their own interests and research. Each collection could be viewed online through a web- and mobile-friendly permalink and was meant to be shared with the world.

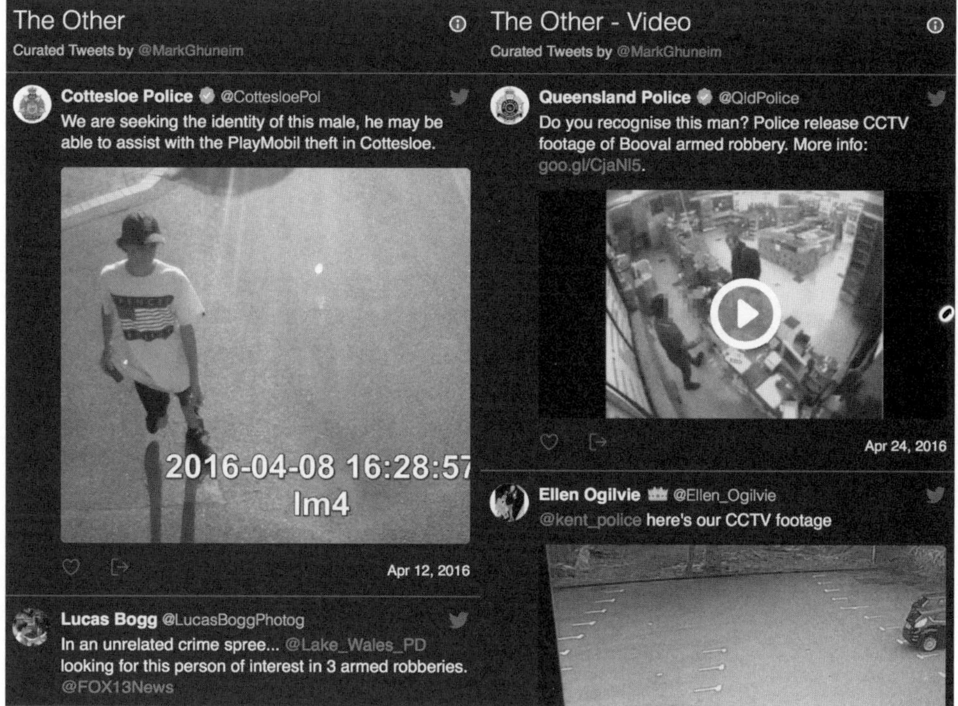

As Zeynep Tufekci, the self-styled "techno-sociologist," points out, as with most conversational settings, social media does not make much sense taken out of context. One has to be immersed in the social-media experience to fully appreciate its conversational nuance. She argues that "close up, it's alive and brimming with humanity," while from a distance, it's not easy to represent or empathize with the experience of being fully immersed in online conversations.[3]

Creating theme-based search parameters that would work "from a distance" and over time, without losing the necessary context, was one of the students' great challenges. As digital-culture writer Jacob Silverman put it, "Someone is always updating more often or rising to the top by virtue of retweets, re-shares, or some opaque algorithmic calculation."[4]

3 Zeynep Tufekci, "Social Media's Small, Positive Role in Human Relationships," *Atlantic*, April 25, 2012.

4 Jacob Silverman, "'Pics or It Didn't Happen'—The Mantra of the Instagram Era," *Guardian*, February 26, 2015, https://www.theguardian.com/news/2015/feb/26/pics-or-it-didnt-happen-mantra-instagram-era-facebook-twitter.

Students quickly realized that disconnected threads made for disconnected reading and viewing experiences, and updates and posts were often obsolete and irrelevant as soon as they were posted. To counteract such results, they spent many hours fine-tuning the search parameters to return relevant images for their collections, and creating tight filters to sift out repetitive, off-topic, unwelcome, or inappropriate content.

A central question throughout the process was: Did we want to curate feeds that were interesting and on-topic, or did we want to genuinely reflect how people use the social platforms as a form of cultural exploration? After all, visitors would exercise free and personal judgment on the value of the content.

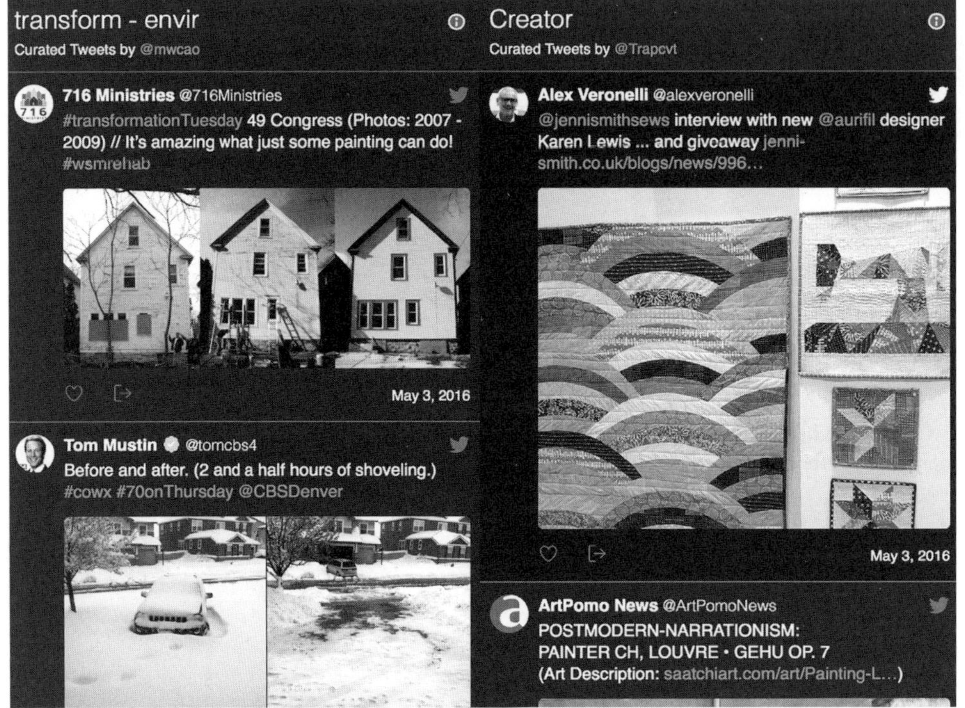

This relative lack of control inserted a new degree of uncertainty into the curatorial process. In some ways, the process of sorting through vast amounts of online information and presenting that data in a meaningful and organized way around a specific collection is comparable to a museum curator's task when organizing an exhibition. But even the accurate deployment of APIs and search terms offered limited control as to the kinds of images that would be revealed to visitors to the museum, upending the traditional dynamic between curator and audience. As Jay Rosen put it, "The people formerly known as the audience are those who [are] on the receiving end of a media system."[5] The real-time curation project underscored the fact that a media savvy

5 Jay Rosen, "The People Formerly Known as the Audience," *PressThink*, June 27, 2006, http://archive.pressthink.org/2006/06/27/ppl_frmr.html.

audience is no longer a passive one, and also that "curating" is an essential function of how people use social platforms. In some ways, social media has made everybody a curator.

The question remains as to whether it is possible to impose curatorial order on a stream of data. As critic Sean O'Hagan pointed out in the *Guardian*, referring to the show's social-media elements and real-time streams, their "curatorially imposed order ... possibly negates their fractured nature."[6] Perhaps there is no longer any curating outside and beyond the media experience.

6 Sean O'Hagan, "The Digital Age Reshapes Our Notion of Photography. Not Everyone Is Happy...," *Guardian*, July 2, 2016, https://www.theguardian.com/artanddesign/2016/jul/02/photography-no-longer-just-prints-on-the-wall.

REFLECTION: MAKING *PUBLIC/PRIVATE/PORTRAIT*, ROMKE HOOGWAERTS

Independent publisher Romke Hoogwaerts was invited by Charlotte Cotton to create a special issue of his *Mossless* publication that responded to the themes of *Public, Private, Secret*. The ensuing *Public/Private/Portrait* was published to coincide with the opening of the new ICP Museum; here Hoogwaerts describes his curatorial and editorial process.

After five years of publishing photography books independently under the name *Mossless*, I told people at the 2015 New York Art Book Fair that it would be my last year behind a booth—for a little while at least. I'd had so much fun with it, experimenting with different formats and interviewing hundreds of photographers, but I wanted a change. On the last day of the fair, Charlotte Cotton came to my table and asked if I wanted to collaborate on a book to be copublished by *Mossless* and ICP. I immediately regretted telling people I was going to hang up my hat.

The next issue of *Mossless*, an idea I'd shelved, was going to be all about portraiture. It was a stiflingly broad concept. Once Charlotte told me about the ICP's plans to investigate the concepts of publicness and privacy in their opening exhibition at the new Bowery location, a perfect melding of ideas came to light. Through our many conversations, the title *Public/Private/Portrait* was born, one that, funnily enough, I'd thought of weeks before hearing the exhibition's similar title. The book was unlike any other I'd made, with a huge amount of text and an array of distinct features, such as perforated pages, an oversize format, and a reflective cover. It gave me an opportunity to work with designer Elana Schlenker, who had impressed me not just with her imaginative design style, but also her industrious work ethic in creating *Gratuitous Type*, a magazine of her own. Hers was exactly the right kind of spirit for this elaborate project.

The list of photographers that came together for this project was astounding and it became diverse in an organic manner. Their work was produced in countries that included Egypt, the Netherlands, France, Germany, Georgia, Malaysia, South Africa, and the United States. Most of the contributors were photographers and artists who work independently of the large market forces in photography. A number of them traveled online to gather their source material, using video chats, Google Street View, appropriated Instagram images, and so on. Their projects spanned a magnificent spectrum of imaginative approaches to photography. I want to thank all of the artists once again for allowing me to publish them. Their collaboration and disposition were key to the success of the publication.

The first half of the book showcased the photographs, while the second half was an assemblage of complementary texts, sixty-seven in all. We talked to Anouk Kruithof about her sculptural appropriations of blurry TSA Instagram mugshots. We commissioned Alexis Anais Avedisian

Gonzalo Bénard, from *B Shot By A Stranger*, 2016

to write about Signe Pierce's "reality experiments." We asked David A. Banks to write about how political campaigns cleverly implemented selfie culture into their strategies.

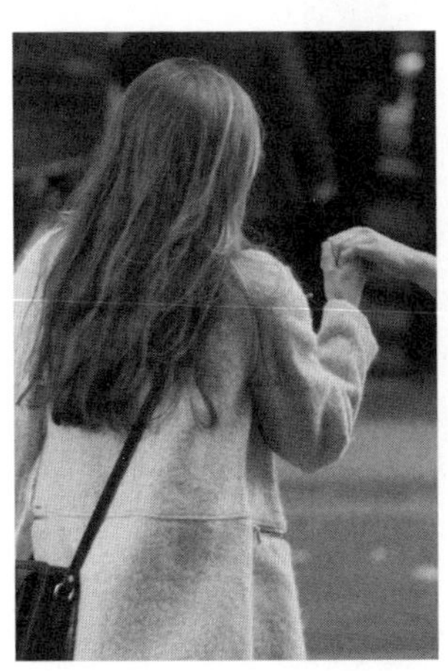
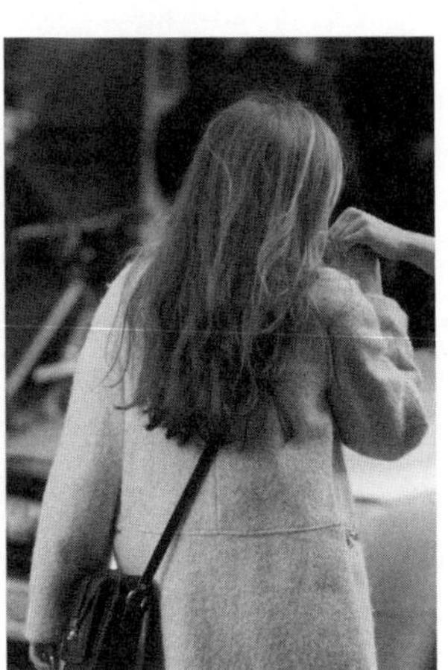
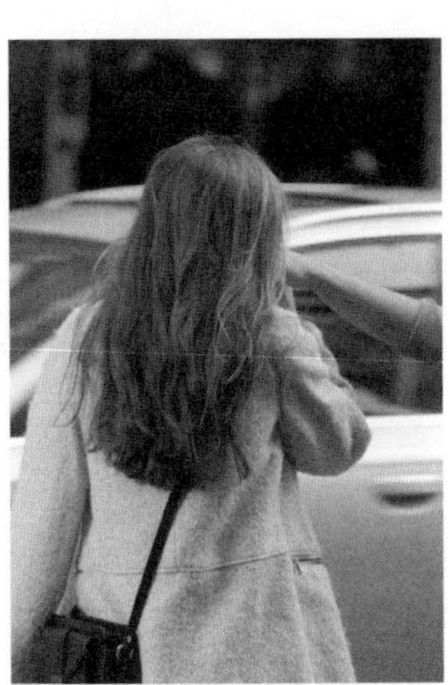

Nina Perlman, *Kissed His Hand*, 2013

We paired Molly Soda and Arvida Byström to discuss privacy intrusions online. Ashley McNelis commented on the work of Jason Hanasik and Alex Matzke, two photographers shining light on delicate aspects of the private lives of individuals in the military. Matthew Leifheit spoke at length with Rachel Stern about her self-portraits that reflect different versions of herself. Our final feature was an interview with Stacy Kranitz about her controversial use of transgressive and fictitious self-portraiture within her documentary photography.

Looking back at the interviews and texts, the volume presents a compelling cascade of thoughtful conversations and connections between the different bodies of work. Every artist emphasized different aspects of the larger theme: The video *American Reflexxx* (2013) documents a performance by Signe Pierce in Florida in which civilians attacked her while she wore a mirror mask. It provides heft to the argument that anonymity does not necessarily make one safe, not even from other citizens. In contrast, Caroline Tompkins turned her camera toward men who catcalled her, forcing their likenesses into a public, recorded permanence. Anka Gujabidze and Wendy Red Star both toyed with public interpretations of their cultures—a beleaguered rural Georgian mining community and Native American identity, respectively—by cleverly incorporating stock imagery into their work. Nabil Boutros demonstrated the malleability of identity when he posed as different socioeconomic or professional types found in Egypt. Photographers Lisa Lindvay and Isadora Kosofsky showed that private stories of struggle are far more

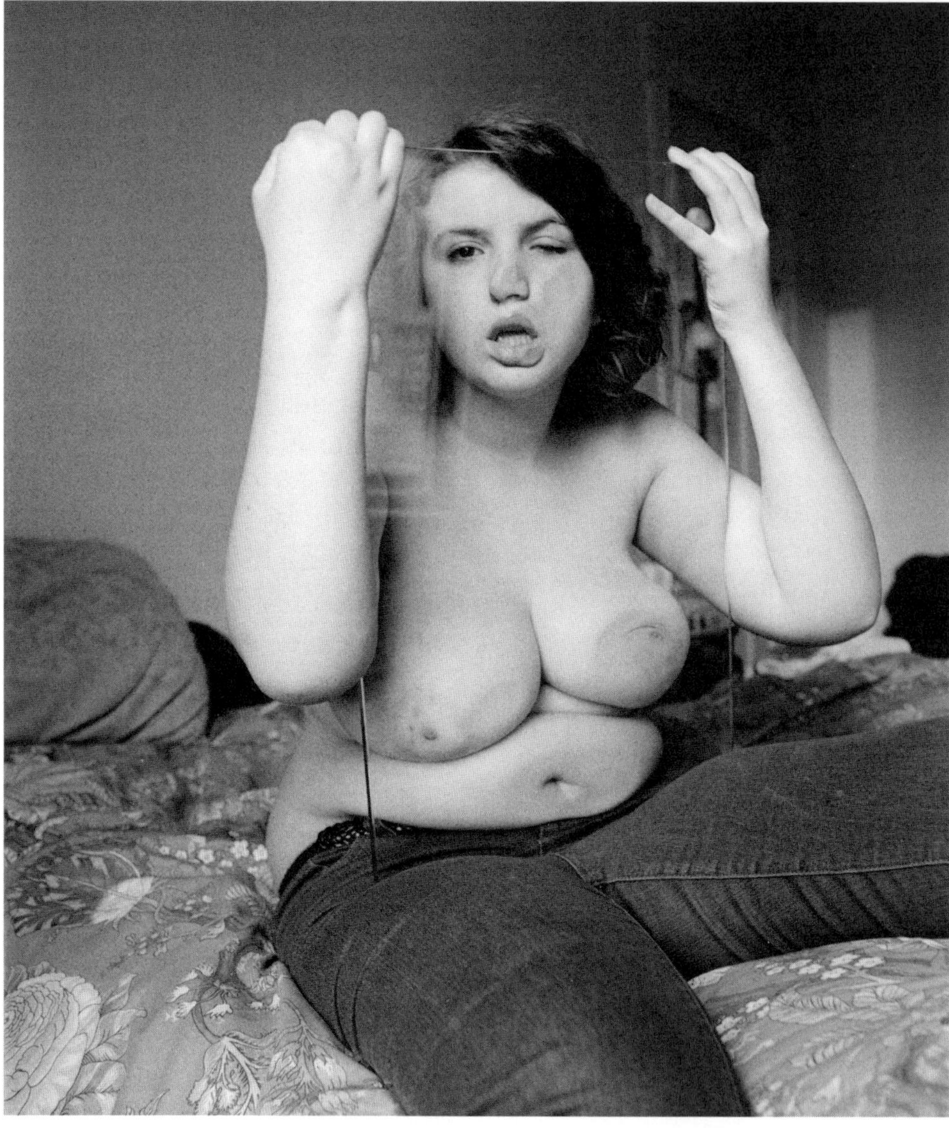

Leah Edelman-Brier, *Pressed Face*, 2014

complex than they might seem on the surface. Rollin Leonard's portrait of Faith Holland depicted Holland through hundreds of globs of water on a glass plane, creating numerous iterations of her face.

The introduction to *Public/Private/ Portrait* proposes that the published works speak to "leaking boundaries, moving in a kind of quicksand dynamic, that create a 'boundarylessness' between ideas of public and private." The word *boundarylessness* is uniquely apt, as the concept of privacy has evolved tremendously over the last two decades. While privacy as a social construct has never been a static concept, the recent acceleration of its transformation has become a source of anxiety for many, if not all of us. How that anxiety manifests is different for everyone. For instance, in her interview with Matthew Leifheit, performative photographer Rachel Stern spoke openly about how transgressions of privacy evoke conflicting emotional states: "I want everyone to adore me, but I don't want to talk to anyone."

In my research about the history of privacy and publicness, and in the making of this book, it became clear to me that we live in a unique moment: there is no legitimate consensus on where the line between public and private rests. We might, for instance, be standing in the middle of a public street and still operate within a supposedly private intellectual space through our phones. The social politics of a scenario as simple as that are still undefined. After all, how can any kind of moral concept take root within a culture if sweeping changes to its underlying technology threaten to make it redundant within just a few years? Furthermore, with the rise of artificial intelligence and augmented reality, identity politics as a whole—a set of ideas inherently entangled with publicness and the display of the self—are going to be shaken up even more dramatically. The mere thought of it makes me nervous, but I am eager to discover what artists will make of it.

REFLECTION: URGENT ARCHIVES, PAUL SOULELLIS

Paul Soulellis began the Library of the Printed Web in 2013, publishing newsprint magazines that curated artists' responses to the web in printed form. In 2016, Soulellis was invited to create *Printed Web 4*, which drew together artists working with issues of identity and privacy; this was published for the opening of *Public, Private, Secret*. Here, Soulellis reflects upon the recent history of artists corralling online archives and the way in which this now-pivotal artistic act and the premise of *Public, Private, Secret* feel altered by the turn of recent social and political events.

How do we choose what to preserve? Any text, image, threaded conversation, or tweet may be considered a valuable artifact in today's post-truth condition. While the pressure to save and accumulate is immense, so is our need to curate and amplify particular messages. After the most recent US presidential election, I saw people printing tweets and carrying them high above their heads at protests. Bernie Sanders brought a large, printed tweet to the Senate floor during one debate on healthcare. This act of drawing from digital archives and displaying printed material publicly serves as a material reminder, or proof: at this particular moment, something was said. As each utterance is broadcast, indexed, and archived into our hyperreal state, printing still seems to be one way to control—or at least resist—the narrative.

Printing has always been political. The act of transferring material to paper carries with it a charge, a potential transfer of state—from private to public, from speech to text, from one copy to many. These affordances of the printed page come very close to the definition of publishing itself. Contained within "making public" are paper's properties of exposing, giving visibility, circulating, and saving. Printing *digital* material is especially fraught with this charge, because embedded within it is a particular instinct to pause and preserve what might otherwise be lost—to downshift from fast to slow, to resist the speed and ephemerality of digital flow.

This call to examine digital archives has always been at the heart of the Library of the Printed Web. When I founded the project in 2013, it was to collect artists' books and zines around a very simple idea: network culture articulated as printed artifact. My interest was centered around artists asking questions about speed and materiality in this context, as well as themes such as authorship, aura, and accessibility.

I would identify that period, roughly from 2008 to 2015, as post-iPhone and pre-Trump. It was the time when the network began to get personal, to build our trust, to travel with us, to reveal itself in more surprising places. It was the time of the new aesthetic, a term coined by artist James Bridle around 2012, referring to "a way of seeing that seemed to reveal a blurring between 'the real' and 'the digital,' the physical and the virtual, the human and the machine."[1] It was also the beginning of total network saturation, as artists and designers learned to construct identity, negotiate presence, and present work in truly networked space.

We began to carry the browser around with us all day, and to sleep beside it at night. What did it now mean to see it on paper? How did screen-based work change when printed in this uncanny way? And what opportunities did web-to-print afford for distribution, platforms, and audience? For a while, it seemed crucial that we acknowledge spaces like the Instagram account and the Reddit thread and text messaging as legitimate venues for writing, publishing, and artistic practice. The hierarchy between web page and printed page had become less fixed, and Printed Web was a fitting venue to perform and celebrate this slippery condition.

ICP's *Public, Private, Secret* exhibition opened to the public on the same day that the Brexit vote was cast, and one month before Trump was officially nominated as the Republican candidate for the US presidency. Installed in the museum's new lobby on the Bowery that evening were all of the newsprint pages of *Printed Web 4*, copublished with the International Center of Photography Museum. Looking back now, it's impossible not to see this installation—and perhaps the entire *Public, Private, Secret* exhibition—within a larger context of sociopolitical angst and turmoil. I curated the work in *Printed Web 4* around the exhibition's theme, so this sixty-four-page tabloid-size publication now seems like a particularly good

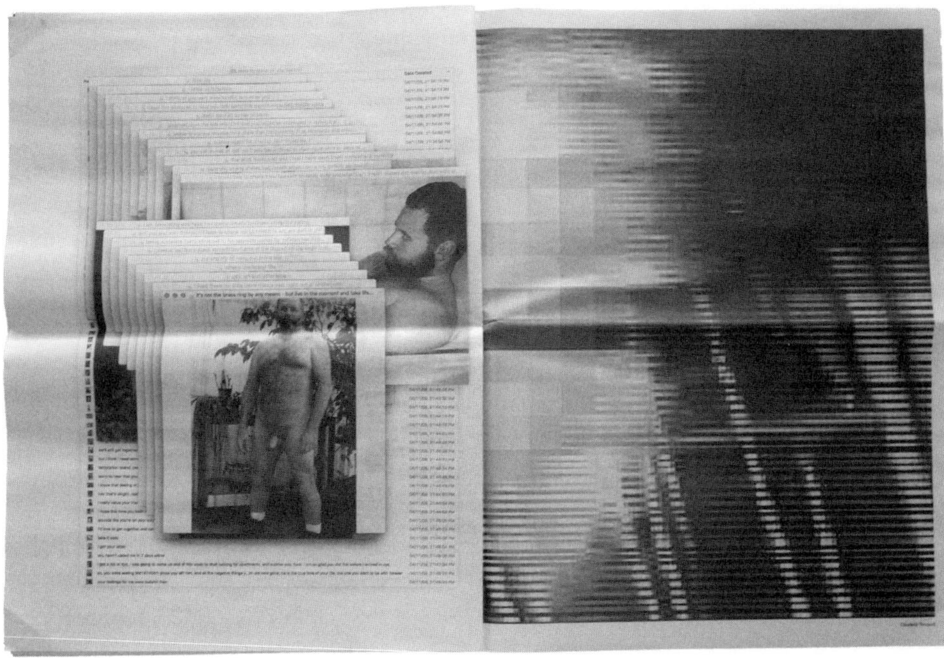

Printed Web 4 (Christopher Clary & Elisabeth Tonnard), 2016

1 James Bridle, "#sxaesthetic," *booktwo* (blog), March 15, 2012, booktwo.org/notebook/sxaesthetic/.

lens for viewing artists who worked with issues of identity, privacy, and digital archives at the very moment when #fakenews first appeared.

Many of the artists in the issue suggested that the current state of the image was precarious and anxious. They did this through the use of found material and an acute interrogation of the digital archive: Angela Genusa's *Throne* (2016) presents hundreds of JPG snapshots of US military personnel posing on Saddam Hussein's throne. The images are part of a larger digital archive assembled by the artist from various online locations. Wolfgang Plöger's *Accused* (2016) consists of four tightly cropped, silhouetted images. Each depicts a person accused of criminal activity, photographed in public while hiding their face behind paper. Eva and Franco Mattes's *The Others* (2011) features fifty-one images from a collection of ten thousand photographs taken from random personal computers; the original authors and subjects remain unacknowledged and, most likely, unaware. Elisabeth Tonnard's *Geldermalsen riots* work (2016) consists of two zoomed-in images, each of a person who rioted at a proposed refugee center in the Netherlands. The blurred photographs, taken from surveillance footage, were originally published by the local authorities to force the rioters to publicly identify themselves. Christopher Clary's centerfold project, *sorry to dump on you like this.zip* (2016), shows an arrangement of found images of men taken from gay porn sites. The work is part of the artist's ongoing effort to disperse a large collection of online porn that he accumulated over many years.

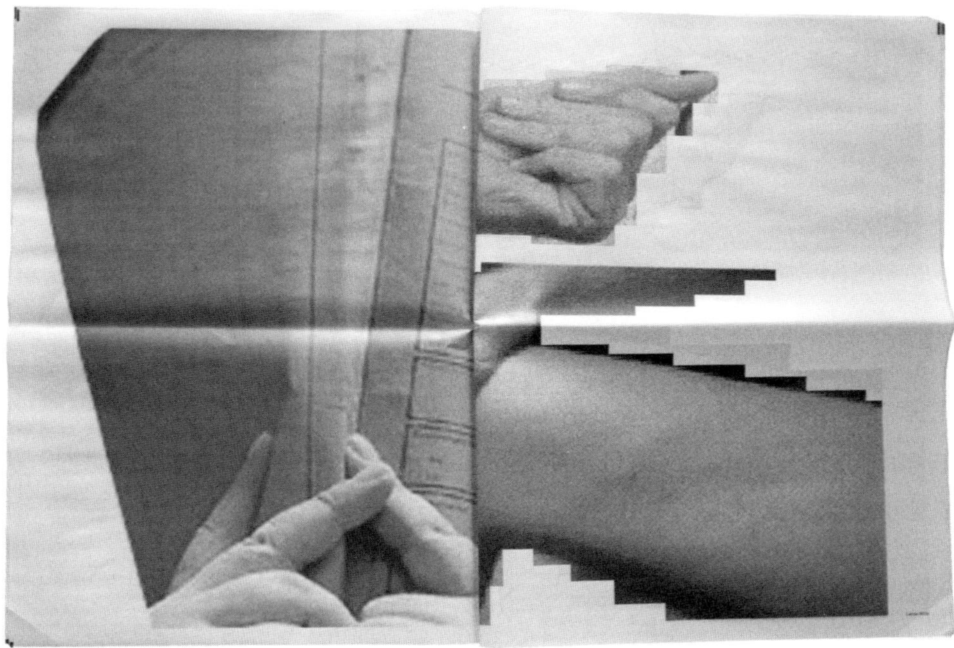

Printed Web 4 (Wolfgang Plöger & Lorna Mills), 2016

I once tried to identify each of the artists in Library of the Printed Web—there are now several hundred—by the types of actions they enacted in their web-to-print work: grabbing, hunting, or transforming the material in a performative way. These acts are nothing new; they seem like basic collage tactics now, not unlike how the cubists worked a hundred years ago. As a rubric for understanding contemporary artistic practice in and around digital archives, formal moves like these no longer suffice; we now need to look deeper at the power structures that flow into and out of works of appropriation. Who owns the platform? Who profits as the work circulates?

Post-Trump, it's difficult to see the word *grabbing* and not recognize an imperialist move. Taking material in a way that disturbs authorship remains an intriguing strategy for artistic practice, but not without these urgent questions: Who controls the narrative? To what end will the found material be used? Does the act of appropriation work to reveal an imbalance of power, or amplify an underrepresented voice, or expose a site of oppression? Might the work even repair or stitch together broken relations?

Library of the Printed Web was recently acquired by the Museum of Modern Art Library. I'm seeing the project from a different perspective now, absorbed into the ultimate archive of artists' publications: at a critical distance, removed from my control, and in the context of a much larger timeline. More than a year after the installation of *Printed Web 4* at *Public, Private, Secret*, the project serves as a kind of cultural marker, pointing us more directly toward inherent anxieties embedded in our culture of accumulation. The condition of total saturation has arrived, and it's not going anywhere. As we struggle to make sense of all of our material, questions around agency, trust, surveillance, automation, and labor seem imperative now. The collective need to know, print, share, track, preserve, and interrogate our archives is doubtless an urgent one. The question now is not whether but how to mobilize curatorial practice as a strategy of resistance.

REFLECTION: BELONGING IN THE MESS, JOHANNA HEDVA

As director of advocacy for the Processing Foundation, Johanna Hedva curated a series of events with the foundation's 2016 fellows, the Digital Citizens Lab, Claire Kearney-Volpe, and Tega Brain. The presence of the Processing Foundation's mission of promoting software literacy in diverse communities was an important marker of *Public, Private, Secret*'s narration of the inequities within digital control and visibility. Here, Hedva offers a personal reading of open-source culture and the need for individualized resistance to the digital status quo.

I'm an outsider—no matter the community. I'm an American living in Berlin. I'm disabled, yet my disabilities are invisible. I pass as white, having inherited all of my mother's Czech and German genes, and none of my father's Korean ones, which makes me an outsider to Asian American and POC communities, and also an outsider in white communities, neither all the way in nor out. I'm an outsider in queer and trans communities because, although I am genderqueer, I serve a lot of femme realness and use she/her pronouns, and, although queer, I'm currently partnered with a cis man; all of which, it goes without saying, make me an outsider in the straight cis world, which is to say, it's complicated. In my work, I write and perform: writing is the medium of my art practice, and performance is the context for my writing; so I don't fit easily into the art or performance worlds (where the visual is the most prominent signifier of meaning), nor the literary world (where the materiality of language is often still kept separate from the visual and the embodied). And in my work for the Processing Foundation, as director of advocacy, I am not a coder, or even somewhat technically inclined, preferring books to screens. I don't even have a phone. In fact, my primary day job is as a witch, giving astrology and tarot readings, having conversations with the dead—an outsider, then, even to this world of the living.

So, a good question is: what's a disabled, queer, Korean-American writer-performer-witch doing as a director for an open-source software project? The way I like to think of an answer is to refigure the terms that would signify a particular position in an identity politic as terms that indicate a practice, a method. Disability, queerness, open source not as identities, or groups I belong to, but as modes of doing, of how I practice myself.

Being an outsider means that the question of theory and practice—how practice is affected by theory, how theory is constructed by practice—becomes the most important one. Membership to particular groups and experiences is often predicated on the visual—whether someone "looks like" they belong or not—which means that my membership to most groups must rely on something else. My belonging has more to do with how I enact that group's politic, which is to say, less *that* I "walk the walk" and more *how*.

The question of theory and practice is also the central question of open source. In a way, open source could be said to be a philosophy of how to practice a theory of utopia, a demonstration in how to make a community, as a community. In its aims of collaboration and shared labor, and of making software nonproprietary and free, open source is a proposal for how software can operate beyond the terms of its commercial value, but rather, in its social, cultural, creative, and political value.

To participate in the community of open source, you have to do something. You have to be a maker. Unlike proprietary software, which requires only a purchase of the license for you to be a "member," open source demands that you get your hands dirty, that you become an active part of the project itself. It's not enough just to buy your way in. You have to devote your time, your attention and intention, and it's not enough to think through whatever issues arise, or to merely talk about them. Something has to be *done*, which is another way of saying that something has to be made.

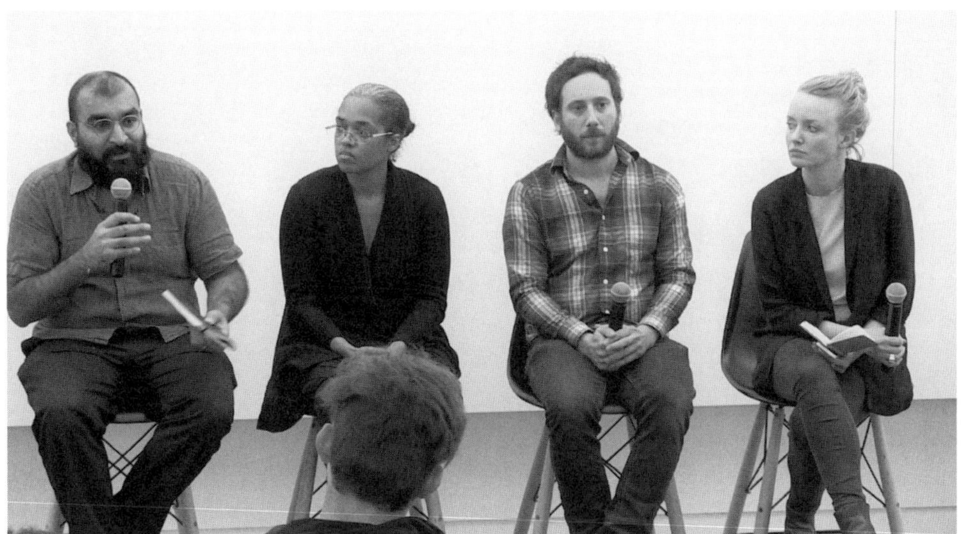

Learning to Teach panel discussion, hosted by Tega Brain, in collaboration with the Processing Foundation and the School for Poetic Computation, ICP Museum, November 30, 2016

Within open source, the capitalist mandate of time equaling money rings false. It's exposed for the bankrupt, exploitative analogy that it is. Time and money—as the world is being forced to confront in ever starker terms—are not equivalent within institutions of power, no matter how much those institutions insist they are. Such institutions operate upon systems that are white-supremacist, imperial-colonial, neoliberal, ableist, cis-heteronormative, and patriarchal—all of which are attempts to reduce the irreducible complexity of humanity down to objects whose sole purpose is economic—manageable—their edges and details shaved away, pegs in all manner of shapes being forced into identical holes.

I don't claim to know the answers for how to solve these problems. But the most salient response I can summon has to do with scale. It seems that the problem lies primarily in the capitalist inertia of scaling everything up, while relying on the paradox of infinite growth that organizes resources in terms of scarcity. When the world is organized according to such a paradox, the scale becomes skewed: it means that infinite growth does in fact happen, but only to a few, since the rest of us, laboring within the system of scarcity, are what provides those few with the resources required to get to the top of the pyramid. I think this is why I've always found resonance in open source: because of its relentless insistence on human-scaled labor, and its skepticism and rejection of vertically scaled hierarchies, it is less about ascending to the top of the mountain and more about working the soil of the land. (I often say that the only thing I'm willing to scale up under capitalism is my hair.)

Another good question: Is it possible for artists to subvert, or transgress, or resist these institutions of power? Should resistance be a part of an artist's practice? If so, how? At this moment in twenty-first-century global capitalism, is it even possible *not* to collude with the forms of power that oppress?

Though it may seem daunting and preposterous, I live my life under the belief that the answer to those questions is yes: yes, artists must necessarily be attempting a practice of resistance. The reason artists must resist is because art is not only about talking and thinking, or about buying one's way into a group, but it's about doing, building, and making: theory and practice.

This is not to say we will all arrive at a solution any time soon; in fact, I would argue that the very notion of arriving at a solution, as though the process will culminate and thus, stop, is a fantasy, and a dangerous one. The process of making, the struggle itself, seems to me the best we can hope for. Like I said, there's something in open source that relies on an image of utopia—and we all know how problematic and dangerous the fantasy of utopia can be. But the hope that I draw from open source comes less from its utopian impulses and more from the way—the means—in which it struggles toward them.

Resistance can take many forms: it can interrogate, explode, trick, prank, mourn. But primarily, it is about the practice of theory, which is to say, the struggle of doing and making. As

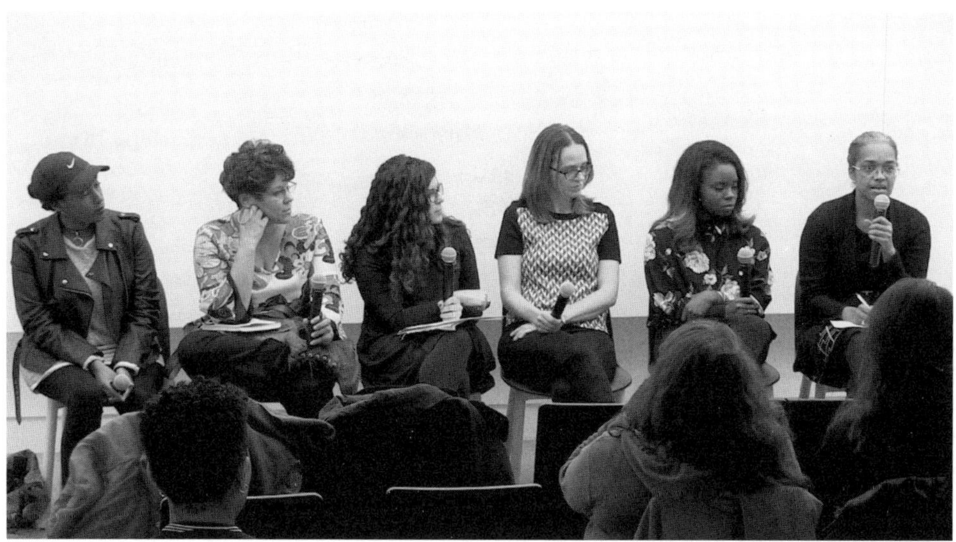

Coding Comic and STEM Teaching panel discussion, hosted by the Digital Citizens Lab, in collaboration with the Processing Foundation, ICP Museum, October 26, 2016

Dawn Lundy Martin writes, "Only in the space of discomfort can we be truly creativity [*sic*] ... Mastery is an attempt to dominate the artwork, to weaken it. It is lording our skills over the artwork. If we were to live in that space of always getting it exactly right, we might not be so interested in the process. Many of us prefer it to hurt a little."[1]

Struggle is inherent to and defining for resistance; struggle gives resistance its definition, linguistically and in terms of its edges, where its edges bump up against the thing it's pushing back against. This place of encounter is a place of friction, messy and in between; there are no masters here because we're all standing on the same unstable ground. But such friction is what we need to take action, to be moved to do anything. Which is to say, it's going to be a bumpy ride.

As someone who lives her life at this chaotic convergence point, who's built her house upon the liminal, regularly dealing with the quakes and tumult that arise from the friction, I can tell you that I often long to be on more stable ground. But I don't belong there. I belong to—in—the mess.

1 Dawn Lundy Martin, "A Black Poetics: Against Mastery," *boundary 2* 44, no. 3 (2017): https://doi.org/10.1215/01903659-3898154.

REFLECTION: SPOOKY ACTION FROM A DISTANCE, LUCAS WRENCH

Curator, cryptoparty organizer, and cyberpunk reader Lucas Wrench curated a series of workshops, performances, and artist-led experiences that spoke to the issue of privacy within visual culture. Wrench reflects on the pacing of this live-event program, which ranged from tactical instruction on how to protect your privacy or anonymity to discussions about creative and critical distance from generalized ideas of surveillance and its impact on our lives.

I first learned about plans for the exhibition that would become *Public, Private, Secret* in 2014 over pancakes at Jacks N Joe—A Breakfast All Day Kinda Place, in Los Angeles. At the time I was involved in a number of anti-security state endeavors: organizing a semiofficial cyberpunk reading group, hosting rogue "cryptoparties," and coordinating events like "Becoming Anonymous" and "Cybersecurity for Modern Hellscapes" at Machine Project, an experimental art space in the Echo Park neighborhood of LA. As part of the process, I found myself surrounded by a bizarre coalition of concerned citizens: a UCLA student who spent his summer vacation fighting with Libyan rebels during the Arab Spring; a young artist who always wore a gorilla mask; bio-hackers with microchip implants; a number of mysterious white men who refused to bring any electronic devices to our events, insisting on paying for workshops in cash and under pseudonyms; and, appropriately, an FBI cybercrime investigator, among others. Armed with code names like "Zarathustra," "Helix," and "RootKat," we were only rollerblades away from fulfilling my nineties cyberpunk fantasies, but my libertarian alarm bells started ringing. While surveillance activism benefits from a measure of bipartisan support, in the process we attracted some dubious allies: corporate behemoths like Apple align themselves with defenders of privacy as a means of reinforcing rights to corporate secrecy. WikiLeaks appears to have been instrumental in installing our current neofascist regime. Meanwhile, here in Los Angeles, the same privacy laws that protect celebrities from intrusion by paparazzi have created major obstacles for victims of domestic abuse to present evidence against their abusers.

While I earnestly believe in the value of surveillance literacy—the importance of understanding how these systems function and when and how we might circumvent them—the concealment of identity on which privacy, or anonymity, is premised is difficult to reconcile with traditional activism and civil-rights advocacy. Surveillance is not evenly applied across society. We don't live in a panopticon of neatly distributed suspicion and paranoia. Given that surveillance is for the most part racialized, the cloak of anonymity that empowers some, can reproduce an erasure of identity for those marked as "other," those whom our white-supremacist state pursues in the first place. DREAMers have built a movement out of the refusal to hide in the ways our immigration policy demands. The entire history of civil rights in this country has been based on increasing the visibility of marginalized individuals and communities. While groups like Black bloc, antifa, and the Zapatistas have demonstrated the political potential of tactics such as concealment and anonymity, these strategies don't work across the board. Most political movements will eventually require individuals to make themselves visible, and therefore expose themselves to risk. In practical terms, simply circumventing surveillance is not a sufficient strategy—we need to learn to live within this soup and we aren't going to find the answers under our social-media privacy settings.

Public, Private, Secret and its related programming offered an opportunity to give space to these complications. We avoided framing the workshops around the idea of government surveillance; instead we took as a point of departure a more generous position that favored "privacy in visual culture." This approach led us from a policy-centered discussion to a broader conversation around the values, habits, and social desires that have motivated some four centuries of categorization, quantification, and control. From a programming perspective, the goal was to leave people more conflicted than afraid or reassured. We began with a weekend of more conventional "surveillance programming"—email encryption and anonymous internet-browsing workshops, but as the months progressed we strayed further and further from any kind of concrete, tactical instruction. Franziska Lamprecht and Hajoe Moderegger, otherwise known as the art collective eteam, spent a morning trying to become invisible by way of a novel arrangement of iPads and cheap webcams. Heather Dewey-Hagborg led a primer in DNA phenotyping, in which she taught

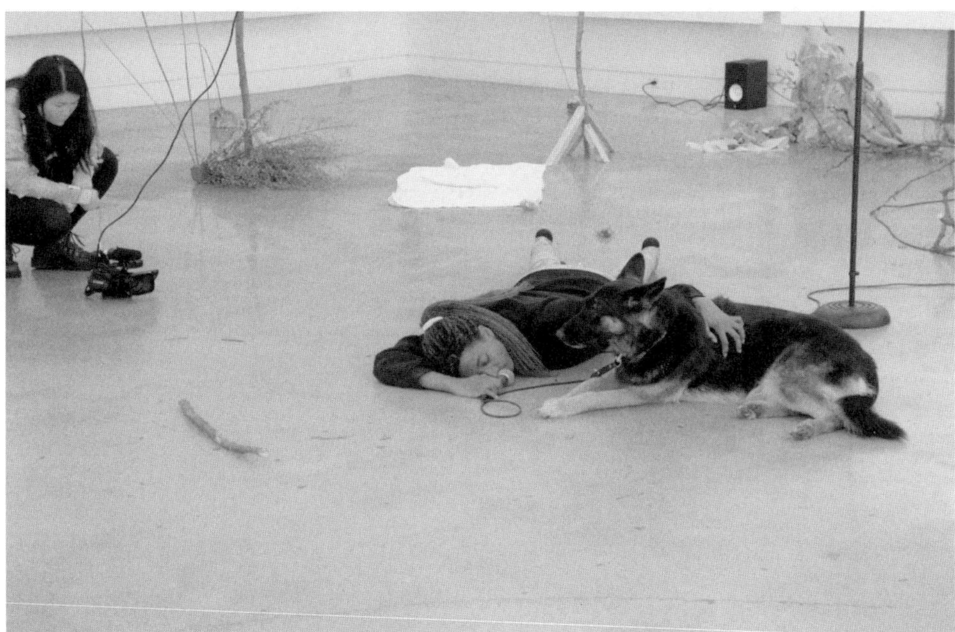

Lex Brown, *Hard Numbers*, performance commissioned by Lucas Wrench for *Public, Private, Secret* (performed at ICP Museum, September 24 and 25, 2016). Photo by Africia Heiderhoff

participants how to take a used piece of gum and turn it into a possible portrait of its chewer. Lex Brown stalked the museum lobby with a hired dog. Dan Phiffer taught kids how to make decentralized "darknets." From week to week, participants were thrown into often conflicting roles—investigator and suspect, under scrutiny and blissfully unknown. The goal was not to impart a comprehensive surveillance education, but to give participants some of the critical distance they needed to locate somewhat technical and abstract processes—bulk data collection, or biometric analysis, for example—within their own moral compass or social values.

How to proceed from here? On the one hand we have the standard trap of futurism: waiting for some kind of technological rapture that will allow us to circumvent systems of capture and control altogether, relieving the burden of complex political upheaval. The internet itself is an "instrument for state oppression and accelerated capitalism" as *Public, Private, Secret* artist Zach Blas observes in the preface of his project *Contra-Internet* (2015–16). Our ambitions run contrary to the infrastructure we inhabit. In this sense, we're talking about truly utopian aspirations that require us to imagine something that has never existed and may not be possible within our current reality—*except*, perhaps, within the thing we call Art. Until artists worked it out, Europeans hadn't realized that if you draw something smaller, it looks as if it's further away. I'm confident we will continue to make valuable and equally perspective-altering contributions to ways of seeing, being seen, and all things in between!

REFLECTION: PICTURES WITHOUT WORDS, JOSEPH MAIDA

Artist and educator Joseph Maida hosted two evening discussions as part of the *Public, Private, Secret* program that focused on past and present-day gender binaries and hierarchies within photographic culture. Maida outlines the prompts that the dynamic of the *Public, Private, Secret* exhibition gave him in the structuring of his events at the ICP Museum, and also muses on the process of reflecting back upon his own photographic practice.

I. Words and Pictures

When I contemplate the ever-growing presence and influence of photography, I cannot readily divorce myself from words. The relationship of photographs to language reflects the bias of a linear history, a narrative that predates the invention of the medium. Long before silver-chloride prints and daguerreotypes, there were pictures: pictograms, to be precise, which represent some of the oldest origins of written language, including Egyptian hieroglyphs and Chinese characters. Once these pictures became words, and these words became trusted holders of meaning, pictures themselves became permanently intertwined with the languages they bore. Even as pictures permeate all aspects of daily life today, we officially remain in an era of spoken and written language. And words, which typically develop from cultural and social histories, require revision over time. The expansion of a common lexicon has proven difficult, however, particularly when it comes to adjusting linguistic hegemony.

That said, in our more personal correspondence, online and on smartphones, we have embraced emojis—a new strain of pictograms—which suggest ways in which language could evolve by giving more agency and independence to photographs and pictures in general. Emojis remind us that just as pictures need words, words, too, need pictures. Social platforms like Instagram and direct messaging, with a seemingly infinite stream of shared images, hint at what thinking and communicating in pictures can be.

II. Public, Private, Secret

The opportunity for artworks of the past to attain new relevance through contemporary reconsideration connects the practices of artists, curators, and scholars alike. The exhibition *Public, Private, Secret* not only acknowledged these intersections through the physical arrangement of works among its mirrored walls, but also deliberately stirred the photographic pot to hold the past accountable. The show invited fresh interpretations of familiar projects, including the charged street portraits in the Women Are Beautiful series by Garry Winogrand.

During the first event I hosted for *Public, Private, Secret,* with work like Winogrand's in mind, I provided an abridged history of nonbinary pronouns as a springboard from which one could revisit and expand the vocabulary used to describe photographs that challenge or reinforce gender stereotypes, or that paradoxically do both. In a room full of viewer-participants, we reconsidered a selection of photographs utilizing this method. Yet, the limitations of our language—and its dominant position in our thought process—remained an obstacle, even as we considered options beyond English, with special guests Yasaman Alipour, Keren Greenberg, and Sabrina Marques, who spoke to the perspectives of their respective native languages: Farsi, Hebrew, and Spanish.

We found that words, with their ability to define and specify, simultaneously limit and contain. This is especially true with gendered language, and in this instance I mean English, which gives us "he" and "she," but no singular pronoun to refer to a person without assigning male or female gender. (Every language has advantages and disadvantages in terms of how it disbands or reinforces the gender binary, either through specific words, or through the expectation of the language to be performed according to male or female gender.) The lack of a nonbinary singular pronoun apart from "it" in English proves problematic not only grammatically, in instances when a subject's gender is unknown, but also in cases where the subject's gender is both male and female, or neither, or lies somewhere in the middle. In the case of the former, men were historically given precedence using the default "he" to refer to a singular individual, reinforcing the grasp of the patriarchy. In the latter instances, some transgender, genderqueer, and intersex individuals have been kept lexically invisible due to the language's inability to accurately acknowledge them.

III. Singular They

For over two centuries, writers of English grammar guides, academic texts, and letters to the editor have highlighted arguments for and against a common-gender, singular pronoun, including "they." In his recent scholarship, linguist Dennis Baron cites such primary sources, noting that while the first coiners of nonbinary pronouns were concerned with grammatical correctness as early as 1792, the political and social implications of such pronouns did not fully move to the fore until the end of the nineteenth century, with the growing momentum of women's rights and suffrage.[1] In an 1882 article titled "A New Pronoun Wanted," a writer to the *Memphis Free Trade* refuses to use "he" to mean "she" when grammatical correctness calls for a singular pronoun:

> *Why should it not be the duty of woman's rights to supply this, the needed term? As the laws of grammar now stand, the use of "he" when "she" may be meant is an outrage upon the dignity, and an encroachment upon the rights, of woman. It is quite as important that they should stand equal with men in the grammars as before the law.*[2]

As with many modern social movements, feminism laid the groundwork for recognizing overlooked, discredited,

1 Dennis Baron, "The Words That Failed: A Chronology of Early Nonbinary Pronouns," http://www.english.illinois.edu/-people-/faculty/debaron/essays/epicene.htm.

2 "A New Pronoun Wanted," *Daily Arkansas Gazette*, May 7, 1882.

and marginalized groups, and for changing power dynamics through an insistence on equal representation and a shift in language.

This is not to say that adapting new language has ever come easily, even if the history of the singular "they" suggests that the grammatical repurposing of a familiar word is lighter on society than the coinage of a new one. In his 1871 book *Words and Their Uses, Past and Present*, American writer Richard Grant White makes a familiar case against the coinage of a new common-gender pronoun. A correspondent to White implores:

> *We must have a word to take the place of he or she, his or her, him or her, etc.... As the French make the little word en answer a great many purposes, suppose we take the same word, give it an English pronunciation (or any other word), and make it answer for any and every case of that kind, and thus tend to simplify the language.*

To which White bluntly objects:

> *First, the thing can't be done; last, it is not at all necessary or desirable that it should be done.... Man, as in the word mankind, is used in a general sense for the species. Any objection to this use of man, and of the relative pronoun, is for the consideration of the next Woman's Rights Convention.... With he, she, it, and we, and one, and some, we have no need of en or any other outlandish pronoun.*[3]

Thirteen years later, in 1884, pronoun coinage was in the air, bringing us "hi," "le," "his'er," "ip," and "thon," among others. "Thon," a singular nonbinary pronoun blending *that* and *one*, gained notable momentum and was even included in *Funk and Wagnalls Standard Dictionary* in 1898, as well as *Webster's Second New International Dictionary* in 1934. "Thon" was, however, quietly dropped from *Webster's Third* and quickly forgotten, a similar fate of all new words put forward to fill the aforementioned singular nonbinary pronoun gap.[4] Scottish linguist and philosopher Alexander Bain made a clear and practical case for "they" as a singular pronoun in 1879,[5] but it took well over a hundred years for this pronoun to gain official recognition in the English language despite it colloquial use since the 1300s.[6] In 2015, the American Dialect Society remarkably voted singular "they" its "word of the year," noting its "emerging use as a pronoun to refer to a known person, often as a conscious choice by a person rejecting the traditional gender binary of he and she."[7]

Nonbinary pronouns, including singular "they," can serve as models not only for expanding language but also for embracing the wonderfully ambiguous nature of photographs, which can reveal something or someone whom we cannot accurately name within the limits of our daily lexicon. Just as we have better understood photography throughout its history thanks to the arguments constructed with written and spoken language, "speaking" and "writing"

3 Richard Grant White, *Words and Their Uses, Past and Present: A Study of the English Language* (New York: Sheldon & Co., 1871), pp. 241–42.
4 Dennis Baron, *Grammar and Gender* (New Haven, CT: Yale University Press, 1986), p. 201.
5 Alexander Bain, *Higher English Grammar* (New York: H. Holt & Co., 1879), pp. 310–11.
6 Merriam-Webster, "Singular 'They,'" https://www.merriam-webster.com/words-at-play/singular-nonbinary-they.
7 American Dialect Society, "2015 Word of the Year Is Singular 'They,'" http://www.americandialect.org/2015-word-of-the-year-is-singular-they.

with photographs—making use of their remarkable plasticity—can broaden how we produce, use, and understand our vocabularies.

IV. Toward Ambiguity

Public, Private, Secret and the events I hosted presented an opportunity to reconsider my engagement with overlapping territory in my own practice over the last two decades, namely, photography, image, language, and gender. The kinship I felt with this exhibition's unabashed ambiguity—offering simultaneous paths toward approaching art and media from the past and present for a vision of the future—resonates with my own attempts to go beyond the limits of language and bias as I learn from experience and revisit my past.

As *Public, Private, Secret* challenged the boundaries of a white-cubed institution and its former identity from within its new walls, I, too, have sought to reread photography—including my own—to embrace fluidity, development, and change. Pictures can be the strongest invitation to reimagine, or reinvent, language that expresses what we see and feel, especially when what they present exists beyond the scope of what we immediately recognize or know how to name.

In the spirit of expanding thinking, seeing, and speaking, we can revise the adage "a picture is worth a thousand words" to "a picture is worth a thousand *new* words" that can, collectively, help us unpack the ambiguous, liminal space that photography brilliantly occupies. In light of this discussion, I've selected twelve pictures from my archive, taken at different times, to provide a departure point for a rereading of my work based on photographic communication and the possibilities of extending language. I encourage you, the reader-viewer, to consider how you look at these photographs and, if possible, try to see without words, allowing a visual and photographic discourse to be self-sufficient. And if you must use language, which you inevitably will, attempt to expand it. To quote Walker Evans quoting Herman Melville while introducing a selection of uncaptioned archival stock photographs published in *Fortune* in May 1947: "It may pay you to incline with Herman Melville to 'let the ambiguous procession of events reveal their own ambiguousness.'"

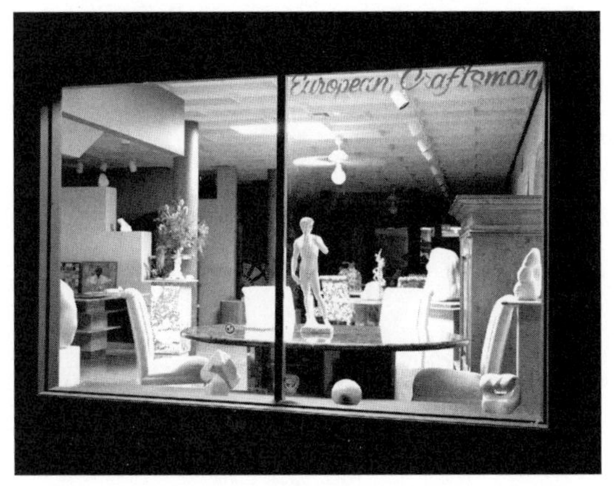
European Craftsman

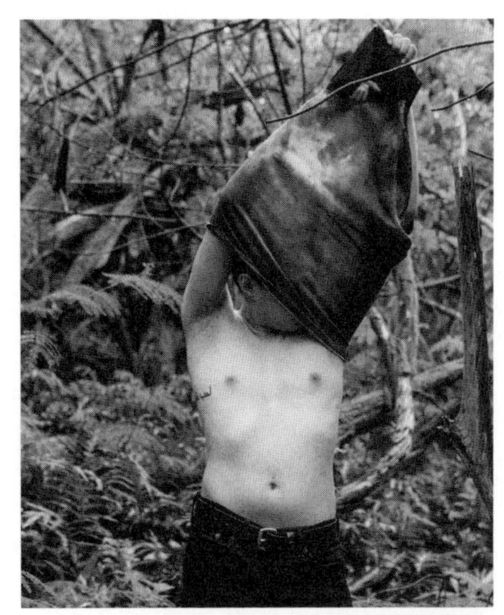

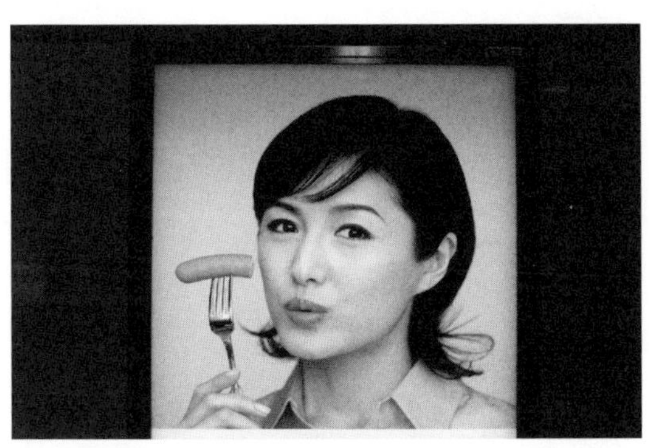

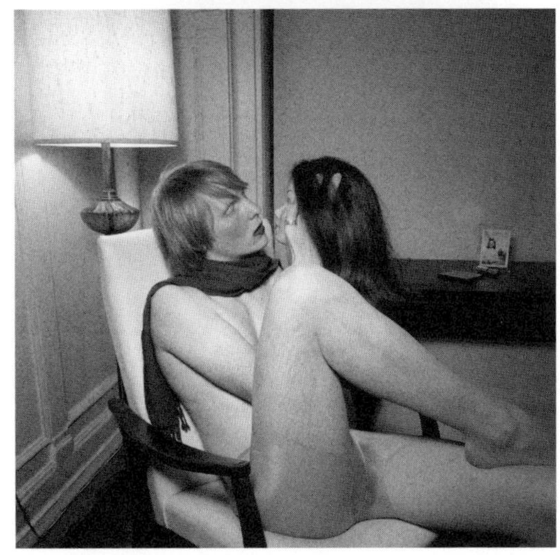

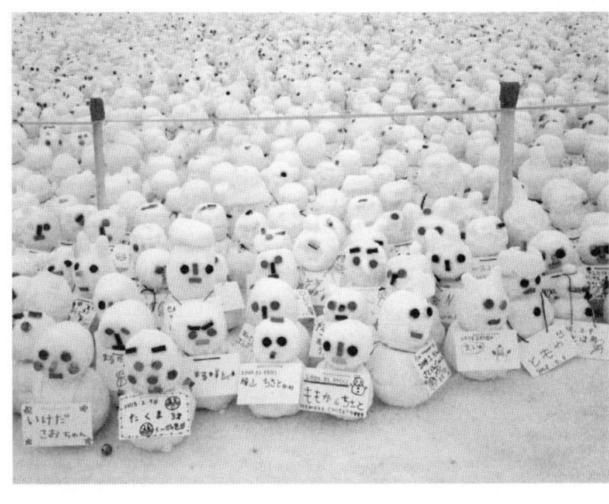

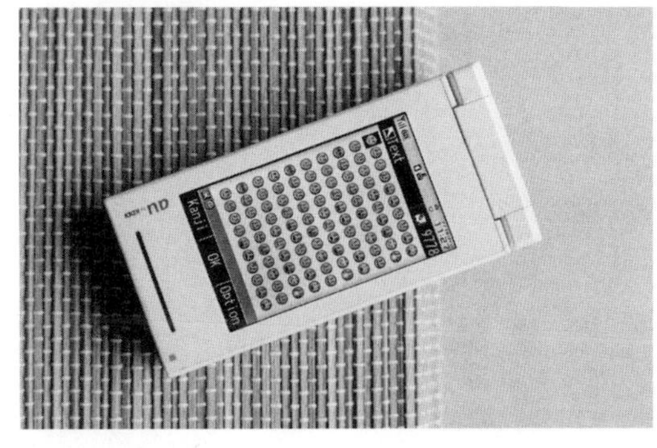
Text
Kanji
OK
Option

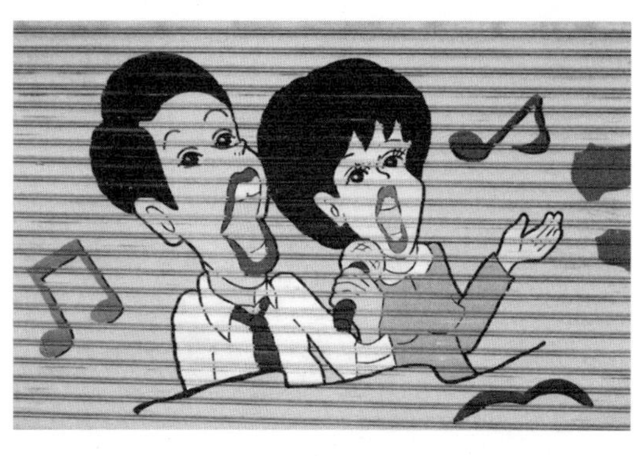

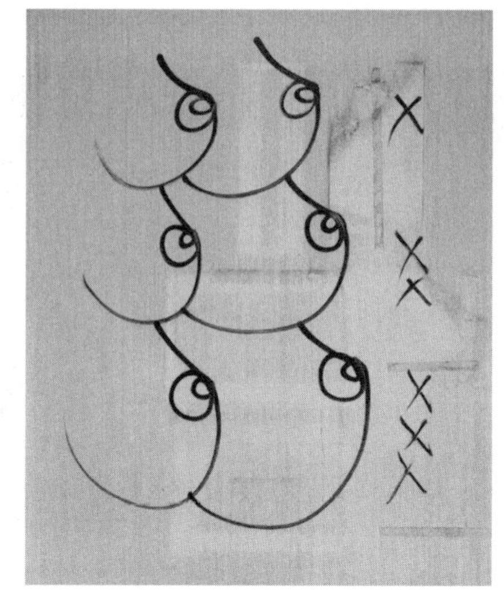

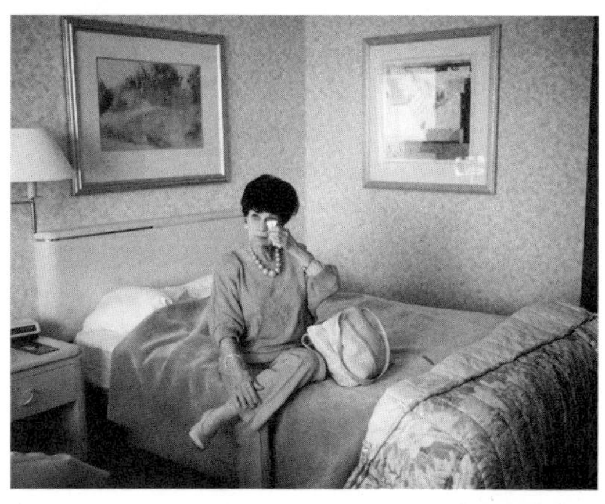

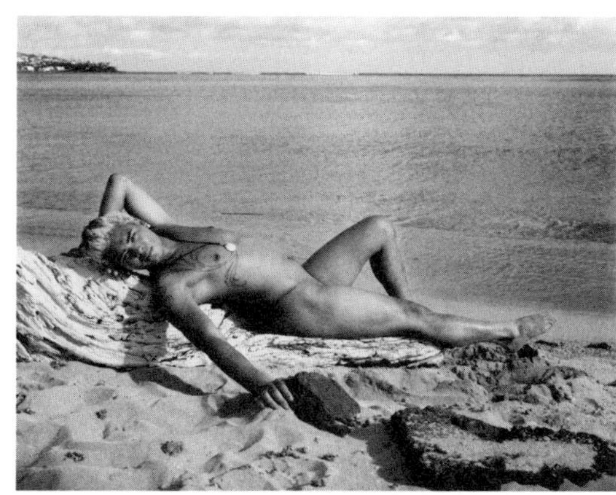

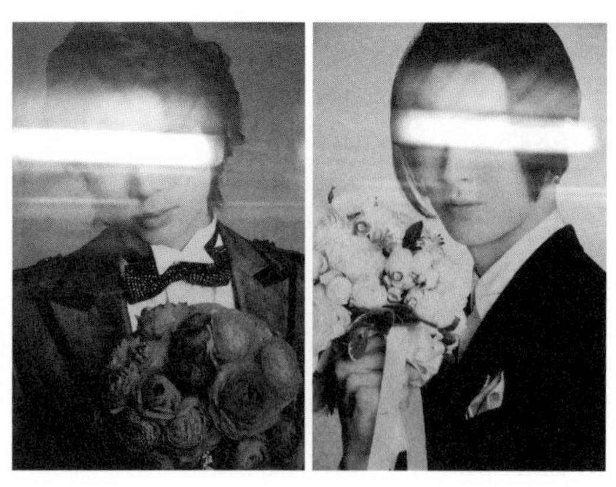

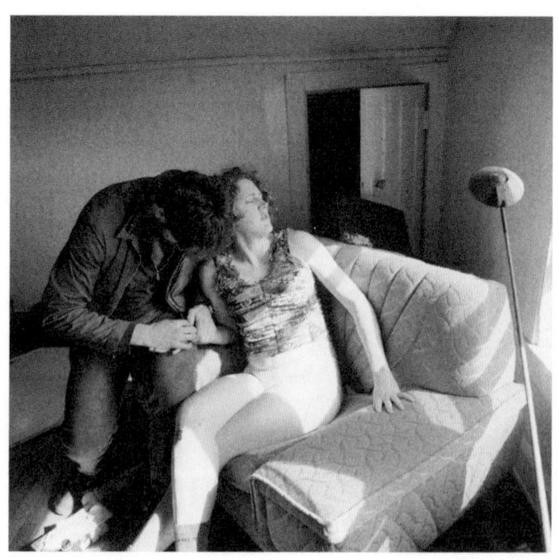

REFLECTION: REDEFINING WHAT AND WHO WE SEE AND DON'T SEE, LACY AUSTIN

As director of ICP's Community Programs, Lacy Austin was critical in forging connections between *Public, Private, Secret* and participants in ICP's youth and community-based initiatives. These programs, which included tours, workshops, educator trainings, classes, and community partnerships, significantly expanded the reach of the exhibition by bringing its urgent issues into conversations with a wider, more diverse, and often younger audience. In her account below, Austin speaks in detail about some of the initiatives, shares first-hand reactions to the discussions engendered by the exhibition, and reflects on its lasting effects.

What and who is made public, private, secret—and how do we navigate these layered identities both externally and internally in a world where not everyone's voice and story is valued and seen? Since its founding in 1974 by Cornell Capa, the International Center of Photography has explored the power of images to change the way we see and understand ourselves, each other, and the world around us. As ICP's director of community programs over the past sixteen years, it has been a privilege to participate in such critical progress. ICP's Community Programs serve over ten thousand students and teachers annually through onsite museum education initiatives and youth classes, as well as offsite through partnerships with schools and social-service organizations in underserved communities. The programs foster self and community empowerment through the interdisciplinary teaching of photography, visual literacy, critical thinking, writing, and public speaking.

As student Raymond Jimenez shares, "Photography is the way I see the world, and the only way I can understand it." Our goal is to give young people tools to express themselves, tell their stories with pride, believe in their dreams, and make a difference. We are especially committed to youth from communities whose voices are too often unseen, unheard, and/or misrepresented—across lines of culture, class, gender, sexual orientation—and to providing platforms for their stories to be honored and amplified.

When Charlotte Cotton and I first met, she not only embraced the value of the programs and the stories of our communities, but envisioned an exhibition and a space that would allow them to come to life in unprecedented ways. *Public, Private, Secret* offered a unique opportunity to discuss its important themes with our diverse audiences and then to showcase work by our communities for the first time ever in our museum. Through daily tours, rotating exhibitions on the poster wall, and a teen class inspired by the exhibition, a statement was made that everyone's voice and story are valuable and deserve to be heard and seen.

Our Museum Education program led daily activities, including tours, workshops, and events for educators. These resources introduced visitors to our exhibitions while building visual literacy and critical thinking skills. Guided tours led by museum educators were conducted in an inquiry-based discussion format, encouraging audience members to consider multiple interpretations and meanings. The diversity of artists and artworks on display offered an entry point for a much broader audience than usual. In reflecting on her guided tours, museum educator Ifétayo Abdus-Salam said,

> *Discussing the* PPS *exhibition was a profoundly enlightening exploration into the ways technology has altered our understanding of public and private spaces. It was especially interesting to observe how ideologies of what is to be considered public and private varied based on the age group having the discussion. One line of conversation that continues to stand out is the observation of the use of the photographic image and the publication of one's self as represented historically through the work of Sojourner Truth and Frederick Douglass, and contemporarily by Kim Kardashian West.*

From children to seniors, further discussions around what it means to define yourself and who has access to seeing and telling their own story remain invaluable in our memory. Works ranging from Sojourner Truth's *I Sell the Shadow to Support the Substance* (1864) to Rashid Johnson's *Self-Portrait with My Hair Parted Like Frederick Douglass* (2003) and Lyle Ashton Harris's *Appunti per L'Afro-Barocco* (2015) offered a more diverse range of visitors the opportunity to see their own reflection through the work; and to feel an integral part of the conversation meant a tremendous amount to many of our visitors and students. It remains critical for us to be a space for reflection and advocacy based on how many individuals and communities continue to fight for the right to be seen and heard justly, and to work toward changing that.

The expansive program for *Public, Private, Secret* also incorporated voices from our Community Partnerships into the exhibition itself through its poster wall. Located on the first floor of the museum, which is open to the public and free of charge, it featured artists' projects and education-based initiatives on a rotating basis throughout the run of the show. The wall highlighted three of our initiatives, including our Community Partnership ICP at THE POINT; our Teen Academy class "My Roots, Our City" in partnership with the Tenement Museum; and one of our Neighborhood Collaborations, the Bowery Mission. Marina, one of the exhibiting artists from the Bowery Mission, said, "I feel empowered as I see my future unfolding and my ideas and goals manifesting."

Another exhibiting artist, Roy Baizan, an alumnus from ICP at THE POINT who is now an ICP staff member, expanded on this idea: "My images challenge negative misconceptions about my community by documenting and sharing my own personal experiences and representing a positive side that is often overlooked by popular media. I try to show solutions to problems. I show what I know is true." By allowing our diverse communities to create their own image(s) and then to present those images in the museum, the traditional hierarchy and ownership of output was redefined and democratized.

We also brought the exhibition to life within our Teen Academy program. Inspired by *PPS*, we offered a course on social media, to our families and friends, to each other—and on the other, the private lives we try to lead

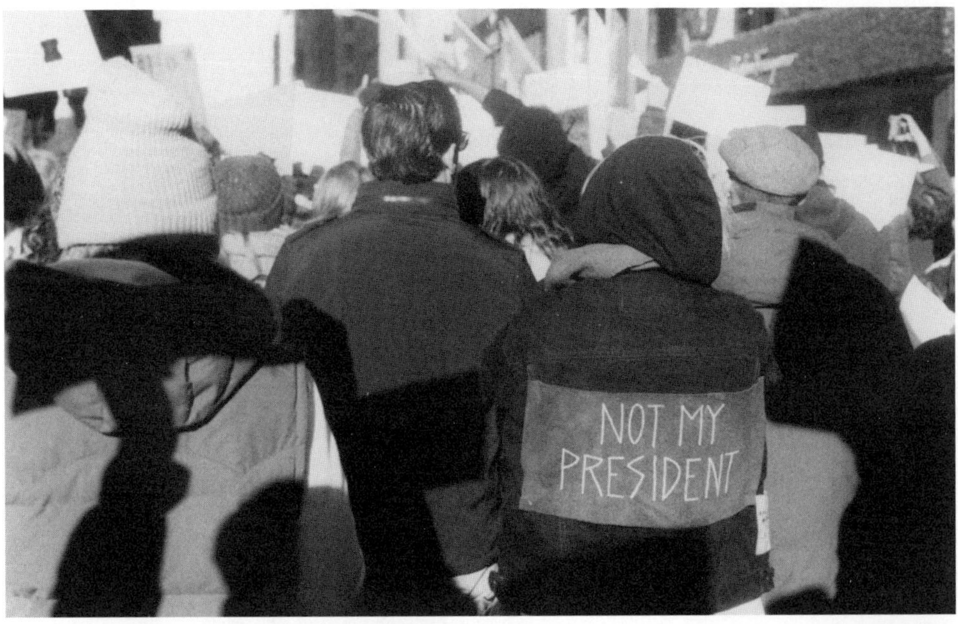

Nubia Celis-Etienne, Untitled, 2016

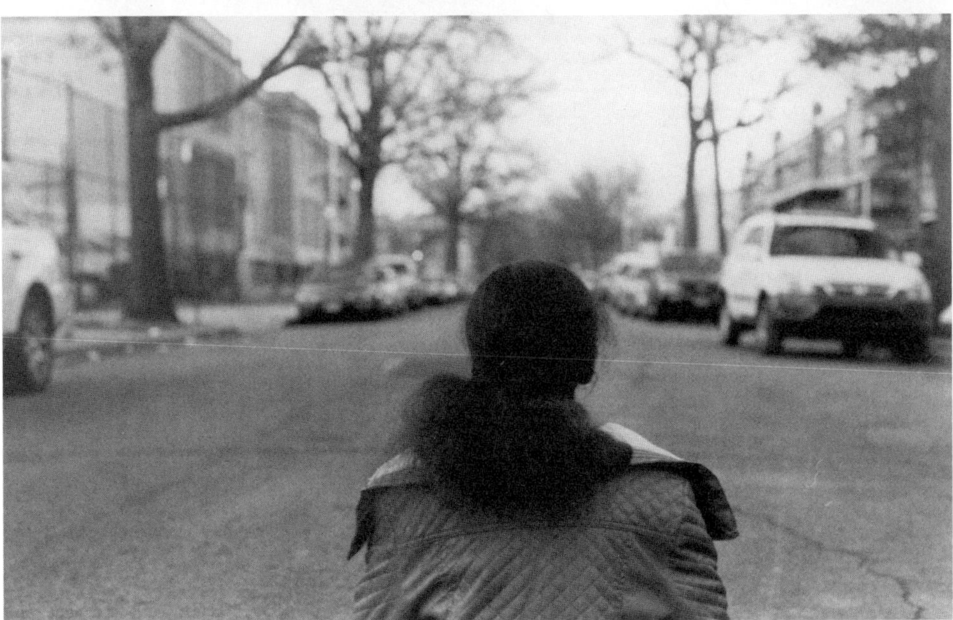

Nicole Chow, Untitled, 2016

that examined the work of exhibiting artists and other artists whose work focuses on similar themes. Students reflected on the duality of identity: on the one hand, the version we present to the outside world— outside of the gaze of society. Incorporating concepts drawn from performance and installation art, as well as traditional darkroom photographic methods, students created their own image-based projects exploring boundaries between fiction and documentation. As faculty member Doran Walot pointed out,

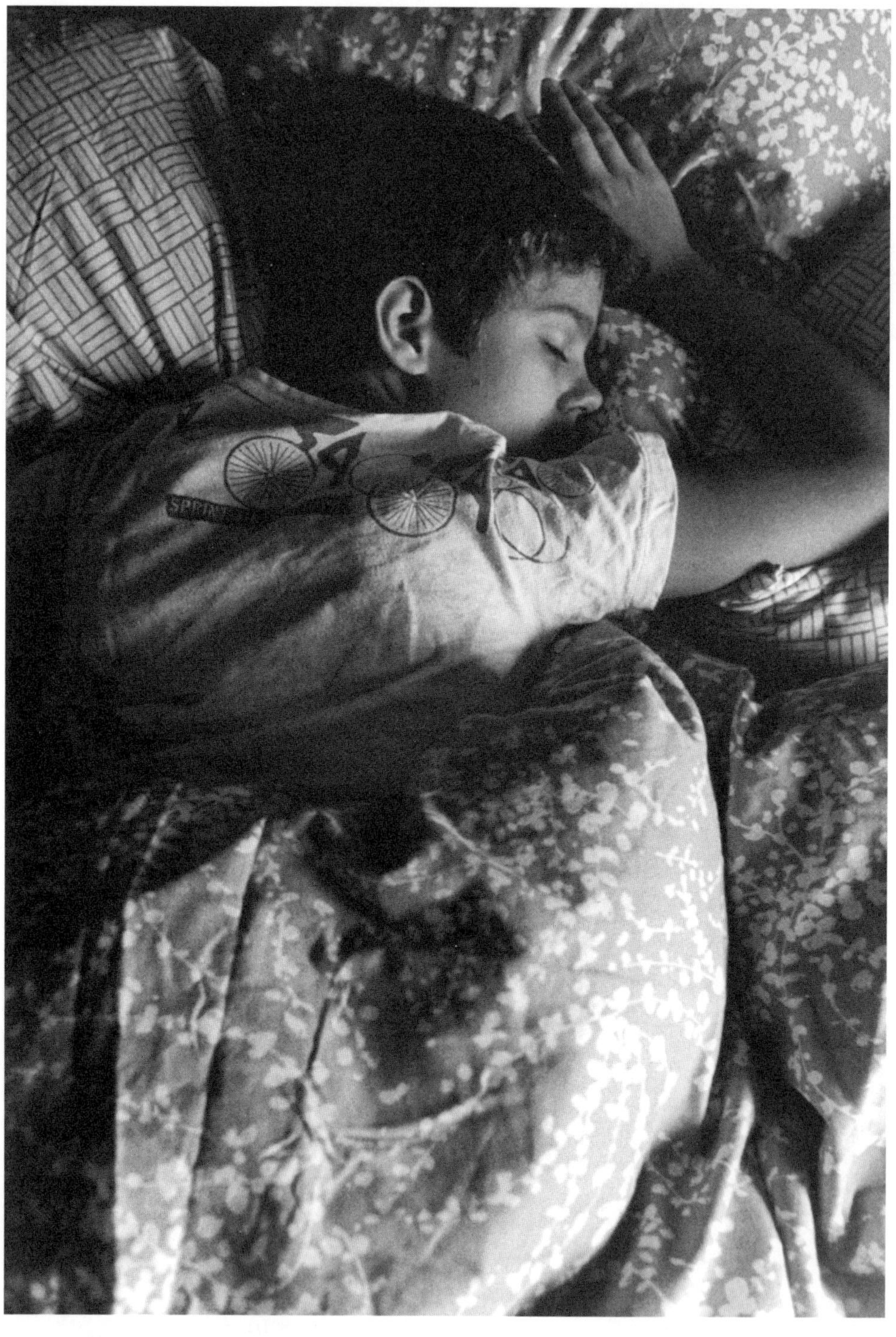

Annika Heegard, Untitled, 2016

Who is more familiar with the code-switching of contemporary identity than a modern teenager? A high school student has to wear many masks while trying to discover their own personhood—for their parents, for their teachers, with their peers, on social media, in church, in their bedroom. By providing a safe space to experiment with the movable concepts of identity across media—including analog photography, installation, and performance—we gave students the opportunity to either directly reflect their own experiences, or to create fictional spaces where public, private, and secret worlds could bleed together.

Given the scarcity of safe and supportive environments for young people to express themselves, the work created in this class was especially important.

In reflecting back, *Public, Private, Secret* was hardly just an exhibition. We experienced it throughout Community Programs as a springboard for profound reflection on and participation in critical issues of our time. By removing barriers to access and creating a safe and inclusive environment for private expression that could, if desired, be channeled more publicly, what and who we see and don't see changes: the voices of our youth and underserved communities—so often underrepresented and misrepresented—were seen and heard more clearly and loudly. It is our continued resolve to create such necessary spaces for self-exploration and expression, which challenge and redefine identities on one's own terms, and build community from the inside out. The uniquely inclusive and participatory model of this exhibition has already influenced and will continue to influence how we imagine spaces for exhibition and education, and ultimately how we see and value ourselves and each other.

Back
Poster Wall Displays
Live Events
Acknowledgments
Colophon

POSTER WALL DISPLAYS

The poster wall at the ICP Museum on the Bowery featured a rotating schedule of physical displays in the free-access space, including artist projects, ICP School and Community Programs presentations, and announcements about ICP's partnerships and exhibitions.

June 2–26, 2016: Paul Soulellis, *Printed Web 4*
ICP-commissioned issue of Soulellis's ongoing publication series

June 28–July 3: Romke Hoogwaerts, *Mossless 4: Public/Private/Portrait*
ICP collaboration with Hoogwaerts's photography magazine

July 5–10: *The Ties That Bind*
ICP–Bard MFA class of 2016 exhibition, on view at Baxter Street at the Camera Club of New York

July 12–17: Paul Soulellis, *Printed Web 4*

July 19–31: Paolo Cirio, *Overexposed*
A series (2015) comprising nine photographs of CIA, FBI, and NSA officials, taken from social media and rendered in Cirio's graffiti-style print technique

August 2–7: *Another Kind of Paradise*
ICP School's various one-year certificate programs' student exhibition, on view at the ICP School

August 9–14: *Winning the White House: From Press Prints to Selfies*
ICP exhibition on view at Southampton Arts Center

August 16–21: *My Roots, Our City*
ICP Teen Academy class, in collaboration with the Tenement Museum, New York

August 23–28: *Winning the White House: From Press Prints to Selfies*
ICP exhibition on view at Southampton Arts Center

August 30–September 11: *Voyeurism, Surveillance, and Identity in the Cinema*
Film series partnership with Anthology Film Archives, New York

September 13–25: Mark Ghuneim, *Surveillance Index Edition One*
A publication (2016) indexing one hundred books related to surveillance photography

September 27–October 2: *The Future Perfect*
ICP alumni exhibition on view at the ICP School

October 4–9: *Bronx Eyes*
ICP at THE POINT student exhibition at THE POINT Community Development Corporation

October 11–16: Daphne Chan, *Transparency: The Gender Identity Project*

An immersive transmedia work (2015–) that explores agency, identity, and representation in the LGBTQ+ community

October 18–23: *Radical Networks*

An annual conference in collaboration with Eyebeam, encouraging empowered engagement with the internet and networked technology

October 25–November 6: Joy Episalla, *144 Years*

A series of portraits (2016), each an amalgam of the faces of thirty-three women who have won their party's nomination for the US presidency since 1872

November 8–13: *Winning the White House: From Press Prints to Selfies*

ICP exhibition on view at ICP Mana, Jersey City

November 15–20: *ICP New Media Narratives*

ICP New Media Narratives program 2016 students' responses to the real-time curation in *Public, Private, Secret*

November 22–December 4: Natasha Caruana, *Married Man*

A series (2008–9) documenting Caruana's dates with married men over the course of one year

December 6–11: *ICP Neighborhood Collaboration with The Bowery Mission*

An exhibition of photographic portraits and personal statements by workshop students from The Bowery Mission

December 13–18: *ICP–Bard MFA Program*

ICP's 2016 MFA candidates' responses to the themes of *Public, Private, Secret*

December 20–25: *ICP General Studies Program*

ICP General Studies Program 2016 students' work in response to *Public, Private, Secret*

Unless otherwise noted, all events took place at the ICP Museum at 250 Bowery, New York, in 2016.

Ultraconcentrated: Image, Media, Software, lecture by Casey Reas, September 7, 2016

Gathering source material from newspapers, social-media profiles, broadcast television, and YouTube searches, Los Angeles–based artist and educator Casey Reas created a series of software-based collages that manifest his personal confrontations with media. Reas spoke about his projects from 2012 to the present.

Reas is a cofounder of the Processing Foundation, whose mission is to promote software literacy within the visual arts and visual literacy within technology-related fields—and to make these fields accessible to diverse communities.

PGP Email Encryption, workshop hosted by Dan Bustillo, Tim Schwartz, and Lucas Wrench of LA Cryptoparty, in collaboration with Machine Project, September 10, 2016

In this three-hour, role-play-based workshop, participants learned to safely and securely communicate via encrypted email, using the initial communications between whistle-blower Edward Snowden and journalist Laura Poitras as their guide. To address the uncertainty of whether their communications were secure, participants were invited to assume the roles of both whistle-blower and journalist as they reenacted the first emails between the two and learned the steps required for smuggling national secrets.

Becoming Anonymous, workshop hosted by Dan Bustillo, Tim Schwartz, and Lucas Wrench of LA Cryptoparty, in collaboration with Machine Project, September 11, 2016

Becoming Anonymous was a workshop aimed at sorting through the murky world of online privacy. With a focus on secure internet browsing, participants learned to use a set of online tools designed to limit and block surveillance of their online browsing. Participants delved into the processes by examining what information is gathered on them as internet users, and learned how simple shifts in online behavior could dramatically affect the online data they made available about themselves.

The "Singular They," reading group hosted by Joseph Maida, September 22, 2016

Tracing the histories of both photography and nonbinary pronouns, this conversation was driven by a reconsideration of historically celebrated photographs in which the genders of the subjects, photographers, and viewers determine how we see and read their meaning. The group revised their approaches to word usage in order to evaluate photographs and consider the promises, paradoxes, and shortcomings in seeing, naming, and understanding gender today.

Hard Numbers, live performance by Lex Brown, in collaboration with Machine Project, September 24 and 25, 2016

Lex Brown, artist and author of the book *My Wet Hot Drone Summer* (2015), presented *Hard Numbers*, a partly scripted, partly improvised live performance. Commissioned for *Public, Private, Secret*, Brown's performance touched on refugeeism, camouflage, personal privacy, commodification, racism, and criminality.

Hoods, John Edmonds in conversation with Antwaun Sargent, September 28, 2016

Photographer and writer John Edmonds presented his photographic portrait series Hoods, which evolved from a personal exploration of reclusiveness and a broader investigation of the intersection of art, politics, and black identity. Edmonds then discussed the work with writer and critic Antwaun Sargent.

Real People Fight the Swipe, lecture by Susie Lee, October 5, 2016

Social media has changed the way we think about visibility, intimacy, and self-representation and has reshaped our personal boundaries. Susie Lee, visual artist, CEO, and former entrepreneur-in-residence at NEW INC, guided the audience through the ubiquitous "shopping-for-humans" online social model and presented an alternative—a way of closely connecting people through technology—with her award-winning dating app Siren.

An Evening with Ron Galella, hosted by Anthology Film Archives, October 13, 2016

The International Center of Photography and Anthology Film Archives hosted an evening with legendary American paparazzo Ron Galella. The program included a screening of *Smash His Camera* (2010), the award-winning HBO film directed by documentarian Leon Gast, and was followed by a Q&A and book signing with Galella.

A Third Look, conversation hosted by Joseph Maida, October 13, 2016

Taking the hegemonic male gaze of twentieth-century American photography as his prompt, Joseph Maida proposed a reevaluation of Garry Winogrand's renowned 1970s street photographs Women Are Beautiful as well as Lee Friedlander's nudes of women in domestic spaces. Maida introduced and discussed his latest series, A Third Look, to reconsider these masters' photographs as provocative opportunities to address past gender binaries and hierarchies in the wake of contemporary feminist, multicultural, and queer perspectives.

Investigative Practices 101, workshop hosted by Anne Elizabeth Moore, in collaboration with Machine Project, October 15, 2016

Investigative Practices 101 was a three-hour investigative-journalism workshop intended to empower participants with the tools to begin pursuing journalistic investigations of their own. Anne Elizabeth Moore led participants through the basic steps of any amateur investigation, from formulating initial questions and identifying involved parties to basic interviewing techniques and journalistic etiquette. Participants learned to use a set of online tools and databases to locate documents relevant to their investigation.

Trans Culture through Media, conversation hosted by Daphne Chan, with Michel Bellici, Pêche Di, Ceyenne Doroshow, and Jes Tom, October 19, 2016

Based on Daphne Chan's research surrounding her work Transparency: The Gender Identity Project, Chan participated in a conversation with Brooklyn-based artist and healer Michel Bellici; model and Trans Models agency founder Pêche Di; activist, author, and former sex worker Ceyenne Doroshow; and queer stand-up comic Jes Tom.

Radical Networks, reading group hosted by Eyebeam, October 20, 2016

Radical Networks is an annual conference organized by Sarah Grant, Amelia Marzec, Erica Kermani, and Eyebeam. It brings together practitioners who analyze and use accessible networking technologies to understand methods of control.

How to Disappear, workshop hosted by Eteam, in collaboration with Machine Project, October 22 and 23, 2016

Half philosophical exercise, and half skills-based experience, participants in this drop-in event explored ideas of disappearance, camouflage, and invisibility, including how to make digital and physical objects disappear, and even how to make themselves vanish.

Coding Comic and STEM Teaching, conversation hosted by the Digital Citizens Lab, in collaboration with the Processing Foundation, October 26, 2016

The Digital Citizens Lab is a design collective with a focus on civic technology and on creating tools and resources for educators to meet the needs of historically underserved children of color. They presented their Coding Comic project and, with invited educators, discussed strategies and challenges related to teaching STEM (science, technology, engineering, and math) and STEAM (adding art) in schools. Participants included: the Digital Citizens Lab (Sharon Lee De La Cruz, Leslie Martinez, Evan Chin-hsuan Wu); Salome Asega; De Angela Duff; Gwen Hyman; Clarisa James; LaJuné McMillian; and Elizabeth Waters.

Our Net, workshop hosted by Dan Phiffer, in collaboration with Machine Project and Eyebeam, November 5 and 6, 2016

The Our Net workshop enabled participants to develop private networks that exist independently of the internet. The goal was to leave the workshop with enhanced digital literacy and an understanding of privacy on the internet, including its origins and history.

Accessible Technology, lecture by Claire Kearney-Volpe and Chancey Fleet, in collaboration with the Processing Foundation, November 9, 2016 (canceled)

Claire Kearney-Volpe and Chancey Fleet prepared a lecture that demonstrated the process of learning to code that is used by blind and partially sighted people.

Learning to Teach, conversation hosted by Tega Brain, in collaboration with the Processing Foundation and the School for Poetic Computation, November 30, 2016

Tega Brain (School for Poetic Computation) hosted a conversation with educators De Angela Duff (New York University), Aankit Patel (Department of Education), and David Sheinkopf (Pioneer Works), focusing on pedagogy and tools for developing interdisciplinary computational arts practices in universities, high schools, and creative communities. Brain was a 2016 Processing Foundation fellow.

Stranger Visions, workshop hosted by Heather Dewey-Hagborg, in collaboration with Machine Project, December 10 and 11, 2016

The participants in this workshop were taken through the creative stages behind Heather Dewey-Hagborg's Stranger Visions project, which consists of a series of sculpture-portraits made by the artist following the analysis of genetic material collected in public spaces. The work, which draws on methods used in science and the field of information gathering, seeks to highlight current social issues such as DNA data banking. Participants generated portraits based on their own interpretations and analyses of genetic data found online.

Voyeurism, Surveillance, and Identity in the Cinema, film series, July through December 2016

ICP and Anthology Film Archives inaugurated an ongoing collaboration with the reopening of the ICP Museum on the Bowery and the launch of *Public, Private, Secret*. AFA organized two film series inspired by the exhibition. Combining classics like *Rear Window*, *Peeping Tom*, *Blow-Up*, and *The Conversation* with experimental films, documentaries, and video art, the series demonstrate how central these ideas have been throughout the history of the cinema.

Films screened: *Rear Window* (Alfred Hitchcock,1954); *Peeping Tom* (Michael Powell, 1960); *Paul Swan* (Andy Warhol, 1965); *Blow-Up* (Michelangelo Antonioni, 1966); *David Holzman's Diary* (Jim McBride, 1967); *Portrait of Jason* (Shirley Clarke, 1967); *Rape* (Yoko Ono and John Lennon, 1969); *The Continuing Story of Carel and Ferd* (Arthur Ginsberg, 1972); *The Conversation* (Francis Ford Coppola, 1974); *The Model Couple* (William Klein, 1977); *Blow Out* (Brian De Palma, 1981); *Body Double* (Brian De Palma, 1984); *The Family Album* (Alan Berliner, 1986); *A Short Film About Love* (Krzysztof Kieślowski, 1988); *Doin' Time in Times Square* (Charlie Ahearn, 1991); *Notes from the Basement* (Rainer Frimmel, 1993–2000); *The Sleepers* (Amie Siegel, 1999); *Prison Images* (Harun Farocki, 2000); *Confessions of a Sociopath* (Joe Gibbons, 2001); *Tearoom* (William E. Jones, 2007); *Citizenfour* (Laura Poitras, 2014).

Short films screened: *Outer and Inner Space* (Andy Warhol, 1965); *People Near Here* (Ron Finne, 1969), *Two Faces* (Hermine Freed, 1972); *Now* (Lynda Benglis, 1973); *Hannah Wilke through the Large Glass* (Hannah Wilke, 1976); *Spying* (Joe Gibbons, 1977–78); *The Woman Next Door* (Burt Barr, 1984); *Dirty Film* (Alan Sondheim, 1990), *I Thought I Was Seeing Convicts* (Harun Farocki, 2000); *In Order Not to Be Here* (Deborah Stratman, 2002); *The Conversation, Brooklyn* (Michel Auder, 2003); *Unfinished* (Sophie Calle, 2005).

ACKNOWLEDGMENTS

From the outset, *Public, Private, Secret* has been a deeply collaborative effort, thanks to the inimitable spirits of Marina Chao and Pauline Vermare. Together, we thank all of the artists, thinkers, and curators who contributed their knowledge and work to this project, and to our colleagues at ICP in 2015 to 2016, and Aperture in 2017, who so brilliantly supported us.

Thank you to the keen-minded authors who contributed the seven stellar essays to this book, bringing their knowledgeable perspectives to bear on the subject of personal privacy: Marisa Olson, Lucas Wrench, David A. Banks, Ben Burbridge, Dan Bustillo, Sarah Tuck, and Daniel Rubinstein.

Thank you to the artists Zach Blas, Ann Hirsch, Martine Syms, Shelly Silver, Nancy Burson, John Houck, Kate Cooper, Stefan Ruiz, Merry Alpern, Trevor Paglen, Doug Rickard, Jon Rafman, Natalie Bookchin, and Lyle Ashton Harris (with Parissah Lin), who so thoughtfully responded to the interview questions of Marina Chao, Paula Kupfer, Pauline Vermare, and Lucas Wrench.

The exhibition, live program of events, copublications, and this book's manifestations of *Public, Private, Secret* hinged on our collaborations with Todd Rouhe and Maria Ibañez de Sendadiano of common room, David Reinfurt, Mark Ghuneim, Elizabeth Kilroy, Romke Hoogwaerts, Paul Soulellis, Johanna Hedva, Lucas Wrench, Joseph Maida, and Lacy Austin. Thank you for taking the time to reflect back upon what you took away from the ideas that we enacted together.

My respect for Geoff Han, who created the graphic identity of ICP Museum's 250 Bowery location, the *Public, Private, Secret* exhibition, and this book, knows no bounds. I am grateful in perpetuity for his talent for rendering a clear and meaningful translation of the project's concept in exhibition and book form, and for the stellar work Immanuel Yang has undertaken in the realization of this book.

Thank you to Chris Boot and Lesley Martin for instigating this book, and for providing such a great team, with Associate Editor Samantha Marlow, production organizers True Sims and Nelson Chan, Senior Text Editor Susan Ciccotti, proofreader Sally Knapp, and Aperture Work Scholars Marisa Sottos and Lucas Vasilko. Kudos to Paula Kupfer, who copyedited and so elegantly polished every word of the *Public, Private, Secret* exhibition texts and this book.

Thank you to Sheila Bergman, executive director, UCR/ARTSblock; Joanna Szupinska-Myers, curator of exhibitions; and Kathryn Poindexter, assistant curator at the California Museum of Photography, and the faculty and students of University of California, Riverside, for inviting us to rethink and recalibrate *Public, Private, Secret*, culminating in an exhibition, September 2019 through January 2020.

This book was made possible by a grant from Metabolic Studio. I am deeply indebted to Lauren Bon for her collegiate kindnesses to me over the past decade, and the inspiration Metabolic Studio gives to many in their quest to create on a scale that society has the capacity to destroy.

Charlotte Cotton

Public, Private, Secret
On Photography &
the Configuration of Self
By Charlotte Cotton
With Marina Chao and
Pauline Vermare

Associate Editor: Samantha Marlow
Graphic Design: Geoff Han
Design Assistant: Immanuel Yang
Production: True Sims, Nelson Chan
Senior Text Editor: Susan Ciccotti
Copy Editor: Paula Kupfer
Proofreader: Sally Knapp
Work Scholars: Marisa Sottos, Lucas Vasilko

Additional staff of the Aperture book program includes: Chris Boot, Executive Director; Lesley A. Martin, Creative Director; Amelia Lang, Associate Publisher; Taia Kwinter, Managing Editor; Kellie McLaughlin, Director of Sales and Marketing; Richard Gregg, Sales Director, Books

Copublished by Aperture and the International Center of Photography

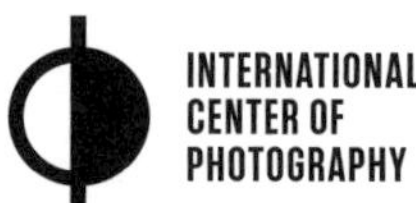

Exhibition schedule: International Center of Photography, New York, June 23, 2016–January 8, 2017

University of California, Riverside, September 2019–January 2020

Typeset in Permanent, created by Laurenz Brunner

First edition, 2018
Printed by Midas in China
10 9 8 7 6 5 4 3 2 1

Library of Congress Cataloging-in-Publication Data

Names: Cotton, Charlotte, editor.
Title: Public, Private, Secret: on Photography and the Configuration of Self /by Charlotte Cotton with Marina Chao and Pauline Vermare; contributions by Lacy Austin, David A. Banks, Ben Burbridge, Dan Bustillo, common room, Mark Ghuneim, Johanna Hedva, Romke Hoogwaerts, Elizabeth Kilroy, Joseph Maida, Marisa Olson, David Reinfurt, Daniel Rubinstein, Paul Soulellis, Sarah Tuck, and Lucas Wrench; interviews with Merry Alpern, Zach Blas, Natalie Bookchin, Nancy Burson, Kate Cooper, Lyle Ashton Harris, Ann Hirsch, John Houck, Trevor Paglen, Jon Rafman, Doug Rickard, Stefan Ruiz, Shelly Silver, and Martine Syms.
Description: First edition. | New York, N.Y. : Aperture Foundation, 2018.
Identifiers: LCCN 2017052464 | ISBN 9781597114387 (pbk. with flaps : alk. paper)
Subjects: LCSH: Photography—Psychological aspects. | Self. | Expression (Philosophy) | Photographers—Interviews.
Classification: LCC TR183 .P84 2018 | DDC 770—dc23
LC record available at https://lccn.loc.gov/2017052464

To order Aperture books, contact:
+1 212.946.7154
orders@aperture.org

For information about Aperture trade distribution worldwide, visit: aperture.org/distribution

aperture
Aperture Foundation
547 West 27th Street
4th Floor
New York, N.Y. 10001
aperture.org

Aperture, a not-for-profit foundation, connects the photo community and its audiences with the most inspiring work, the sharpest ideas, and with each other—in print, in person, and online.